Harvest of Want

Conflict and Social Change Series

Series Editors
Scott Whiteford and William Derman
Michigan State University

Harvest of Want: Hunger and Food Security in Central America and Mexico, edited by Scott Whiteford and Anne E. Ferguson

Singing with Sai Baba: The Politics of Revitalization in Trinidad, Morton Klass

Struggling for Survival: Workers, Women, and Class on a Nicaraguan State Farm, Gary Ruchwarger

The Spiral Road: Change in a Chinese Village Through the Eyes of a Communist Party Leader, Huang Shu-min

Kilowatts and Crisis: Hydroelectric Power and Social Dislocation in Eastern Panama, Alaka Wali

Deep Water: Development and Change in Pacific Village Fisheries, Margaret Critchlow Rodman

FORTHCOMING

Computers and Culture: New Information Technology and Social Change in England, David Hakken and Barbara Andrews

Surviving Drought and Development: Ariaal Pastoralists of Northern Kenya, Elliot Fratkin

The Bushman Myth: The Making of a Namibian Underclass, Robert J. Gordon

The Myth of the Male Breadwinner: Women, Industrialization, and State Policy in the Caribbean, Helen I. Safa

Literacy and People's Power in a Mozambican Factory, Judith Marshall

Harvest of Want

Hunger and Food Security in Central America and Mexico

EDITED BY

Scott Whiteford and Anne E. Ferguson

Westview Press

BOULDER • SAN FRANCISCO • OXFORD

Conflict and Social Change Series

Copyright © 1991 by Westview Press, Inc.

Published in 1991 in the United States of America by Westview Press, Inc., 5500 Central Avenue, Boulder, Colorado 80301, and in the United Kingdom by Westview Press, 36 Lonsdale Road, Summertown, Oxford OX2 7EW

Library of Congress Cataloging-in-Publication Data
Harvest of want : hunger and food security in Central America and
  Mexico / edited by Scott Whiteford and Anne E. Ferguson.
    p. cm. — (Conflict and social change series)
  Includes index.
  ISBN 0-8133-7986-5
  1. Food supply—Central America. 2. Food supply—Mexico.
3. Nutrition policy—Central America. 4. Nutrition policy—Mexico.
I. Whiteford, Scott, 1942–   . II. Ferguson, Anne E.
III. Series.
HD9014.C462H37 1991
363.8′09728—dc20
                                                               91-10878
                                                               CIP

Printed and bound in the United States of America

The paper used in this publication meets the requirements of the American National Standard for Permanence of Paper for Printed Library Materials Z39.48-1984.

10   9   8   7   6   5   4   3   2   1

Contents

1

Social Dimensions of Food Security and Hunger: An Overview

Scott Whiteford and Anne E. Ferguson

Wars, revolts, and revolutions have been fought in Central America and Mexico over access to land. This is not surprising given the richness of the land and the overwhelming importance of agriculture for export earnings, employment, and food availability in the region. Despite abundant arable land, skilled farmers, and a conducive climate, however, malnutrition is a major problem. Current estimates are that three out of four children in Central America are malnourished and that the percentage of these children is growing faster than is the population as a whole (Barry 1987, xiv). In Mexico by 1980 it was reported that "ninety percent of the rural population suffers from a severe deficiency of calories and protein; a quarter of the entire Mexican population subsists on farms 25 percent to 40 percent below recommended minimal levels" (Esteva 1983, 13), even though the country is a major producer of agricultural products.

The chapters in this book explore the broad range of social factors that play a role in creating this scale of hunger and malnutrition. These factors stem from national social and economic structures and power relationships, many of which originated during the colonial period. The concentration of power in the hands of a small number of elite families, in part a colonial legacy, has been challenged repeatedly in the region, but only in Mexico and Nicaragua have revolutions led to significant restructuring and broad-based land reforms.

The internal social and economic structures of countries in the region link these countries to the broader world system. As a result of the expansion of industrial capitalism in Europe and the United States, Central America and to a lesser degree, Mexico, were incorporated into the world system as primary producers of agricultural products. As we shall see, this legacy has been difficult to escape, even in countries such as Mexico and Nicaragua, which have undergone profound social and economic transformations during this century.

Food Security

Conventional definitions of food security stress that enough food must be available to meet market demands without severe shortages or price fluctuations occurring. The issue of distribution—whether all groups in a society have access to sufficient food—is often side-stepped in discussions of food security. As Barraclough and Utting (1987, 3) contend, however, the capacity to make food available to the whole population is an important component in the food-security equation. Other traits of a secure food system include autonomy, reliability, and sustainability. Such a system should have the autonomy necessary to reduce vulnerability to market fluctuations and external political pressures. It should also be reliable in the sense that it is able to buffer fluctuations in food production, imports, storage, and distribution caused by weather, changes in pricing structures, import capacity, and the like. Finally, a secure food system should be sustainable in that soils and other aspects of the natural ecosystem are preserved rather than depleted (Barraclough and Scott 1987). As we shall see, food systems in most Central American countries are profoundly lacking in these elements.

Two points concerning food security deserve initial consideration. First, although declines in per capita food production in the Central American and Caribbean region have occurred in the past decade, generally speaking sufficient food could be produced, or acquired, to meet the nutritional needs of the population. The contributors to this volume demonstrate how hunger and malnutrition may exist simultaneously with growth in agricultural production, especially if this output is destined for the export market. Thus, the key issue is not a technical one related to agricultural production practices but rather a more fundamental one involving the allocation of resources and the political will to provide for all groups in the society. In this sense, the degree of food security achieved reflects the broad distribution of power and resources. Where these are highly skewed, as they are in much of Central America, many families experience food insecurity—they are excluded from access to the resources necessary to produce sufficient food and lack the purchasing power to acquire it.

Second, although they are closely interrelated, food self-sufficiency and food security are not synonymous concepts. In some cases, food security can be achieved in the absence of food self-sufficiency. For example, nations like Japan provide adequate supplies of food to meet their people's needs even though they depend on food imports. Other countries, like Brazil, may be capable of meeting their population's food needs but may export so much that many go hungry. Although food security is possible in the absence of food self-sufficiency, as Hollist and Tullis (1987, 1) point out, in many instances the rural poor are not likely to eat well unless they produce adequate amounts of their own food. Thus, though some food needs may be met through imports, a degree of autonomous production capacity is usually desirable.

In the chapter "Food Security and Regional Development," Jack Corbett identifies two approaches to the creation of food-security systems at the national level. One centers on the principle of supply and the other emphasizes consumption as the organizing focus. Corbett contrasts these approaches and the tensions that integrate and divide them in Mexico and Central America. He points out that with the exception of Nicaragua, the production-based approach has dominated in the region.

For our purposes, then, food security means that there is dependable access to food—supplied through ecologically sound agricultural techniques and, when necessary, imports—to meet the nutritional requirements of all individuals and groups within a country.

The Roots of Food Insecurity
in Mexico and Central America

The contributors to this volume point to a series of factors that have generated food insecurity throughout much of Central America and Mexico: extreme socioeconomic and political inequality; war and the large-scale displacement of peoples; the international debt crisis; over-emphasis on export agriculture and ineffective support in the form of credit, services, and technologies for food-crop producers; over-reliance on food imports; poorly developed mechanisms for distributing food to those most in need; and processes of environmental degradation. In our discussion, we explore three broad, interrelated issues that encompass many of these causes: agricultural export-led growth strategies and their impact on food production; the depletion of the natural resource base resulting from these development strategies; and the effects of militarization, violence, and the growing number of refugees on food security.

The Agricultural Export-Led Growth Strategy and Its Food Production Consequences

In Mexico and Central America, governments have a long history of pursuing agricultural policies that support the expansion of export crops and livestock production. The chapter by Robert Williams in this volume, "Land, Labor, and the Crisis in Central America," argues that the current crisis in Central America can be traced to processes that evolved from basic structural inequalities, the enclosure of traditional peasant lands, and the modernization of agricultural labor relations resulting from this export focus. Liberal economic measures pursued by many Central American governments during the late nineteenth century resulted in the privatization of many community-owned properties in an effort to stimulate production of export crops, particularly coffee. These and other measures to promote exports led to the concentration of property in the hands of a small minority and to the progressive marginalization and poverty of much of the rural population. Many families lost access to land and came to depend more and more on seasonal wage labor on large estates.

After the Great Depression and especially after World War II, governments, still ascribing to an export orientation, made efforts to diversify the export base and a number of additional commodities, particularly cotton, sugar, and beef, were added to the traditional exports of the region. In part as a result of these efforts, during the 1960s and 1970s Central American economies experienced rapid economic growth. Between 1950 and the mid-1970s agro-exports grew at about 8 percent per year, and rates of growth for the region were among the highest in Latin America (Barraclough and Scott 1987, 39). However, these growth rates improved the standard of living of only a small proportion of the population, primarily middle-class urban dwellers. Few of the benefits reached peasants and plantation workers in the rural areas, and hence, many families saw little change in their condition as land and access to capital and other resources continued to be highly concentrated.

Martin Diskin examines the outcome of this pattern of economic growth in his chapter, "Lack of Access to Land and Food in El Salvador." He notes that although El Salvador's economy grew rapidly during the 1960s and 1970s, this growth was accompanied by little improvement in the well-being of the majority of the population. A statement by the president of the Salvadoran National Association of Private Enterprises (ANEP) reflected the political will to maintain the concentration of power and resources in the hands of the few. When asked when the benefits of growth would reach more people, he suggested that a sustained annual growth rate of 35 percent was first necessary. As Diskin demonstrates, such trickle-down strategies often founder because there is no clear point at which the national wealth begins to be more evenly distributed, responsibility for such redistribution usually rests in the hands of those who profit from current distribution systems, and few if any mechanisms exist to ensure that benefits reach a wide segment of the population.

The chapter "Land, Malnutrition, and Health: The Dilemmas of Development in Guatemala" by Kjell Enge and Pilar Martinez-Enge examines the relationships between economic growth, a highly skewed concentration of wealth, and the poverty of the rural and predominately indigenous population. They point out that Guatemala has the worst distribution of income in Central America, the concentration of land-holdings is the least equitable in the region, the rate of malnutrition continues to climb, and the infant mortality rate is one of the highest in Latin America, comparable to that of Haiti.

Throughout Central America, the rise in oil prices coupled with the drop in commodity prices and the growing debt burden brought a slowing of economic growth in the late 1970s and 1980s. Popular insurrections in Nicaragua, El Salvador, and Guatemala reflected massive discontent with existing political and economic structures that had excluded the majority from benefiting from economic growth.

The Mexican economic crisis did not emerge until the 1980s, but conditions in most rural areas before that time were harsh due to lack of government support, a deteriorating resource base, and limited access to land. During the 1970s the Mexican government, optimistically predicting high oil revenues, expanded programs by borrowing money on the international market. During the 1970s and early 1980s these programs included SAM (Sistema Alimentario Mexicano), an integrated program of food production, distribution, and consumption; and PIDER, a large-scale investment program for rural development.

By 1982 a series of factors indicated a crisis was emerging, one that would have a tremendous impact on both urban and rural populations. The Mexican debt had reached $62 billion, export earnings were falling, and inflation was accelerating. Between 1979 and 1985 the value of Mexico's food imports was greater than agricultural exports (Barkin 1987, 271). Oil prices fell drastically in 1986 at a time when the nation was still recovering from the earthquake of 1985. The impact of the crisis on the urban and rural poor was devastating. Inflation accelerated rapidly, wages declined, and development programs were curtailed.

The government responded by implementing fiscal austerity programs and cutting back on spending. Major reductions were made in government programs in agriculture, public works, and transportation. Subsidies for basic consumer goods were cut, increasing costs for the poor. Significantly, the sectors most affected did not revolt against the government, although it is clear that the government and the *Partido Revolucionario Institutional* (PRI) did lose credibility. Instead, households developed strategies to diversify incomes. The chapter by Billie DeWalt and Kathleen DeWalt,

"The Results of Mexican Agricultural and Food Policy: Debt, Drugs, and Illegal Aliens," in this volume describes many of the diversification strategies peasants used to cope with the crisis and their food needs.

As a solution to the current economic stagnation, heavy debt burdens, and civil unrest, the Mexican and Central American governments, with the exception of Nicaragua, have chosen more of the same—increasing the emphasis on the agricultural export sector and seeking means to diversify their export base to generate larger amounts of foreign exchange. Ironically, in Central America part of the debt that brought on the crisis was created by heavy borrowing to expand export agriculture in the first place, and the debt continues to grow more rapidly than the exports (Brockett 1988, 62).

The Role of Foreign Assistance. Governments in the region are supported in their efforts to promote export-led growth by a wide array of international donors and lending institutions. During the 1980s, Central America experienced a tremendous growth in development assistance, much of it from the United States as a part of its efforts to stabilize the region's governments and pacify its populations to prevent popular uprisings similar to the Sandinista takeover in Nicaragua in 1979. Between 1946 and 1979, U.S. economic aid to the region totaled $1,898.3 million; during the 1980–1986 period alone it increased by more than one third, reaching $3,191.5 million (Barry and Preusch 1988, xv). In addition to U.S. assistance, the World Bank and the Inter-American Development Bank also provide considerable economic support to the region.

U.S. bilateral assistance to Central America takes many forms, including that delivered through the Agency for International Development (AID), the Export-Import Bank, the United States Information Agency, and various other organizations. AID itself administers three types of bilateral economic support: development assistance, Public Law 480 (PL480) food aid, and Economic Support Funds (ESF).

The PL480 and ESF programs mushroomed during the 1980s, growing from $11 million in 1979 to nearly $650 million in 1986 (Barry and Preusch 1988, 23). These two categories of assistance are aimed at stabilizing governments and pacifying populations rather than at initiating the structural reforms necessary for equitable distribution and development. Economic Support Funds aid, delivered in the form of cash transfers, meets immediate government funding needs. In El Salvador, for example, these funds are used to cover balance-of-payment deficits, to rebuild infrastructure damaged in the civil war, and to fund government operating expenses, thus freeing up moneys for the war effort (Barry and Preusch 1988, 29).

The Title I program makes it possible for U.S. agricultural commodities to be either given or sold at very low prices to foreign governments.

The commodities may be distributed directly by receiving government agencies, but they are usually bought by private processing companies. This program relieves recipient country governments of the need to use scarce foreign exchange for food imports and generates local revenue for the sale of the surpluses. Between 1980 and 1988, Title I program aid to Central American countries, particularly El Salvador, Guatemala, and Honduras, was more than $600 million, in contrast to only $10 million in food aid between 1954 and 1979 (Garst and Barry 1990, 18).

In El Salvador, in particular, dependency on food aid reached tremendous proportions. Barraclough and Scott (1987, 21) reported that approximately one third of the country's cereals—including 27 percent of the maize and 32 percent of the rice—and half of the edible oil and dairy products were provided through food aid. Graft and corruption accompanied many of these food transfers (Barraclough and Scott 1987, 80). The food-aid programs have often been a disincentive for local grain producers who have been unable to compete with the subsidized imports. The result is a growing dependence on food imports coupled with an incentive to export. There is little evidence that Title I has contributed to long-term alleviation of hunger in the region (Garst and Barry 1990, 92).

Before the Nicaraguan Revolution, Nicaragua was importing more than 210,000 tons of grain from the United States, much of it financed by the inexpensive credit system of the U.S. government. Ninety percent of the national credit was allocated to large growers for the production of export crops (Collins, Lappe, and Allen 1982, 107). Prior to the revolution in 1979, it is estimated that "over half the country's children suffered from under-nutrition and about 15 percent were seriously undernourished" (Barraclough et al. 1988, 33). After the revolution, food imports from the United States were curtailed by the Reagan administration and a trade embargo was imposed. Nicaragua turned to other nations for credit and technical services and redesigned its food production and distribution systems. One component of the program was a shift from importing wheat to growing more corn and domestic food crops. The chapter by Veronica Frenkel in this volume, "The Dilemmas of Food Security in a Revolutionary Context: Nicaragua, 1979–1986," examines the programs developed by Nicaragua after the revolution to increase national self-sufficiency in food production, more equitably distribute land and food, and maintain export production.

In large part, AID and other donor funding in Central America is used to support private-sector, export-led development strategies in industry and agriculture. The Caribbean Basin Initiative (CBI) illustrates the development philosophy underlying many of these programs. Its overall thrusts are to increase agriculture and industrial exports, attract foreign capital, and strengthen local businesses. To accomplish these ends, several measures have been adopted including state divestiture of public-sector enterprises, removal of price controls on basic goods, cutbacks on social services, increases in sales taxes, modifications in labor legislation, expansion of infrastructure, and reductions in import tariffs and export taxes. In essence, the goal of the CBI aid package is to improve the private-sector business climate in the familiar, but yet-to-be supported, expectation that the benefits derived will eventually improve the living standards of the majority.

In agriculture, development initiatives sponsored by AID, the World Bank, and other economic assistance agencies with the support of the International Monetary Fund (IMF) have emphasized private, usually large-scale commercial production of cotton, coffee, bananas, sugar, and beef. More recently, in a second wave to diversify exports winter vegetables, flowers, spices, and citrus have received priority as a means of generating needed foreign exchange. In their chapter, Billie DeWalt and Kathleen DeWalt examine some of the nutritional ramifications of macro-economic policies advocated by the IMF and other international donor and lending institutions for dealing with the debt crisis. The policies examined are land reform, the application of modern agricultural technologies, and the promotion of exports. Because of the long history of these reform measures in Mexico, the DeWalts' case history illustrates the potential long-term effects of these policies on food production and nutritional status elsewhere in the region.

The expansion of the livestock industry represents one of the major development initiatives promoted by national governments and donors alike over the past 25 years in Mexico and Central America. Three chapters in this volume touch on the effects of the promotion of this industry: "The Political Economy of Environmental Destruction: Food Security in Southern Honduras" by Susan Stonich; "From *Gallo Pinto* to 'Jack's Snacks': Observations on Dietary Change in a Rural Costa Rican Village" by Michael Whiteford; and the DeWalt and DeWalt chapter. These authors document how forest and crop lands have been progressively turned into pastures or used for the production of feed grains. They explore some of the food-security and nutrition consequences of these alterations in land-use patterns, showing that the poor rarely reap any long-term benefits.

Large amounts of investment capital have been allocated to the livestock industry in Central America since 1960, much of it supplied by international donors and lending institutions (Leonard 1987, 88–89; Barry and Preusch 1988). Leonard indicates that during the early 1970s approximately one half of all agricultural credit in Costa Rica went to support the livestock industry; in Panama 40 percent of total agricultural credit provided in 1977 was invested in this sector (1987, 88–89). Brown (1988, 9) finds that since 1963 the World Bank has provided more credit for livestock in Central America than for any other kind of agricultural activity.

As a result of this influx of development assistance, beef production grew rapidly in Central America, with annual production increasing from an average of 153,000 metric tons in the early 1960s to over 350,000 metric tons in 1980 (Leonard 1987, 87). This increase was accompanied by growth in beef exports from Central America: In the early 1960s only 22 percent of total beef production was exported; by the early 1970s this had expanded to over 40 percent (Leonard 1987, 87). Although exports grew, per capita consumption of beef rose only slightly in the region as a whole and in some countries—El Salvador and Nicaragua—consumption of beef actually declined between 1960 and 1980.

Similar to the other major commodity exports, beef production is subject to fluctuations in international market demand, and producers must compete with other suppliers of the same commodity. Demand for beef in the United States, long the major market for Central American cattle exports, has declined significantly in the past decade. Consequently, cattle production in Central America and Mexico is increasingly dependent on domestic markets. As beef loses its position as a major generator of foreign exchange, much of the economic rationale for specializing in cattle is eroded because, as Leonard notes, "other agricultural uses of the land could generate far more employment and would either bring greater export revenues or produce greater amounts of food" (1987, 88). In Mexico, as grain production increases, a greater and greater percentage is being used for animal feed to provide beef for the middle and upper classes. Meanwhile, a large portion of the population goes hungry (DeWalt 1985, 53–54; Barkin, Batt, and DeWalt 1990).

Biotechnology has initiated a new wave of fundamental change in agriculture, one with uncertain social and economic consequences for the populations in Mexico, Central America, and elsewhere in the developing world (Buttel, Kenney, and Kloppenberg 1985; Messer and Heywood 1988). Since the late 1970s relationships between the public and private sector in the U.S. agricultural establishment have been altered, and it is likely that in the future trade relationships among nations will be affected as the potential for production of substitutes for tropical crops increases (Doyle 1985; Juma 1989; Kloppenberg 1988). Although the new technologies may reduce the cost of production of many food and export crops, in the process they may undercut the ability of the small-scale producers to compete, generating increased proletarianization, semi-proletarianization, and urbanization.

Land Allocation: Implications for Food Production and Nutritional Status. Land is the traditional base of power in Central America and Mexico. During this century only Nicaragua and Mexico have implemented significant agrarian reform programs that reduced the degree of land concentration. Elsewhere in the region property ownership is highly skewed, with a small number of families owning a major share of the farmland. For example, Guatemala reportedly has the most unequal distribution of land in Latin America. In 1982, a USAID study documented that less than 3 percent of farms occupied 65 percent of the farmland and 88 percent of farms were too small to provide for the needs of a family. In 1979, an estimated 25 percent of the population was landless, up from 15 percent in 1950 (Barraclough and Scott 1987, 50–51). Since the early 1960s even Costa Rica, once known for its large number of family-sized farms, has experienced a growing concentration of land accompanying the expansion of coffee and beef production for the export market.

Lands used to grow export crops or to raise livestock are usually among the most productive and fertile. Consequently, as peasants have been displaced by the spread of commercialized, export-oriented agriculture, they and the food crops they grow have been relegated to marginal, rainfed, and unimproved areas. As we shall see, this process of displacement affects not only food production but also the quality of the environment and the long-term sustainability of the natural resource base. Barry reported that 80 percent of the farmers in Central America did not have enough land to feed their families. Landlessness had tripled since 1960; 85 percent of the best land was owned by elites and used for export crops, and 45 percent of the arable land was used for grazing cattle (Barry 1987, xiv).

Food crop production has been marginalized in other ways as well. In comparison with coffee, cattle, cotton, winter vegetables, and other major export crops, such basic staples as maize and beans have been given little government or donor support. Agricultural research and extension efforts by national governments and international lenders have supported the export sector, and little in the way of research, credit, or services has reached the small-scale, semi-commercialized, or subsistence producers who are responsible for most of the food production.

Reflecting these trends, food production between 1960 and 1980 in much of Mexico and Central America barely kept pace with population growth. Per capita food production increased by less than 10 percent in Central America between 1960 and 1980 and has been declining since the 1970s, a trend that continued into the 1980s. Drawing on recent UN Food and Agricultural Organization figures, Leonard (1987, 82) reports that for the Latin American/Caribbean region as a whole, per capita cereal production increased by 60 percent between 1975 and 1981, but for Central America itself per capita production actually decreased by more than 8 percent. Using Comisión Económica para América Latina (CEPAL) figures, Redclift (1989, 367) shows that between 1964 and 1983 Costa Rica, El Salvador, and Nicaragua all witnessed a fall in their per capita food production; Guatemala, Mexico, and Honduras made slight gains.

As food production for domestic consumption has stagnated or declined, reliance on food imports, and by some countries on food aid, has grown, increasing the vulnerability of the region's food system. Food imports in Central America have risen to over 750,000 tons (Barry 1987, xvi). Barraclough and Scott (1987, 21) report that in 1983 the value of imports as a proportion of that of agricultural exports was approximately 40 percent in El Salvador and Costa Rica, 53 percent in Nicaragua, and 30 percent in Guatemala and Honduras. Mexico also has become increasingly dependent on imported beans, wheat, and corn. By the early 1980s, Mexico was importing large amounts of basic grains. For example, in 1979 nearly 69 percent of the wheat consumed was imported (Otero 1989, 295). Changes in prices, credit, and consumption patterns have somewhat reduced the reliance on imports of basic grains, but as Mexico moves into the 1990s, large-scale importation of grains looms as a long-term problem.

Although reliance on food imports has grown, nations in the region have found their importing capacities compromised by declines in the value of many of their export commodities. Terms of trade for coffee, cotton, sugar, beef, and other exports have deteriorated significantly during the 1980s with severe consequences for the poor. The sugar industry provides an example of changes in these trade relationships. The development of artificial sweeteners, the production of sugar from corn, and the powerful sugar lobby in the United States have all led to major reductions in U.S. imports of sugar from Latin America and to a general fall in world sugar prices. Although many Latin American countries are cutting back production, extensive areas are still planted in sugar cane because of capital investment in the sugar complexes, many of which are controlled by large corporations. Meanwhile, wages have been cut, and the purchasing power of workers has been reduced in an effort to make sugar competitive on the world market. Only in Nicaragua, as Frenkel's chapter indicates, has this overall pattern been significantly reversed.

Frenkel's chapter and the chapter by Jonathan Fox, "Popular Participation and Access to Food: Mexico's Community Food Councils," are significant because they highlight the importance of distributional issues in the food-security equation. Many Latin American governments have adopted a policy of keeping food prices low. These low prices are clearly important in the battle against hunger and malnutrition; they are also significant to government leaders for other reasons. It is easier to keep industrial wages down if food is cheap, and lower wages in turn serve to attract industrial investment and stimulate growth. Equally important, governments in the region see the growing urban population as powerful and potentially disruptive, and governments fear that rising food prices may generate revolt (Timmer 1986). As a result, strategies have been developed to keep prices down, including low payments to farmers for staples, massive importation of basic grains, subsidization of the sale of food products, and development of elaborate food-distribution agencies.

In her chapter, María Verónica Frenkel examines efforts by the Nicaraguan government to guarantee prices that stimulate producers to grow staples but that also are low enough for consumers. These policies have undergone adjustment as the terms of trade shifted away from an advantage to the farmers, who at times even found it cheaper to buy their own food from government subsidized stores than to grow it themselves. Frenkel examines government efforts to reduce the cost of marketing, the complications in the marketing and distribution system generated by initial Sandinista government policies, and subsequent adjustments in pricing and market controls made by the government to stimulate production. Many of these government efforts were undermined by the contra war—and by U.S. support for this militarization.

Empowerment and control of the food distribution network are the subjects of Jonathan Fox's chapter. He focuses on food subsidy programs, arguing that these have received less study than have other measures to improve access to food, such as land reform and employment generation. Using the case of Mexico's community food councils, Fox illustrates how government can design a food-subsidy program to attack poverty and hunger in the face of increasing economic austerity. He finds that the program was most successful at encouraging participation where peasants already were mobilized or where the conditions for such mobilization existed. In Mexico, these were the areas with large indigenous populations, particularly the state of Oaxaca. Overall, the chapter makes an important contribution by examining how beneficiaries can influence the nature of the program and by considering how scarce resources can be allocated efficiently and equitably. Although it is clear that effective mechanisms were developed by beneficiary organizations in Mexico, many of the internal conflicts over power intensified as state resources became increasingly scarce.

The autonomy and dependability of systems of production and distribution in most of Central America and increasingly in Mexico have declined, a process that is reflected by nutrition indicators. Barraclough and Scott (1987, 20) reported that in Central America, Costa Rica was the only country that theoretically could meet its population's calorie requirements throughout the year and still have a small surplus for market purposes. In Nicaragua, calorie needs could be met but there would be no market surplus. In Guatemala, El Salvador, and Honduras food availability was not sufficient to meet minimum requirements. In no Central American country were protein requirements satisfied. In Mexico the economic crisis led to a further deterioration in food security. Rural diets "already less rich in protein than those in urban areas, relied increasingly on corn and beans and substitutes with little nutritional content" (Grindle 1989, 197).

By reflecting per capita calorie availability at the national level, these figures mask a far more serious reality. Calories and food are not distributed equally among the population or over seasons, and although the nutritional needs of children in middle- and upper-class families are more than satisfied throughout the year, large numbers of children in poor households suffer from both chronic and seasonal malnutrition.

Food Insecurity and Environmental Degradation

The rapid destruction of natural resources in Latin America has suddenly caught the attention of policymakers and scholars. Awareness is growing of the multiple links between the region's development process, the resulting high levels of poverty, and environmental degradation. At the same time that our understanding of the relationships between these processes grows, so do pressures grow to exploit the region's resources. The debt crisis, population growth, and the desperate need of rural peoples to sustain their families have all led to efforts to increase foreign exchange earnings. These efforts in turn have led to the staggering scale and speed of environmental destruction. Redclift (1989, 309) reports that three quarters of rainfed cropland is affected by desertification in Latin America, and in Central America the problem is mounting. In El Salvador, for example, more than 50 percent of the arable land is badly eroded (Leonard 1987, xi).

The expansion of export crops and the inequality in land tenure in Central America and Mexico have forced thousands of subsistence-oriented sharecroppers, squatters, and others off the land. Those who remain often find themselves relegated to more marginal, steeply sloped lands that are easily degraded. The resulting severe soil erosion and other forms of environmental degradation have decreased crop yields at a time when peasants face severe economic hardships. This process of marginalization of peasant producers has generated hunger, reduced national food production, and systematically destroyed the resource base.

The health of the natural environment has become a critical dimension of food insecurity in many countries of the region.

Particularly dramatic alterations in land-use patterns in Central America have occurred since the 1960s as a result of the promotion of the livestock industry discussed earlier. Much of the forest cover in the region has disappeared, resulting in a loss of species diversity, increases in soil erosion, and siltation of rivers and streams. Using Food and Agriculture Organization (FAO) statistics, Leonard (1987, 99) reports that of the approximately 510,000 square kilometers of land in the region, 61 percent was in forests and woodlands and about 25 percent was devoted to agriculture in 1960. By 1980, in contrast, only about 40 percent of the land area was forested, 13 percent was being cultivated, and 22 percent was in permanent pasture. As Leonard suggests, these figures may actually underestimate the area devoted to cattle raising. The data include only those lands used exclusively for pasture during the past five years and do not take into account lands cleared for pasture but initially used for crop production, a pattern that occurs frequently in Central America.

Some of the most fertile lands in Central America are currently used for cattle grazing. Roughly two-thirds of the flat, fertile Pacific coastal strip of Central America is being used for beef rather than for crop production, and there are indications that many of the large-scale producers who occupy this land do not manage their operations efficiently (Leonard 1987, 171). Overall, until recently many of the production gains in the export sector were achieved by expanding the amount of land under cultivation rather than by intensifying or improving land-use practices (Leonard 1987, 80). With regard to the livestock sector, few improved grasses have been introduced, and the stocking rates and the nutritional level of the cattle are reportedly low. Recent studies suggest that small-scale beef production integrated with other farming activities is more productive than many of the large-scale operations (Leonard 1987, 91).

The chapter by Susan Stonich on food security and environmental degradation in Honduras contributes to our understanding of the relationship between poverty, government policy, and environmental concerns. Stonich documents a critical set of interrelationships among land tenure, unemployment, demography, and poverty. Her conclusions point to the difficulty of implementing a policy of sustainable development. As she indicates, efforts to achieve long-term ecological sustainability conflict with the forces of capitalist accumulation and the most powerful actors in the national and international society.

Environmental degradation is a problem in many areas of Mexico as well. Water pollution, erosion, and salinization have all affected the food production system. As in Central America, the expansion of livestock production has increased the pace of deforestation, which in turn has had an impact on the environment. Irrigation systems play a greater role in Mexico than they do in Central America, with consequences for the environment. In their chapter in this volume, Billie DeWalt and Kathleen DeWalt discuss the massive investment in irrigation infrastructure, which represents between 70 and 99 percent of the total Mexican agricultural budget between 1940 and 1979. Although irrigation has made major increases in agricultural production possible, it has also resulted in growing salinization and siltation in the areas where it has been employed. Already, over 1 million acres of land that was formerly cultivated is no longer usable because of these ecological consequences. Rehabilitation will have to be undertaken in the historical centers of indigenous irrigation such as the Tehuacan Valley and in the newly developed river basin systems (Whiteford 1986; Enge and Whiteford 1989). Estimates are that more than 2.5 million acres will need to be reclaimed or they will be abandoned by 1990 (Yates 1981, 64).

Militarization, Violence, and Refugees: Implications for Food Security

Food insecurity is intimately related to the process of militarization that has occurred in Central America over the past decades. Conflicts in the region have taken more than 260,000 lives and led to the displacement of 2 million people.

Although the 1980s has witnessed a massive military buildup in Central America, the process has a long history. Central American military spending increased sevenfold between 1952 and 1983 (Deyer 1986, 4). Between 1980 and 1985 the United States spent $2.3 billion for military aid in the area, a tremendous increase over previous amounts.

The tragic human cost of the conflict is startling. In El Salvador, for example, more than 70,000 people have been killed since 1979, and thousands of families have fled their homes, many leaving the country. The nation has suffered $2 billion in damages to infrastructure and production units including highways, electrical and communication equipment, and plantations (Rohter 1989, 30).

This violence plays an important role in generating food insecurity in the region. It has displaced thousands of families from their communities and traditional agricultural lands, and it has robbed the region of key food producers who are killed or injured or who leave the area to participate in or avoid paramilitary actions. Further, countries are faced with the problem of feeding the growing refugee population. The scale of the displacement is staggering. By 1989 there were more than

872,000 displaced people in Central America itself and another 893,000 who had left the region (UNHCR 1989, 20).

The figures for individual countries, particularly El Salvador, Guatemala, and Nicaragua, tell a tragic tale. Between 25 and 29 percent of the Salvadoran population has been displaced by the violence and military conflict. In his chapter in this volume, Martin Diskin points to the great inequity in power relationships and landholding that exists in the country, the deteriorating state of the peasantry, and repression as factors generating this displacement. Yet, ironically, the refugees remain central to El Salvador's economy. By sending $350–$600 million annually back to family and friends, the refugees, rather than export crops, are the country's biggest source of foreign exchange (Barraclough and Scott 1987, 27–28).

In Guatemala, between 3 and 7.5 percent of the population are displaced. More than 40,000 refugees, most of whom are Indian peasants, have fled to Mexico and are living in refugee camps in Chiapas. Another 60,000 Guatemalans may be living in Mexico clandestinely (Durand 1984, 90). As the chapter by Kjell Enge and Pilar Martinez-Enge indicates, the indigenous population has been systematically excluded from access to new lands and deprived of their traditional landholdings. One of the outcomes of this process has been hunger, poor health, and resistance. The resistance on the part of major segments of the indigenous population has resulted in protracted military conflict with the national government. Military operations and armed conflict in turn have generated food insecurity and malnutrition as villages were destroyed and thousands of people were killed or forced to become refugees.

In Nicaragua also war has led to the displacement of thousands of peasants from military zones. As many as 43,000 Nicaraguans have migrated to Honduras where they have settled in refugee camps or been incorporated in the contra war effort. Possibly twice this number of Nicaraguans have fled to Costa Rica, and between 40,000 and 80,000 have moved to the United States (HMP 1989, 21). At the same time Nicaragua has received more than 17,000 Salvadoran and 1,000 Guatemalan refugees (Barton 1986, 27).

Mexico has also felt the effects of this violence, particularly through the massive migration of displaced Central Americans across its borders. In addition to the thousands of Guatemalans, more than 120,000 Salvadorans have sought refuge in Mexico. As the chapter by Billie DeWalt and Kathleen DeWalt illustrates, however, the consequences of uneven development in Mexico have contributed to growing unrest there and to a steady stream of migrants heading north across the border to the United States.

Conclusion

If food security means that there is dependable access to food to satisfy the nutritional requirements of all individuals and groups within a nation, such security is a long way from attainment in most Central American countries and is increasingly undermined for different reasons in Nicaragua and Mexico. The skewed distribution of resources and power in Guatemala, El Salvador, and Honduras and growing disparities in Mexico and Costa Rica have been bolstered by development strategies emphasizing growth and diversification of export crop production. In many countries in the region the results have been declines in food-crop production, growing dependence on food imports and food aid, environmental degradation, and increases in hunger and malnutrition.

In large measure, these outcomes result from conscious choices and allocations of resources on the part of power-holders, not from production-oriented agricultural constraints that can be addressed through technological innovations. In the final chapter of this volume, "Food Security and Regional Development," Jack Corbett makes this point when he discusses the alliance of interests between capitalist, large-scale agriculture and scientific research. Agricultural exports like beef, cotton, sugar, coffee, and newer entries such as vegetables and spices have received the bulk of scientific investigation, extension, and credit support. Output of these crops has grown in recent decades at the same time that food production has stagnated or declined. Further, although the majority of the population has not benefited from this use of resources, members of the middle and upper classes within and outside the region have profited substantially.

Clearly, the roots of the hunger and malnutrition so prevalent in the region are political and social in nature and are intertwined with issues of empowerment, equity, and the distribution of resources in society. Corbett, Diskin, Stonich, and Enge and Martinez-Enge raise concerns about what can be accomplished under existing political structures in countries such as Guatemala, Honduras, and El Salvador. They suggest that there is little likelihood that elites, faced with challenges to their positions, will implement significant adjustments in wage rates, adopt small-scale, producer-oriented development strategies, or opt for measures that will conserve natural resources. These authors suggest that instead of policies of redistribution of resources and power, more energetic accumulation on the part of elites may be the likely outcome. In Nicaragua, in contrast, where the political will existed to address many of the most pressing problems, the U.S.-backed contra war severely damaged the economy and slowed progress.

Empowerment at the local level, such as that which has taken place in Nicaragua since 1978, is a key element in solving the pressing problems of hunger and malnutrition in the region. Barraclough and Utting (1987) rightly indicate that unless the poor are involved in the process of problem identification and resolution it is unlikely that efforts to benefit them will succeed. However, the poor are not a homogeneous category, and attention needs to be paid to differentiating among the needs and interests of various constituencies. Perhaps most neglected in this sense are the urban poor, especially women. In Central America, much of the research continues to focus on rural populations and social structures even though migration to cities has increased dramatically in recent decades and the number of female-headed households is growing (Thomson 1986; Bossen 1984). Provisioning strategies used by women require additional research. Studies need to be carried out on the nutritional and health ramifications of the division of labor and the allocation of resources and responsibilities within households (Poats, Schmink, and Spring 1988; Bolton et al. 1989; Ashby and Gomez 1985; Dwyer and Bruce 1988; Wilk 1989). The results of these studies can be used to better inform food-security discussions at the policy level.

Although local participation and empowerment are important, by themselves they are insufficient in addressing the problems of hunger and malnutrition. The authors in this volume document the highly complex nature of the factors that create food insecurity. These factors often transcend neighborhood, community, or regional organizational domains and require state-level interventions both internally with regard to the redistribution of power and resources and externally with regard to international commodity marketing structures. As the authors suggest, the elimination of hunger has been difficult in Mexico and Central America because food security as we have defined it here has seldom been a goal of the state or of international donor agencies that have promoted policies of comparative advantage and agricultural export-led growth. Yet, ultimately, the destinies of these nations depend on fashioning means by which the poor share in a development process that enhances their well-being. Food security is one of the most telling ways in which such a commitment on the part of the state can be gauged.

References and Bibliography

Ashby, J., and S. Gomez
  1985   *Women, Agriculture and Rural Development in Latin America.* Cali, Colombia: International Fertilizer Development Center/Centro International de Agricultura Tropical.

Barkin, D.
1987   "The End of Food Self-Sufficiency in Mexico." *Latin American Perspectives* 14(3): 271–297.
Barkin, D., R. L. Batt, and B. DeWalt
1990   *Food Crops vs. Feed Crops: Global Substitution of Grains in Production.* Boulder: Lynne Rienner Pub.
Barraclough, S.L., and M. Scott
1987   *The Rich Have Already Eaten: Roots of Catastrophe in Central America.* Amsterdam: Transnational Institute.
Barraclough, S.L., and P. Utting
1987   *Food Security Trends and Prospects in Latin America.* Working Paper no. 99. Notre Dame: Helen Kellogg Institute for International Studies, University of Notre Dame.
Barraclough, S.L., A. van Bruren, A. Gariazzo, A. Sundarman, and P. Utting
1988   *Aid that Counts. The Western Contribution to Development and Survival in Nicaragua.* Amsterdam: Transnational Institute.
Barry, T.
1987   *Roots of Rebellion: Land and Hunger in Central America.* Boston: South End Press.
Barry, T., and D. Preusch
1988   *The Soft War. The Uses and Abuses of U.S. Economic Aid in Central America.* New York: Grove Press.
Barton, M.
1986   "Refugees in Central America: What Lies Ahead." *Refugees* 31:19–27.
Bolton, P.C. Kendall, E. Leontsini, and C. Whitaker
1989   "Health Technologies and Women of the Third World." In *The Women and International Development Annual*, vol. 1, edited by R. Gallin, M. Aronoff, and A. Ferguson. Boulder: Westview Press.
Bossen, L.H.
1984   *The Redivision of Labor.* Albany: State University of New York Press.
Brockett, C.D.
1988   *Land, Power, and Poverty: Agrarian Transformation and Political Conflict in Central America.* Boston: Unwin Hyman.
Brown, L.R.
1988   "Poverty and Environmental Degradation: Basic Concerns for U.S. Cooperation with Developing Countries." Paper presented at Michigan State University.
Buttel, F.H., M. Kenney, and J. Kloppenberg
1985   "From Green Revolution to Biorevolution: Some Observations on the Changing Technological Base of Economic Transformation in the Third World." *Economic Development and Cultural Change* 34(1): 31–55.
Collins, J., F.M. Lappe, and N. Allen
1982   *What Difference Could a Revolution Make? Food and Farming in the New Nicaragua.* San Francisco: Institute for Food and Development Policy.
DeWalt, B.R.
1985   "Mexico's Second Green Revolution: Food for Feed." *Mexican Studies* 1(1): 29–60.

Deyer, S.
  1986   *Military Expenditures in Third-World Countries: The Economic Effects.*
          Boston: Routledge and Kegan Paul.
Doyle, J.
  1985   *Altered Harvest. Agriculture, Genetics, and the Fate of the World's Food
          Supply.* New York: Penguin Books.
Durand, D.
  1984   "Killing Time Which Kills Us." *Refugees* 6:9–11.
Dwyer, D., and J. Bruce
  1988   *A Home Divided. Women and Income in the Third World.* Stanford:
          Stanford University Press.
Enge, K., and C. Whiteford
  1989   *The Keepers of Water and Earth: Mexican Rural Social Organization and
          Irrigation.* Austin: University of Texas Press.
Esteva, G.
  1983   *The Struggle for Rural Mexico.* South Handley, Mass.: Bergin and
          Garvey Publishers.
Garst, R., and T. Barry
  1990   *Feeding the Crisis: U.S. Food Aid and Farm Policy in Central America.*
          Lincoln: University of Nebraska Press.
Grindle, M.
  1989   "The Response to Austerity: Political and Economic Strategies of
          Mexico's Rural Poor." In *Lost Promises: Debt, Austerity, and Development
          in Latin America*, edited by W. Canak. Boulder: Westview Press.
Hemispheric Migration Project (HMP)
  1989   *Central American Refugees: Workshop Report—Central American Refugee
          Research Recommendations for Policy.* Washington, D.C.: Georgetown
          University.
Hollist, W.L., and F.L. Tullis
  1987   *Pursuing Food Security. Strategies and Obstacles in Africa, Asia, Latin
          America, and the Middle East.* Boulder: Lynne Rienner Pub.
Juma, C.
  1989   *The Gene Hunters: Biotechnology and the Scramble for Seeds.* Princeton:
          Princeton University Press.
Kloppenberg, J., ed.
  1988   *First the Seed: The Political Economy of Plant Biotechnology: 1492–2000.*
          Cambridge: Cambridge University Press.
Leonard, H.J.
  1987   *Natural Resources and Economic Development in Central America. A
          Regional Environmental Profile.* New Brunswick: Transaction Books.
Messer, E., and P. Heywood
  1988   "Hunger and the 'Green-Gene' Revolution." In *The Future of Hunger.*
          Boston: World Hunger Program, Brown University.
Otero, G.
  1989   "Agrarian Reform in Mexico: Capitalism and the State." In *Searching
          for Agrarian Reform in Latin America*, edited by W. Thiessenhusen.
          Madison: University of Wisconsin Press.

Poats, S.V., M. Schmink, and A. Spring (eds.)
   1988   *Gender Issues in Farming Systems Research and Extension.* Boulder: Westview Press.
Redclift, M.
   1989   "The Environmental Consequences of Latin America's Agricultural Development: Some Thoughts on the Brundtland Commission Report." *World Development* 17(3): 365–377.
Rohter, L.
   1989   "El Salvador Striving to Regain Prosperity." *New York Times*, October 23: 30.
Timmer, C.P.
   1986   "A Framework for Policy Analysis." In *Food Policy: Framework for Analysis and Action*, edited by C. Mann and B. Huddleston. Bloomington: University of Indiana Press.
Thomson, M.
   1986   *Women of El Salvador. The Price of Freedom.* Philadelphia: Institute for the Study of Human Issues.
UNHCR (United Nations High Commission for Refugees)
   1989   "Dossier." *Refugees* 62:20.
Whiteford, S.
   1986   "Agriculture, Irrigation, and Salinization in the Mexicali Valley." *Mexican Forum, Special Issue.* Austin: University of Texas.
Wilk, R.R.
   1989   *The Household Economy: Reconsidering the Domestic Mode of Production.* Boulder: Westview Press.
Yates, P.L.
   1981   *Mexico's Agricultural Dilemma.* Tucson: University of Arizona Press.

2

Land, Labor, and the Crisis in Central America

Robert G. Williams

The wave of unrest that hit Central America during the 1970s and 1980s fits into a more general pattern of peasant uprisings that stretches back to the early colonial period, but the more recent crisis has been different in at least one important way. Unlike previous rebellions, the recent revolutions have not been so easily crushed with quick applications of terror. When traditional repressive measures were applied in the 1970s, people responded to government repression in a fundamentally different way than in prior uprisings. Instead of dividing the opposition, terror in the 1970s united the various opposition forces. Instead of forcing people into submission, repression in the 1970s made people fight harder.

The recent crisis in Central America stems from two fundamental forces: one, a traditional enclosure of peasant lands; the other, a modernization of agricultural labor relations. Both of these forces gathered momentum in the 1950s and 1960s due to the rapid growth and diversification of Central American agricultural exports. Together these forces increased the vulnerability of the Central American economy and further divided the society. When natural disasters and economic shocks

The post–World War II material in this essay comes from the book by the same author, *Export Agriculture and the Crisis in Central America* (Chapel Hill: University of North Carolina Press, 1986). Earlier historical material comes from a work in progress titled, "States and Social Evolution: An Inquiry into Coffee and the Rise of National Governments in Central America." In addition to thanking the University of North Carolina Press for permission to reprint sections of *Export Agriculture*, the author wishes to thank Jefferson Boyer, Marc Edelman, and Carol Smith for critiques of earlier versions of this chapter. All errors and omissions remain the responsibility of the author.

hit in the 1970s, the region experienced a social upheaval of astonishing proportions.

This chapter will first explore the underlying causes of the conflict, and then it will proceed to the immediate causes. Later, the policies of the five Central American governments will be compared in an attempt to explain why Nicaragua, El Salvador, and Guatemala experienced civil wars, but Honduras and Costa Rica did not. The essay will conclude with an assessment of the implications of current U.S. policy for long-run stability in the region.

Land and the Crisis

At the bottom of the recent crisis is a centuries-old struggle over land. What makes this struggle incomprehensible to most North Americans is that Central Americans hold two diametrically opposed views of the purpose of land.

From the perspective of the elites, land is for export. Elites recognize that over the centuries Central America's ability to import modern technologies and luxury goods has depended upon foreign exchange earnings from agricultural exports. The wealthy in Central America reflect with great pride on their ancestors, who carved from inhospitable territory the plantations of indigo, coffee, and other export crops. For most elites today, the ability to import luxuries, to go on shopping tours to Miami, and to educate their children in the United States, rests on titles to export estates. Furthermore, these titles define a family's relative social status.[1] But the titles to export estates mean far more than luxuries and social status; they represent civilization itself.

Perhaps the most beautiful physical embodiment of the elite view of land can be found in the San José Opera House. In the 1890s, this gemlike miniature of the Paris Opera House was constructed by Costa Rica's coffee elite. Materials and craftsmen were imported from Europe with foreign exchange earned from the coffee boom of the late nineteenth century. On the ceiling over the marble staircase is a triptych painted by European artists. The center panel depicts the bustling port of Limon with boxes of coffee, sugar, and other cargo on the docks in the foreground and merchant vessels with flags waving in the background. To the right of the docks is a grove of coffee trees where Rubenesque maidens of European descent blush as they pluck the red berries. The panel on the left shows a stand of sugar cane, and the panel on the right boasts a huge black man toting a stalk of bananas. Decidedly absent from all three panels are corn, beans, and rice. Land is for export.

In contrast, peasants believe land is for life. If a peasant family is going hungry and there is idle land nearby, it is a god-given duty to clear the land, burn the brush, and plant corn. In so doing, an ancient tradition is revived and the seed for future generations is sown. The act is at once practical and religious. In the *Popol Vuh* of the Maya, god created man from corn dough. By planting seed, humans are able to nourish themselves, and when they die, they return to the soil to become nourishment for the corn of future generations. Once land is cleared and put into productive use, it is a denial of life, a sin, for anyone else to claim that land. Even after more than a century of land-titling, peasants in peripheral areas today still cannot afford to obtain legal titles to their lands. Rights to land in these areas are governed by usufruct. Those who have put the land into use have a claim that is usually respected by other peasants. Land is for life.

Conflict has been the norm along the shifting borders between the two systems of land use. The struggle is more intense than a fight over territory because land and labor are intricately entwined. Elites discovered very early that if abundant lands were available to peasants, it would be difficult to secure a labor force. By denying peasants access to the best lands, elites could obtain labor. Thus, from the peasant perspective, the seizure of land by elites has a dual meaning. On the one hand, it means the denial of a life-giving force. On the other, it symbolizes enslavement.

Through the centuries, landowners have found that unless the idle perimeters of an estate are constantly guarded, peasant squatters will invade. Once the land is cleared and planted in corn and beans, the peasants are difficult to budge, for from their perspective, the land is theirs. Armies in Central America have been maintained not so much to guard the national borders from invasion by neighboring armies as to guard the borders of the export estates from invasion by peasants. If a large landowner is having trouble evicting peasant squatters, the local militia or unit of the national army is contacted, and it is the duty of that unit to obey the landlord's wishes. Landowners who have not had the stomach to apply terror at the appropriate times have lost substantial portions of their inherited properties to peasants. Hesitation is viewed by other elites as a sign of personal weakness and a danger to the whole system of labor and land control. Individuals who have surrendered their lands to peasants have become objects of derision at the country club or the opera house.

The conflict between the two systems of land use has exerted an ever-present force on the Central American landscape since the conquest, but during certain critical junctures in the history of the region the pressure has built to produce mass uprisings, which are followed by land reform and/or wholesale massacres of the poor. These uprisings are not random, but follow a pattern.

When favorable conditions in the world market create opportunities for a new export crop, elites use their influence in the state to acquire land suitable for growing that crop. Peasants who have cleared those lands are pushed off to make way for exports. At this stage there is local resistance from the peasants, but in most cases the peasants are not organized, so the resistance can be crushed quickly by military means, sometimes allowing for a long period of export expansion. At a later date, however, when natural or economic shocks disrupt the structures of control, peasants seize the opportunity and move onto the idle portions of the previously expropriated lands to reclaim them for subsistence production.

This wavelike pattern repeated itself at least two times during the colonial period,[2] but the most relevant period for understanding the recent unrest began in the 1850s and 1860s and lasted until the Great Depression when mass uprisings were brutally crushed.

During the coffee boom of the latter half of the nineteenth century, many of the modern-day structures of production were introduced, including private titling of land and the modern system of seasonal wage labor for harvesting. Out of national differences in the development of coffee there emerged differences in the structures of state control that persist until today. In Costa Rica and Honduras, the coffee boom took place relatively peacefully with small farmers participating in its production and elites capturing profits through the ownership of coffee-processing mills, export houses, and financial institutions (Hall 1978; Stone 1971). This development of small-scale producers created the basis for government structures that were more sensitive to the needs of small farmers. In Guatemala, El Salvador, and Nicaragua, however, elites acquired large coffee farms by expropriating lands belonging to the peasantry[3] (Cambranes 1985; Mosk 1955; Browning 1971; Levy 1873; Wheelock 1980). In these three countries state structures emerged that reinforced in a more monolithic way the dictates of the coffee oligarchy (Williams forthcoming; Paige 1985).

During the expansion phase of the coffee economy, land-titling laws, eviction laws, and security forces were created as a means of forcing peasants from prime coffee lands. In most cases where cornlands were seized, peasants were caught off-guard and resisted through sabotage and local acts of violence, but in Nicaragua there was a mass uprising in 1881 followed by a nine-month war that killed 5,000 Indians. In all three cases where large coffee estates came to dominate, armies were successful in carrying out evictions, enforcing new labor codes, and repressing peasant dissent, so that a long period of relative calm followed the initial resistance by the peasantry (Browning 1971, 201–219; Jonas and Tobis 1974, 30; Wheelock 1980, 76–78).

When the price of coffee collapsed between 1929 and 1931, it became unprofitable for growers to continue to cultivate and harvest from marginal lands. Workers were laid off, wages were cut, and marginal lands were left idle. Throughout the region peasants and agricultural workers responded to the stress by invading idle lands and striking against wage cuts. In all five countries, national armies were used to repress dissent.[4] The uprisings and repression were strongest, however, in Nicaragua and El Salvador, where the burst of coffee expansion in the 1920s was most intense.

In Nicaragua after the market collapsed, peasants invaded abandoned coffee farms in the northcentral part of the country, and Sandino's army defended the peasants when U.S. Marines or the National Guard were sent in. After Sandino's assassination in 1934, Somoza's National Guard conducted a counter-insurgency sweep of the area, evicting peasants from invaded properties and massacring whole villages where support for Sandino had been strong. Some of the estates were returned to former owners, and other lands—some newly expropriated—fell into the hands of General Somoza and officers of the National Guard (Wheelock 1980, 78–82).

Similarly in El Salvador, the depression disrupted traditional power relations and increased stress on the poor. In 1930 and 1931, peasants and workers formed mass organizations to resist wage cuts and to push for a return of lands seized by the coffee oligarchy. Following an earthquake in 1932, a mass uprising in the coffee districts of western El Salvador was followed by a wholesale massacre of peasants. Between 15,000 and 30,000 peasants, most of them Indians, died (White 1973, 97–101; Anderson 1971).

Unrest in the 1970s and 1980s closely parallels that of the 1930s. The decades preceding the outbreaks of unrest witnessed a remarkable period of export expansion. Exports were stimulated by favorable prices in the world market, but unlike earlier expansions, the U.S. government, the World Bank, and the Inter-American Development Bank directly subsidized export expansion. From 1961 when the Alliance for Progress began and 1973 when the first wave of crisis hit, the volume of coffee and banana exports increased 50 percent and 300 percent, respectively, levels that were roughly maintained by the time of the second wave of crisis in 1978. More importantly, a host of new products were exported during this period. Especially notable were cotton, sugar, and beef. During the 1950s cotton became an important export, and during the 1960s cotton surpassed bananas as the region's second largest earner of foreign exchange. Forty thousand acres were devoted to cotton in 1950; the cotton boom claimed some 1.2 million acres by 1978, when Central American exports made up 8 percent of the world cotton trade.

Following Castro's rise to power in Cuba, Central America was allocated a portion of Cuba's sugar and beef quotas, permitting Central American producers favorable access to the lucrative U.S. market. From 1961 to 1973, sugar and beef exports increased sixfold. By 1978 when the second wave of crisis hit, Central American sugar exports had risen sevenfold over 1961 levels, and beef exports expanded to nine times 1961 levels, making up more than 15 percent of U.S. beef imports (SIECA 1973; SIECA 1981; Williams 1986).

Some exports came to be cultivated on lands already claimed by large landowners, but others pushed over into the domain of the peasants. As happened during previous export booms, when peasant lands were taken in the 1960s violent clashes occurred, but resistance remained local and was successfully dealt with by the use of military force. It was not until the natural and economic shocks of the 1970s that massive land invasions occurred and armies of peasants began to form in the countryside.

Cattle Evictions, Peasant Resistance, and Repression

The export that contributed most to struggles over land was beef. Coffee, bananas, cotton, sugar, and other export crops all required extremely fertile soils for profitable cultivation. For the most part, the lands suitable for these crops had already been claimed by large land-owners during the nineteenth and early twentieth centuries, and therefore the switch to these exports did not immediately trigger peasant resistance. In contrast, cattle could be raised practically anywhere grass would grow. Once they had filled existing haciendas, cattlemen—with help from AID and multilateral lending institutions—extended their pastures into un-titled areas cleared by peasants (Williams 1986, Chaps. 4–6).

In the 1960s, after the first export packing plants had been built, a repeated series of events began to be reported from the cattle boom zones throughout Central America. The following is a typical cattle eviction story. Don Emilio, a local rancher, receives a beef development loan from the national development bank, which in turn received money from AID or a Washington development bank. With the proceeds of the loan, Don Emilio purchases barbed wire, imports purebred Brahman bulls, and hires a team of men. He instructs his men to fence in a cleared area adjacent to his present ranch.[5] The area to be turned into pasture includes a settlement of peasants, who have cleared the land of forests and are raising corn and beans. The peasants are given notice that the land belongs to Don Emilio and they must move.[6] The peasants do not budge. From their perspective, they cleared the land so it is rightfully theirs.[7] Don Emilio's men arrive with guns and repeat the eviction order. The peasants do not move. After repeated threats fail, and after an offer to pay for land improvements is rejected, Don Emilio waits until a week before the corn is ready to pick. At this time, his men turn cattle onto the corn. The cattle begin to munch and trample the corn.[8] The peasants herd the cattle out of the fields and with barbed wire stolen from a section of Don Emilio's fence, they fence in their cornfields. Don Emilio's men cut the fence and turn the cattle back into the cornfields.[9]

After several repetitions demonstrate that the cattle-trampling stage will not succeed, Don Emilio calls for reinforcements from the national guard, the army, or the police in the nearest town. Peasant leaders are arrested and their thatched huts and cornfields are burned.

In the meantime, the peasants have linked up with peasants in nearby settlements, so when the arrests are made a committee is quickly formed to free those in jail and to protest the seizure of lands. Similarly, the peasants have contacted a priest, a lawyer, a schoolteacher, or some other sympathetic townsperson who can read and write Spanish. A list of grievances is drawn up to present to government officials, and a title search is conducted to see if Don Emilio has legal title to the area being enclosed.[10]

Don Emilio links up with other ranchers in the area, and a squad, usually composed of off-duty guardsmen, is formed. The squad proceeds to intimidate the peasant committee and those exhibiting sympathies toward the peasants. Those connected are threatened, and if they continue to support the evicted peasants, they are roughed up, tortured, and sometimes killed.[11] The peasants take their case to the national land court or land-reform agency, and they seek help from national peasant organizations, labor unions, church groups, university student groups, and other potential allies.[12]

The ranchers gather their forces at a national level, uniting with business and large landowner organizations. They pressure the national security forces to halt the peasant movement, they move to purge the land-reform agency of peasant sympathizers, and they pressure the legislature to close any loopholes in the land law through which peasants might reclaim land. And so the conflict escalates.

Depending on a variety of factors, the above-described sequence may be halted at any point or it may build until extreme levels of violence are reached. Often the case ends when Don Emilio offers the peasants a nominal payment for clearing the land and informs them of how difficult it will be if they do not accept the offer. When escalation occurs, it is inevitable that the local security forces will do the bidding of the large ranchers. This has been true of all Central American cattle zones regardless of whether they are located in "democratic" Costa Rica or "despotic" Guatemala. What has differed greatly from time to time and place to place is the way national governments respond to the conflicts.

The way national governments have behaved has been crucial in determining the degree to which conflict escalates. Generally, when peasants have felt that there is some room to pressure the national government to hear their side of the case, the escalation of violence has been dampened. In both Costa Rica and Honduras extreme levels of violence have been reached at a local level (Williams 1986, 180, 184), but national governments have been more successful in presenting a fair image when grievances reach the national level.

In contrast, when peasants perceive the national government siding unconditionally with the large ranchers, peasant armies have formed to defend the territory. For example, the area where Nicaraguan peasants first joined the Sandinista army was the most important cattle boom zone in the country. Two years before the peasant army formed, Somoza's national guard had conducted a counter-insurgency sweep that cleared the area of peasants to make way for large cattle ranches (Williams 1986, 134). Similarly, in Guatemala, the massacre that triggered the participation of Maya Indians in the Guerrilla Army of the Poor was located on the eastern rim of an Indian-dominated area that was being developed by the Guatemalan army for cattle ranching, oil, nickel, and hydroelectric power. This massacre was itself a cattle eviction, whereby a national army detachment was brought in to help ranchers remove Kekchi Indians from a valley that was being developed for the beef export trade (Williams 1986, 147–151).

In summary, wherever export expansion extended over into territory claimed by peasants it called forth a response as ancient as the resistance to the conquest in the sixteenth century. This response was the same whether the crop was cotton, sugar, or coffee. However, because cattle ranching was so extensive and could be undertaken on marginal lands previously untouched by export agriculture, cattle evictions were more often associated with violence than evictions for the other exports. In this way the cattle boom zones of Central America became the scenes of peasant massacres, and in cases where the national governments allowed no room for peasant grievances, peasant armies formed in retaliation. In the sense that the export boom of the 1960s claimed lands believed by the peasants to be rightfully theirs, the crisis of the 1970s and 1980s is but the modern-day repetition of peasant uprisings in the past. But the current uprising far exceeds the intensity of previous ones, a factor that has a material basis not so much in the enclosure of peasant lands as in the modernization of agricultural practices on lands controlled for some time by elites.

Export Expansion, Modernization, and
the Buildup to Crisis

During the 1960s, all of Central America's major exports were modernized to a certain degree, but for a number of reasons, modern agricultural techniques were introduced first and most thoroughly in cotton growing. Cotton's vulnerability to insects required growers to rely on agribusiness dealerships for newly developed pesticides like DDT and toxaphene. Agribusiness dealerships not only supplied insecticides but also chemical fertilizers, hybrid seeds, herbicides, and other modern inputs. Because of cotton's short growing season and heavy cash needs, cotton growers came to depend on short-term bank finance to a much greater extent than growers of other crops. The reliance on bank finance facilitated the introduction of a wide range of inputs.[13] Furthermore, the flat lands of the Pacific coastal plain where cotton came to be cultivated were easily worked with tractors. During the 1950s, there was a shift from oxen to tractors in the cotton belt, and with the tractors came attachments for plowing, cultivating, spraying, and mowing. As news of high yields and high profits spread along the coastal plain, more and more landowners turned their lands into cotton fields, and with the cotton came airplanes, tractors, agrichemicals, and bank finance. For the above reasons, cotton growing came to symbolize man's conquest of nature with modern imported technology. In addition to higher money profits for growers and suppliers, the change in technology had profound effects on people's connections with the land, with markets, and, ultimately, with each other.

Unlike much of the land that was turned into pasture, the land that was turned into cotton fields was prime cropland that had been claimed by large landowners for several generations (Williams 1986, chap. 2). Unlike the case of cattle expansion, the switch from corn to cotton was usually peaceful. It involved the landlord demanding rent in cash instead of the customary corn, a rental arrangement that most peasants could not afford. The move from prime cornlands placed peasants under duress, but it did not normally evoke resistance on their part because, unlike cattle evictions, it did not tamper with their beliefs about rights to land. The landlord had exercised a claim over those properties for years, and the choice to stay or move was placed squarely on the peasants (Williams 1986, chap. 3).

Cotton claimed the highest yielding cornlands in Central America, forcing those who moved to scrape harder for survival. But cotton's contribution to social instability was not so much the way it impoverished people as the way it changed the relationship between the large landowner and his agricultural workforce.

In the era of corn and oxen, the interrelationships between the owner of the estate and the large number of peasant families living permanently on the estate extended well beyond interchanges associated with work. A web of mutual obligations and duties, reinforced by religion, bound landlord to peasant and vice versa. Basically, the landlord was expected to be charitable and look out for his flock in times of stress, and peasants were expected to be humble and to serve their master on earth so that theirs would be the kingdom of heaven in the hereafter.

With the cash influx that cotton brought to the flatlands of Central America, landowners found that much larger money profits could be earned by mechanizing. Bank finance was easy to obtain for cotton cultivation, and with financing, tractors could be obtained. The introduction of tractors rid the landowner of the need for a large staff to care for oxen year round, and agribusiness suppliers offered all sorts of tractor attachments and chemicals that substituted for human labor at other stages of cultivation. Peasants who were once viewed as essential for the prosperity of an estate began to be seen as excess baggage. Landlords did much better profit-wise to retain a small permanent staff of semiskilled tractor drivers on the estate and turn the peasant parcels into cotton fields. Large landowners who did not take the initiative to become growers themselves could double or triple their earnings simply by evicting peasants and renting the land to cotton growers (Satterthwaite 1971, 222–226).

Large pulses of unskilled labor for weeding and thinning could be hired on a part-time basis from the pool of landless workers that appeared in the slums of the coastal towns, along road rights-of-way, and along rocky river channels. At harvest time the labor needs were so great that cotton growers sent recruiters to the slums of the capital cities or to peasant zones in the least accessible and most barren sections of the country. Those recruited for the harvest from the local labor market returned home every night, but those imported from afar spent the duration of their contracts in makeshift barracks on the cotton plantations. In addition to the money saved from the harvest, many workers returned to their highland communities with intestinal parasites, malaria, and disorders associated with insecticide poisoning (Schmid 1967; ICAITI 1977; Bataillon and Lebot 1976, 66–67).

The eviction of permanent laborers from the large estates and the shift to part-time wage labor began in cotton, but it did not remain limited to cotton for very long. When declining cotton prices and insect infestations lowered the profitability of cotton in the late 1960s, growers switched to other crops, but they did not switch back to the old methods of production. Oxen were not returned to the fields, even when landowners switched production back to corn. The same airplanes that had been used to dust the cotton came to be used in the cultivation of sugar cane and rice. The agribusiness dealerships that had been supplying growers with technology for raising cotton inputs continued supplying hybrid seeds, herbicides, pesticides, fertilizer, and tractor attachments for whatever crops farmers decided to grow. In this respect, the cotton revolution was irreversible. By the mid-1960s, coffee growers began using herbicides and other labor-saving techniques, which permitted the mass expulsion of *colonos*, or permanent laborers, from the large coffee estates.[14]

It was poorly understood by landowners that agricultural modernization meant more than an increase in profits. With each tractor purchased came the potential for an expansion of earnings, but only at the loss of the number of subjects under a landlord's direct control. Once the economic basis of paternalistic rule was destroyed, soon thereafter came a dissolution of the religion that had gone with it. Landowners still went to mass in the churches where the old-time religion was preached, and they continued to exercise their old duties toward their house servants and permanent staff, but it no longer made sense to look after the entire flock when the flock was an unruly crowd of seasonal migrants imported from afar, sometimes from a neighboring country.

Nor did it make sense in the new setting for migrant laborers to be humble and serve their masters when the master was no longer a person, but a corporation, and corporate responsibility ended with the payment of a money wage. In the zones where the seasonal migrants congregated, in the slums of the larger towns and capital cities and in the barren stretches yet untouched by commercial agriculture, a new religion took hold. The new Christianity embraced the peasant concept of the right to land for life, and it offered hope for leaving the house of bondage and entering the promised land. The landlord's position in the celestial hierarchy changed. Instead of occupying the place of a benefactor located somewhere between the peasant and God, the landowner found himself in the position of an evil pharaoh. In the place of a reward to be received in heaven, God's kingdom was promised on earth.

During the decade of the 1960s, all sorts of organizations of the poor began to appear. Farmworker organizations began to demand increases in the minimum agricultural wage and improvement in health conditions on the plantations. Slumdweller associations began to demand water, electricity, and a halt to periodic evictions by the police. Peasant leagues began to press for land reform. Problems that were once worked out in a personal give-and-take between landlord and peasant were increasingly pushed into the domain of the state.

In addition to dissolving the glue that once held the rural order together, the modernization of agriculture also increased the instability of the region by making both landlord and agricultural workforce more dependent on a fluctuating market for survival. The landlord not only had the traditional worry of the fluctuating price of the harvested crop but also had new worries about the costs of insecticide, fertilizer, seed, tractors, diesel fuel, parts, wage labor, and credit. The seasonal worker no longer had the security of a small plot to raise food on. Survival became closely tied to the demand for wage labor, the wage rate, and the prices of food, transportation, and other commodities purchased with the money wage.

During years of worldwide prosperity, the mounting tensions from agricultural modernization went practically unnoticed, and governments had sufficient revenues for minor reforms and repression. It was not until the 1970s when the world crisis hit that the export boom's contribution to instability was fully revealed.

U.S. Policy and the Buildup to Crisis

By the time the economic shocks of the 1970s hit, Central America was divided into two hostile camps. At the center of one camp stood the export oligarchy, changed by more than a decade of export-led growth and technological adaptation but clinging ever more desperately to a vision of civilization inherited from the past. At the center of the other camp stood the Central American peasantry, whose way of life had been radically altered by those selfsame pressures of agricultural modernization and export diversification, but whose vision of civilization looked to a future free of the oligarchy.

Throughout the 1960s, U.S. policy toward Central America nourished a monstrous contradiction. On the military front, the oligarchy was provided a modern, well-equipped repression apparatus, capable of gathering intelligence and terrorizing the newly forming grassroots groups and their sympathizers. On the economic front, the wealth of the oligarchy was enhanced by the new opportunities for investment generated by export diversification and modernization. On the other side, Washington's modernization and export diversification program helped create the class of landless peasants and slumdwellers that moved outside of the traditional day-to-day control of the large landowners. It also brought into open dispute territories long claimed by peasants, thereby creating the conditions for the formation of peasant leagues and armed bands of peasants. While a repressive military apparatus was being equipped and trained for the oligarchy, Washington was denying the wishes of the oligarchy by funding land and other social reforms.

Efforts to mediate the conflict between the two camps were made far more difficult by earthquakes, hurricanes, and economic shocks in the

1970s. The shocks struck at the economic bases of both camps, reduced the economic space for compromise, eroded the fiscal capacities of governments to respond, and unleashed fears and hostilities that had accumulated for years.

World System Shocks: Impact on the Elites

For the elites, the world economic crisis exposed the vulnerability of relying on imported inputs and international credit. During the 1950s and 1960s, reliance on bank credit and tractors, hybrid seeds and chemicals, veterinary medicines and other purchased inputs, produced rapid accumulation of wealth. When the crisis hit, dependence on the market spelled disaster.

The two oil price explosions, 1973 to 1975 and late 1977 to 1981, sent fertilizer, pesticide, and tractor fuel prices spiraling upwards, but coffee, cotton, and beef prices were dampened by the most severe worldwide recessions since the 1930s. The acute anxiety felt by elites during the first wave of world crisis was mitigated in 1976 and 1977 by a recovery of prices of agricultural exports. However, when the second round of oil price inflation and recession hit in the late 1970s and early 1980s, anxiety returned to the elite camp. What made the profit squeeze unbearable was the behavior of interest rates. During both waves of world economic crisis, the cost of borrowing funds from the international banking system skyrocketed, a pressure quickly transmitted through local banking systems.

The waves of crisis made the oligarchy more intransigent than ever on the issue of land rights. Many elites found themselves overextended and having to borrow more from the banks. In order to stay afloat, elites had to mortgage more land. To grant a mortgage on a piece of land in Central America, the banker must not only see the title to the property but must be convinced that the titleholder can exercise effective control over that land. Otherwise, in the event of a default, the bank might end up with a piece of property infested with squatters. With pressures for land reform building up, control over idle properties became particularly suspect from the bankers' viewpoint at precisely the time when landowners were demanding more credit.

World economic pressures, completely outside of the control of local elites, reinforced to the point of passion their traditional view of land. Not only did the idle perimeters of their titled estates have to be more heavily guarded against peasant invasions, but land areas open to dispute had to be titled and brought under their control for use as collateral for loans.

The same world economic pressures that made elites cling to an absolutist position regarding land rights also reinforced an absolutist position regarding labor. A sense of helplessness spread through the elite camp as prices of oil, fertilizer, pesticide, tractors, and credit escalated. Practically the only commodity produced locally, and therefore, subject to landowner influence, was wage labor. Any move by farmworkers, government agencies, or USAID that might lessen landowner dominance over the local labor supply had to be resisted.

With the onslaught of the world economic crisis, the oligarchy felt desperate and cornered. To give up one square inch of territory under these conditions was seen as an invitation for the ill-bred to swarm onto the large estates. To make a single concession to organized labor, even in a sector other than agriculture, was seen as an invitation for the seasonal labor force to form unions and raise the agricultural wage. To give up in the slightest way their absolute right to control land and labor came to be seen by the Central American elites as a move down the road toward Cuba. If elites permitted any softening of these inherited rights today, not far down the road they would find themselves with no rights at all.

To hold on to their accustomed way of life, the oligarchy found it increasingly necessary to call on their traditional allies in the security forces. Encroachments by the poor had to be checked, lest the civilization inherited from the past fall into ruin.

World System Shocks: Impact on the Poor

The world crisis hit the poor earlier than it hit the elites. It also hit the poor harder. The elites were at first able to pass on some of their rising costs before recessions dampened export prices, and when the recessions struck, the elites' anxiety could at least be temporarily relieved by bank loans. The average person was not so lucky. With access to land squeezed by two decades of export-led growth, the majority of the Central American population relied directly or indirectly on money wages for survival. Expulsions, mechanization, and rapid population growth produced a market for unskilled labor that was generally glutted. The pool of landless or nearly landless people overflowed national boundaries in search of work, making upward adjustments in wages difficult.

Although money wages were held down by excess supply in regional labor markets, the prices of some of the most important items of consumption were determined by an inflationary world market. Furthermore, with the best lands taken for export crops, Central America could no longer supply its own food needs but had become a regular importer of grain from the world market by the early 1970s.[15]

This internationalization of the market meant a rapid transmission of world food prices through the regional economy. Glutted labor markets and inflated prices of basic necessities drove down real wages, the greatest reductions occurring during waves of world economic crisis or following natural disasters. The precipitous drop in the purchasing power of the money wage placed greatest stress on those with the lowest wages and those with the least access to land, whose money incomes were almost entirely spent on food and transportation, whose prices rose more dramatically than other goods and services (OAS 1978, 251–252; United Nations 1978, 1981).

To avoid starvation, people who had become dependent on money wages had several choices. One choice consisted of the traditional solution: moving onto idle properties to plant food crops. The other choices consisted of pressuring employers for higher wages or pressuring governments to freeze prices of basic foodstuffs, public transportation, and other necessities.

The waves of unrest that shook Central America in the 1970s were triggered by natural and economic shocks of uncommon magnitude, but the way people responded to the shocks was not merely due to the abnormal severity of the disasters. True, the shocks put large numbers of individuals under severe stress at the same time; responses to stress were not merely individualistic, but conditioned by years of experience in collective action. Peasant leagues that had formed during the 1960s to resist enclosures used their acquired skills and connections to coordinate massive land occupations when the disasters of the seventies struck. Farmworker organizations that had sprung up with the shift to seasonal wage labor in the 1960s staged strikes and used their previously developed connections in church and state to pressure for wage adjustments when bursts of inflation hit. Organizations of slumdwellers that grew up along with the slums in the 1960s reorganized to provide earthquake relief when Managua and Guatemala City were leveled in 1972 and 1976.

People in the camp of the poor were not only armed with organizational skills acquired during the preceding decade, but they were also armed with a new theology. If there were idle lands and people going hungry, the new religion saw it as God's will that people use those idle lands to favor life. If wages were no longer sufficient to cover the necessities of life, it was God's will that the peasants organize to raise wages. If earthquakes created shortages of food, it was God's will that people organize to combat hoarding and speculation, work to secure food, and distribute the loaves and the fishes to the needy multitude. If earthly authorities stood in the way of Life, it was God's will that the chosen people, the oppressed children of Israel, defy the authorities.

Government Responses to the Shocks

Similar pressures were felt by elites and the poor across the five-country area, but the nature of the struggles differed substantially from one country to the next. In Nicaragua, El Salvador, and Guatemala, conflicts escalated into full-scale civil wars, but in Costa Rica and Honduras, open rebellions did not take place. One key factor that helps explain this difference is the way national governments responded to pressures from the two camps.

During the first wave of crisis, local police in Honduras and Costa Rica responded to strikes and land invasions with the same repressive measures as their counterparts in other countries. What differed, however, was the greater flexibility of the national governments of Honduras and Costa Rica in dealing with pressures from the camp of the poor.[16] For example, at a time when local security forces were acting on behalf of large landowners, the army general, who was also the president of Honduras, was open to land reform. Between 1973 and 1975, Honduran peasants recovered some 186,000 acres of land by combining land invasions at a local level with coordinated pressures on the national government.[17] Similarly, when local security forces in Costa Rica were jailing strike leaders and burning squatters' huts, the national land-reform agency was mediating numerous cases in favor of peasants. In 1975 alone, the national government of Costa Rica acquired some 40,000 acres of land from United Brands and began turning it over to peasants who had squatted there.[18] Furthermore, in 1974 when prices of food, transport, and other basic necessities skyrocketed, the Costa Rican government responded by raising minimum wages, with the largest adjustments going to agricultural laborers and other low-wage groups (United Nations 1974, 136). These policies infuriated Costa Rican and Honduran landholding elites, but a time bomb was defused because peasants, workers, and slumdwellers did not come to view their national governments as the enemy.

Following the pattern laid down in the late nineteenth century, the governments of Nicaragua, El Salvador, and Guatemala unambiguously reinforced the position of the large landowners. In 1973 and 1974, strikes and protests by Nicaraguan cotton workers, hospital workers, banana workers, slumdweller organizations, and university students were disrupted by the national guard and leaders were arrested. Meanwhile in the countryside, clashes between the national guard and peasants increased.[19] In 1974 and 1975, Salvadoran slumdweller organizations, peasant leagues, trade unions, student groups, and teachers' unions responded to military repression by linking into large coalitions or blocks. At this time, the national military began to disrupt protests by firing directly at crowds and by stepping up the use of death squads. Similarly, in 1973 and 1974, the Guatemalan military responded to the crisis by massacring peasants involved in land takeovers, by attacking public protesters, by arresting labor union, student, and peasant leaders, and by using death squads to assassinate public figures who advocated land and labor reforms.[20] In all three cases, the national governments closed off the possibility of appeal from below, thereby unifying the opposition against a common enemy. By the time of the second wave of crisis these three countries had burst into civil war.

Conclusion

The underlying causes of the current crisis in Central America are old and new. In the sense that today's crisis is a struggle between two incompatible systems of land use, its roots go back to the sixteenth century. In the sense that the poor in Central America today exhibit a greater ideological unity and a greater willingness to challenge the existing order, the causes can be traced to the recent modernization of agriculture, the shift to wage labor, and the consequent breakdown of paternalistic social relations. Both developments increased tensions in the countryside and weakened the social fabric so that when world economic shocks and natural disasters hit in the 1970s, unrest broke out. Where national governments showed flexibility in relieving the stress placed on the poor, social unrest was dampened. When national governments responded with military force, the crisis escalated into war.

Notes

1. Families that have held land for many generations usually claim a higher social status within elite circles than families that have only recently become landholders.

2. More than a decade after the conquest there was a two-year uprising (1537–1539) in El Salvador where Indians invaded haciendas killing the Spanish and their cattle (Browning 1971, 49). The three hundred years of colonial rule witnessed sporadic skirmishes, but large-scale uprisings did not begin until the end of the colonial period and the first two decades of independence when disruptions in ruling circles provided an opening for peasants to reclaim land. Peasants reclaimed land throughout the region during the post-colonial decades, but in El Salvador (1832–1833) and Guatemala (1838–1839) the struggles took the form of mass uprisings (Browning 1971, 142; Jonas 1974, 123–130).

3. Church lands were also expropriated, especially in Guatemala.

4. In Honduras and Costa Rica, the repression was concentrated on the banana plantations.

5. In his study of Southern Honduras, White (1972) found that "many of the larger landowners have title to a small piece of land but have extended the boundaries of their holdings out over adjacent national lands" (1972, 820). In the municipality of Langue, Honduras, Durham (1979) found that a local rancher whose wife had inherited a portion of land with legal title, illegally extended the acreage by enclosing some 5,000 acres of national lands. In a famous cattle eviction case in Guanacaste, Costa Rica, an ITCO (land colonization office) study found that Morice, the local rancher, had only 613 acres legally titled out of a total claim of 5,797 acres (Seligson 1980, 109). Newspaper coverage tells of the same pattern in other sections of Costa Rica. A ranch with 1,500 legally titled acres in a frontier area of north central Costa Rica was reported in 1975 to be claiming 5,000 acres (*La Libertad*, 22 March 1975). Another case was reported where 1,800 of 5,000 claimed acres was legally titled (*La Libertad*, 12 April 1975), and on one 47,000 acre ranch, the president of the republic intervened to stop a local eviction order on the grounds that the peasants were being evicted from "state lands" (*La Libertad*, 22 March 1975).

6. Sometimes a rancher will offer to pay peasants a small sum for having cleared the area of trees. If the peasants accept the payment, they are acknowledging the rancher's right to the area. If the peasants refuse to accept the payment, the rancher will remind them that they have no legal title to the land and that they cannot afford to hire a lawyer and a surveyor to acquire a legal title. If the peasants still do not budge, the escalation of conflict begins.

7. In these cases it is rarely known until a careful title search has been conducted which lands have longstanding titles and which lands are state land, and even then it may be difficult to tell. What is clear in these cases is that the peasants who have been working the land have a strong conviction that it is rightfully theirs and that the ranchers, local police, and local governments have an equally strong conviction that what is being done is, as White (1972, 831) put it, "important for the development of the region."

8. This is a tactic used throughout Central America. For a vivid description of the tactic as it was applied by the fruit company in northern Honduras, see Posas 1981a, 39.

9. In the case studied by Durham (1979), the fences were cut three times.

10. In Namasigue, Honduras, White (1972) found that some of the leaders of the small farmer defense committee knew the municipal documents well because they had held posts in the municipal government registering titles; the peasants were convinced that the land had been the property of the village and that because the village claim had never been legally alienated, the rancher's claim was invalid (1972, 831). Durham (1979) reports that one of the first actions of "Los Baldíos" was to get a sympathetic local lawyer to assist in a title search.

11. White (1972) found that in one community in southern Honduras where peasant resistance had been strong, after the homes had been burned, the head of the rural police had the peasants who resisted "strung up in trees in the patio of their house, beaten, and left to hang until someone dared to come back and cut them down" (1972, 831).

12. In 1959, the federation of university students at the national university in Tegucigalpa, Honduras, helped peasants of the south coast pressure the government to rule in their favor on lands that had been taken into cattle ranching in Monjarás, Choluteca; Posas (1981a) argues that this was a very important ingredient in the success of the action (1981a, 28–35). In Costa Rica, peasants who had been evicted from an expanding cattle ranch sought refuge in the recreation center at the national university, which became the launching pad for a national protest (*La Libertad*, 12 April 1975).

13. By the 1960s, cotton growers used more agricultural credit than any other crop in the major cotton-producing countries.

14. The trigger mechanism for the expulsion of *colonos* in El Salvador was a 1965 law extending the minimum wage to permanent agricultural laborers. Similarly, when social security deductions were extended to permanent agricultural workers in Guatemala, many large landowners used the occasion to expel *colonos* (Bataillon and Lebot 1976, 53). In both cases the process of eviction was already under way when the legislation was passed (Williams 1986, 59).

15. In the 1950s and early 1960s Central America was self-sufficient in basic grains; some wheat was imported and small amounts of corn and beans were exported. By 1970 Central America imported 311,000 metric tons more grain than it exported for a regional grain deficit valued at $26 million. When the first oil shock hit in 1973 net imports of grain had climbed to 504,000 metric tons valued at $63 million, and by 1975 price increases raised the value of net grain imports to $117 million for a volume of 521,000 metric tons. Net imports of basic grains peaked for the 1970s in 1977 when they reached 973,000 metric tons valued at $142 million (SIECA 1981, table 150, 181).

16. At this time, the Honduran and Costa Rican governments behaved more flexibly than their counterparts in the other three countries due to a number of particular factors surrounding the Lopez Arellano and Oduber regimes. A more fundamental reason for the greater openness to small farmers, however, has to do with disparate structures of coffee production. As was pointed out earlier in this chapter, coffee production in Costa Rica and Honduras has traditionally been dominated by small producers, but in Guatemala, El Salvador, and pre-revolutionary Nicaragua, large growers have dominated. Since the latter half of the nineteenth century these differences in economic structure have strongly influenced the structures of the state. For greater elaboration on this point see Williams (forthcoming) and Paige (1985).

17. One-fifth of the land recovered in Honduras during that period was legally titled (Posas 1981b, 83–84).

18. More land disputes were brought before the national land reform agency (ITCO) in 1974 than in any other previous year. Between 1961 and 1975, ITCO resolved in favor of peasants some 118,000 acres of land previously claimed by large holdings and some 60,000 acres of state lands (Barahona Riera 1980, 119, 275).

19. *Latin America*, 25 January 1974.

20. *Latin America*, 1 June 1973; *Latin America*, 3 August 1973; *Latin America*, 10 May 1974; *Latin America*, 16 May 1975.

42

References and Bibliography

Anderson, Thomas
1971   *Matanza: El Salvador's Communist Revolt of 1932*. Lincoln
        of Nebraska Press.
Barahona Riera, Francisco
1980   *Reforma Agraria y Poder Político*. San José: Editorial Univ
        Costa Rica.
Bataillon, Claude, and Ivan Lebot
1976   "Migración Interna y Empleo Agrícola Temporal en Gua
        Estudios Sociales Centroamericanos 13 (Jan.-Apr.): 35–67.
Browning, David
1971   *El Salvador: Landscape and Society*. Oxford: Clarendon Press.
Cambranes, J.C.
1985   *Coffee and Peasants: The Origins of the Modern Plantation Econom*
        Guatemala 1853–97. Stockholm: Tryckop.
Durham, William
1979   *Scarcity and Survival in Central America: The Ecological Origins of*
        Soccer War. Stanford: Stanford University Press.
Hall, Carolyn
1978   *El Café y el Desarrollo Histórico-Geográfico de Costa Rica*. San José:
        Editorial Costa Rica.
ICAITI (Instituto Centroamericano de Investigación y Tecnología Industrial)
1977   *Estudio de las Consecuencias Ambientales y Económicas del Uso de*
        Plaguicides en la Producción de Algodón de Centroamerica. Guatemala:
        ICAITI.
Jonas, Susanne
1974   "Guatemala: Land of Eternal Struggle." In *Latin America: The Struggle*
        with Dependency and Beyond, edited by R. Chilcote and J. Edelstein.
        New York: Schenkman.
Jonas, Susanne, and David Tobis (ed.)
1974   *Guatemala*. New York: North American Congress on Latin America.
Kissinger, Henry, et al.
1984   *Report of the National Bipartisan Commission on Central America*.
        Washington: U.S. Government Printing Office.
La Libertad (San José)
Latin América (London)
Levy, Paul
1873   *Notas Geográficas y Económicas Sobre la República de Nicaragua*. Paris:
        Librería Española de E. Denne Schmitz.
Mosk, Sanford
1955   "The Coffee Economy of Guatemala, 1850–1918." *Inter-American*
        Economic Affairs (Autumn): 6–20.
OAS (Organization of American States)
1978   *Statistical Bulletin* (January-June). Washington, D.C.: OAS.

Paige, Jeffery
   1985   *Coffee and Politics in Central America*. Ann Arbor: University of
           Michigan Center for Research on Social Organization.
Posas, Mario
   1981a   *Conflictos Agrarios y Organización Campesina*. Tegucigalpa: Universidad
           Nacional Autonoma de Honduras.
   1981b   *El Movimiento Campesino Hondureño*. Tegucigalpa: Editorial Guay-
           muras.
Satterthwaite, Ridgway
   1971   "Campesino Agriculture and Hacienda Modernization in Coastal El
           Salvador, 1949–1969." Ph.D. dissertation, University of Wisconsin.
Schmid, Lester
   1967   The Role of Migratory Labor in the Economic Development of Gua-
           temala. *RP#22* Madison: Land Tenure Center.
Seligson, Mitchell
   1980   *Peasants of Costa Rica and the Development of Agrarian Capitalism*.
           Madison: University of Wisconsin Press.
SIECA (Secretaría Permanente del Tratado General de Integración Económica
Centroamericana)
   1973   *El Desarrollo Integrado de Centroamérica en la Presente Decada*. Buenos
           Aires: INTAL/BID.
   1981   *VII Compéndio Estadistoco Centroamericano*. Guatemala: SIECA.
Stone, Samuel
   1971   *La Dinastia de los Conguistadores: La Crisis del Poder en la Costa Rica
           Contemporanea*. San José: Editorial Universitaria Centro Americana.
United Nations
   1974   *Economic Survey of Latin America*. New York: UN.
   1978   *Economic Survey of Latin America*. New York: UN.
   1981   *Economic Survey of Latin America*. New York: UN.
Wheelock Román, Jaime
   1980   *Nicaragua: Imperialismo y dictadura*, Havana: Editorial de Ciencias
           Sociales.
White, Alistair
   1973   *El Salvador*. New York: Praeger.
White, Robert
   1972   "The Adult Education Program of Acción Cultural Popular Hondureña:
           An Evaluation of the Rural Development Potential of the Radio School
           Movement in Honduras," Mimeo. St. Louis, Mo.: St. Louis University
           Department of Anthropology.
Williams, Robert G.
   1986   *Export Agriculture and the Crisis in Central America*. Chapel Hill:
           University of North Carolina Press.
   forthcoming   "States and Social Evolution: An Inquiry into Coffee and the
           Rise of National Governments in Central America."

3

The Political Economy
of Environmental Destruction:
Food Security
in Southern Honduras

Susan C. Stonich

Hunger in Honduras has increased in the 1980s continuing a three-decade-long deterioration of food entitlements to the poor. Between 1950 and 1986, per capita production of domestic foods consumed by the poor—maize, sorghum, and beans—declined by 24 percent, 83 percent, and 44 percent respectively (FAO-PY 1986; SALA 1988). Overall, from the 1960s to 1986, the availability of these domestic foods, calculated in terms of daily per capita supply, declined by 31 percent (World Bank 1988). According to national food balance sheets, between the mid-1960s and the mid-1970s daily per capita available food energy declined 25 percent, reaching 90 percent of the daily average per capita requirement (Valverde 1986). By 1969 according to a survey by the Institute of Nutrition for Central America and Panama (INCAP), rural Honduran families were meeting, on an average, only 89 percent of daily energy requirements (1969). Food consumption surveys carried out by the national planning agency (SAPLAN) indicated that per capita daily energy intakes fell to only 80 percent of daily needs between 1972 and 1979 (1981). Further, CEPAL (1982) estimated that by the early 1980s, 68 percent of Honduran families did not have the purchasing power to satisfy their food requirements. More recently, the results of the national nutritional study conducted jointly in 1986 by the Honduran secretary for public education (SAEH) and by INCAP indicated that 40 percent of first graders in Honduras were more than two standard deviations below the height-for-age ratio of the World Health Organization (WHO) reference population, suggesting widespread undernutrition (SAEH/

INCAP 1987). The downturn that has characterized all Central American economies since then has further exacerbated the hunger that increasingly plagues the Honduran poor (ADAI 1987). Evidence suggests that despite thirty years of economic growth, a majority of Hondurans find themselves less able now than in the mid-1960s to obtain their basic food requirements. Food security continues to elude them, as per capita supplies of staples consumed by the poor have declined and as their capacity to buy food likewise has diminished.

At the same time, there is overwhelming evidence from Honduras (as well as from throughout the rest of Central America) that rates of loss of forests, soils, fisheries, and other crucial natural resources exceed rates of rengeneration and that ensuing consequences such as land degradation, watershed deterioration, and destruction of coastal resources have reached critical levels in many areas (USAID 1981, 1982; Warren 1984; Stonich 1989).

During the 1980s, Central America's military and fiscal crises attracted the world's attention. The findings just mentioned, however, point to two other interrelated and mutually reinforcing emergencies that are potentially more threatening in the long term: an ecological crisis marked by widespread environmental degradation and a human crisis characterized by growing poverty and hunger. The purpose of this chapter is to argue that both of these vital problems can be linked to the patterns of development that have been characteristic of Central America. The main evidence of this interaction comes from Honduras through the integration of national-level data with the results of village- and household-level research from southern Honduras, but as will be shown, the multilevel processes that have occurred in southern Honduras have been widespread in Central America.

Throughout the region, natural resource-based commodities are the principal means of earning desperately needed foreign exchange, and the percentage of the population involved in agriculture remains significant in all countries. Given the importance of natural resource-based commodities, it is not surprising that many development schemes aimed at contributing to the solution of Central American social and economic crises promote the expanded exploitation of the region's natural resources through increased exports of agricultural commodities, forest products, and industrial fisheries. Given the overpowering signs of environmental destruction throughout Central America, it is essential that development schemes be based on an understanding of the interrelationships between the economic changes that are initiated and their environmental and human consequences.

This chapter attempts to add to such an understanding by demonstrating the linkages between international and national strategies aimed

FIGURE 3.1 Research Sites in Southern Honduras

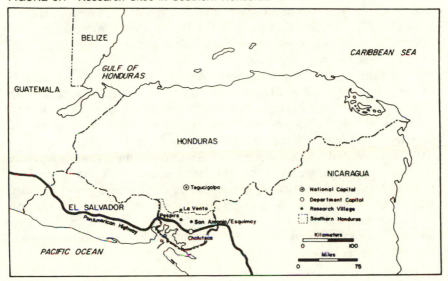

Source: Compiled by author.

at expanding export-oriented agriculture and trends in southern Honduras in agricultural development, environmental deterioration, and food scarcity (Figure 3.1). The chapter shows how the overall pattern of development has generated problems of both food insecurity and environmental destruction. The chapter begins with a discussion of how environmental and food security questions were incorporated into an analysis of the political economy of agricultural development in southern Honduras. This historical, political economy approach shows the close linkages among the dynamics of agricultural development, the associated patterns of capital accumulation, and the external and internal factors that affect environmental integrity and food security. This chapter gives examples that show how larger international and national processes evolve and influence both human and environmental sustainability.

Research Perspective and Methodology

This research used a political economy approach to show the close linkages between social processes, environmental deterioration, and food security. A political economy approach has emerged as one of the major frameworks used to understand agricultural development (De Janvry 1975; Crouch and de Janvry 1980) and ecological change in the Third World (Spooner and Mann 1982; Blaikie 1984; Horowitz and Salem-Murdock 1987; Little 1987; Painter 1987; Schmink and Wood 1987). In this study the political economy model was used to examine the important multilevel and intersystem processes involved in the expansion of capitalist agricultural production and to examine the capitalist approach to production as it relates to changes in the allocation and use of land and as it impacts the regional ecology and food availability.

This political economy framework demonstrates the uneven growth of agriculture in southern Honduras; that is, as commercial agriculture expands, certain commodities become preferentially produced by large capitalist farmers who are more efficient and who also control the available resources. Simultaneously, the small farmers' range of alternatives is reduced as their control of resources diminishes. The results are that an increasing proportion of total agricultural output comes from the capitalist sector while a growing number of resource-poor farm households are pressed to intensify their own agricultural production. The environmental outcomes of these processes have included extensive forest conversion, having as secondary costs both land degradation and watershed deterioration.

The expansion of capitalist agriculture in southern Honduras is shown to be a multilevel process that includes the reorganization of local, regional, national, and international systems of production, distribution, and consumption in order to facilitate the process of capital accumulation. Previous forms of social and economic reproduction are altered as the process and logic of capitalist accumulation spreads. The outcome is that producers at all levels—Honduran small, medium, large farmers, and transnational corporations—often find it in their best interests to move toward the most modern and productive methods of cultivation, management, and marketing, and to turn to the most profitable commodities.

The people of southern Honduras share many general economic, social, and nutritional problems. In order to obtain information about specific and varying economic, farming, cropping, and nutritional systems representative of the area's great environmental diversity, nine communities located in various agroecological zones were chosen for intensive study. They included three agrarian reform communities located on the coastal plains and six communities located in two ecological zones in the highlands.

The methodology integrated ethnographic, survey, and statistical data and documentary sources across multiple levels of analysis. (For more information on the research methodology see DeWalt and DeWalt 1982 and Stonich 1986.) Interviews were administered to an approximately 50 percent random sample of male and female households at least twice (once during the dry season and again during the rainy season) in order to obtain information on seasonal variation in economic/agricultural practices, diet, and nutritional status. Interview responses also reflected changes due to a continuing and worsening drought, increasing militarization, and local concern about the worldwide economic recession that has had a very serious effect throughout Central America. The female interview schedule emphasized economic resources available to women (including information on migration and a labor history), agricultural practices, household composition and family history, reproductive history, group memberships, beliefs about health, and use of health-care facilities. Data concerned more directly with food use were also gathered. A market-basket survey using a list-recall format and twenty-four-hour dietary recall of family meals and for all children under sixty months of age was also administered to women. Anthropometric measures were taken on all children under sixty months of age. The male schedules focused on economic resources available to men, agricultural practices, household agricultural production, migration, and labor history. A sample of households was chosen for more detailed data on household budgets and expenditures. A sample of land parcels was also chosen. These samples provided a means to document and monitor agricultural practices, insect infestations, production, and erosion. These approaches were combined with extensive ethnographic techniques. These included the collection of a sample of economically focused life histories in order to document and understand the economic decision-making processes of women and men as individuals and within households, the changing economic alternatives available to them, and women's and men's predictions about the future outcomes of the choices they were making.

Agricultural Development in Honduras

Except for the banana enclave established at the turn of the century and located along the relatively isolated north coast, the emergence of widespread agrarian capitalism in Honduras did not take place until after World War II. The transformation of Honduran agriculture is best understood in the context of the postwar global capitalist expansion, during which time the industrialized countries established new institutions designed to regulate the international economy, and national security concerns prompted the U.S. government to expand programs of economic and military assistance. Simultaneously, the United States and other industrialized countries promoted capitalist enterprises through increased foreign investment. For the first time, the Honduran government began to play an important role in the national economy and became an instrument of development, creating a variety of state institutions and agencies to expand government services, modernize the country's financial system, and undertake infrastructural projects (White 1977).

For example, the government worked with advisers from the International Monetary Fund to draft and implement a national income tax and to create a central bank and a national development bank. These measures provided revenues for development projects and established the means to channel such revenues into the economy (Posas and del Cid 1981). Critical highways were constructed in the early 1950s that unified the country, expanded the national market, and more effectively integrated agricultural producers into world markets. Simultaneously, the government began to provide credit through the development bank to stimulate the expansion of commercial agriculture aimed at the export market.

Agricultural development aimed at expansion of the export sector has remained a key element in U.S. policies for all of Central America, including Honduras. Such efforts were greatly intensified during the 1960s as part of the Alliance for Progress. This program came about in response to the events of the Cuban Revolution and was intended to improve economic and social conditions in Latin America so that further revolutions would not occur. Throughout Central America, the Alliance for Progress helped to promote the export boom (especially in livestock): export quotas to the United States were increased, promotional efforts were undertaken to stimulate trade and to modernize production, and credit programs were established to help expand the production of export commodities. These programs were all channeled into the region through the large landowners, merchants, and industrialists who made up the elites of the country.

Over a quarter of a century after the beginning of the Alliance for Progress, the United States again attempted to adopt policies to quell the raging conflicts in Central America. The Kissinger Commission Report (1984) recommended that as much as $12 billion in U.S. aid and as much as $6 billion from the World Bank and from other institutions (see Williams 1986, 190) be pumped into Central America during the 1984–1990 period. The promotion of agricultural exports is the principal component of the Kissinger Commission recommendation.

Expansion of Commercial Agriculture
in Southern Honduras

As part of the government's postwar efforts to encourage national economic growth, southern Honduras for the first time was drawn intimately into national, Central American, and foreign (especially U.S.) markets. During the 1950s and early 1960s, the United States, the World Bank, and the Inter-American Development Bank helped fund a variety of projects in the region. Port facilities at Amapala and San Lorenzo were improved; the Pan American Highway linking Nicaragua and El

Salvador with a section connecting it to Tegucigalpa was completed; a system of penetration roads linking the hinterlands to municipal centers and to the Pan American Highway was built; and government supervised bus lines were established (Boyer 1983). This period of intensified public-sector investment coincided with temporary high prices of primary commodities on the world market. Large landowners in the south historically had been unable to respond to favorable economic conditions due to the lack of necessary infrastructure such as transportation, markets, and credit. With the infrastructure now in place these owners found it profitable to expand production for the global market. The terms of trade later became unfavorable, but by that time much of the southern agrarian economy had been transformed.

A domestic capitalist agricultural sector emerged in the south in the 1950s and by the mid-1970s large foreign agricultural enterprises began investing in the area, competing with regional capitalists for land and labor. From mid-century to the 1980s, diversification and growth of agricultural production for export characterized the southern Honduran economy. Cotton, then livestock and sugar were the primary commodities involved in the transformation of the south. By the mid-1970s, these commodities were supplemented by sesame and melons and later by a wider variety of nontraditional exports (CSPE/OEA 1982).

Effects of Agricultural Development on
Food Crop Production for Domestic Consumption

For a time, significant increases in the production and export of basic food crops (maize, sorghum, and beans) occurred. By the early 1960s, under the patterns of trade that emerged as part of the newly established Central American Common Market (CAEM), Honduras was exporting considerable quantities of maize and beans to other Central American countries, especially to El Salvador, in exchange for their manufactured items.

The production of basic grains took place largely on small farms and did not expand at a sufficient rate to keep pace with foreign and increased domestic demand occasioned by population growth and by the growth of the urban centers of Tegucigalpa and San Pedro Sula. This discrepancy resulted in a decreased grain supply in the rural areas by the early 1960s (O'Brien Fonck 1972, 92). Except for grains, most of the market expansion associated with export growth supported large farmers. In the early 1950s, with the exception of coffee, export crops were primarily produced on large farms and the majority of traditional basic grains— the major human food crops—were produced on small farms of less than twenty hectares (OAS 1962). By 1974 (the most recent year for

TABLE 3.1 Population, Area Harvested, Area Harvested per Capita, Total Production, and Production per Capita of Basic Foods (maize, sorghum, beans, and rice) in Honduras: 1952–1986 (area harvested = 1000 hectares = THA, total production = 1000 metric tons = TMT, area harvested per capita = hectares/person, production per capita = kilograms/person)

Year	Population (million)	Maize		Sorghum		Beans		Rice	
		THA	TMT	THA	TMT	THA	TMT	THA	TMT
1952[a]	1.4	254	192	62	51	61	22	11	11
(per capita)		(.185)	(140)	(.04)	(.036)	(.043)	(.016)	(.008)	(.008)
1965[b]	2.0	279	237	60	44	66	30	8	9
(per capita)		(.139)	(118)	(.03)	(.022)	(.032)	(.015)	(.004)	(.005)
1966–71[c]		281	337	32	43	72	48	10	13
1971–76[c]	2.7	294	345	46	48	68	35	15	22
(per capita)		(.111)	(130)	(.017)	(.018)	(.025)	(.013)	(.005)	(.008)
1976–79[c]		411	450	67	43	76	34	16	25
1979–81[d]	3.8	339	407	61	49	72	38	20	35
(per capita)		(.089)	(107)	(.016)	(.013)	(.022)	(.012)	(.005)	(.009)
1984–86[d]	4.37	332	471	38	28	67	40	16	43
(per capita)		(.076)	(107)	(.009)	(.006)	(.015)	(.009)	(.004)	(.009)

[a]Data from DGECH 1954.
[b]Data from DGECH 1968.
[c]Data from SRC 1980.
[d]Data from FAO-PY 1986.

which data were available) such farms still made up 88 percent of all farms and continued to produce more than 70 percent of basic food crops (DGECH 1976). However, between 1952 and 1974, the percentage of cattle raised on small farms declined by 55 percent and the percentage of coffee grown fell by 18 percent reflecting national efforts to expand commercial production of these export-oriented commodities.

Since 1950 there has been a striking stagnation in the production of domestic food crops, but the production of export crops has increased rapidly. As shown in Table 3.1, both the area harvested per capita and the total production per capita of maize, sorghum, and beans fell drastically between 1952 and 1986. More generally, per capita food production indexed at 100 in 1970 fell to 69 by 1986 (World Bank 1988). At the same time, the production—in thousands of metric tons—of the major export crops (bananas, coffee, sugar, and cotton) increased 172 percent (computed from data contained in ECLAC 1987 and FAO-PY 1986) and the production of beef (principally for export) rose 267 percent (computed from data in DGECH 1954; USDA Foreign Agriculture Circulars 1959–1979, and FAO-TY 1982–1986).

The Honduran government has contributed to the stagnation of basic grain-crop production by placing price ceilings on basic staples as a way of maintaining cheap food for the growing urban population. Between

1970 and 1981, real farm prices for maize, beans, rice, sorghum, eggs, milk, chicken, pork, and a variety of other crops declined in spite of stagnating production (Larson 1982). Between 1980 and 1986, real farm prices for corn, sorghum, and beans remained the same or declined (IHMA 1987). At the same time, the government continued to provide subsidies to encourage export agriculture for foreign exchange: consider the disbursement of loan funds allocated by the central bank (BANTRAL) and by the national agricultural development bank (BANADESA). Between 1980 and 1986, over 70 percent of central bank funds was directed to the industrial, commercial, and service sectors; the agricultural sector was allocated approximately 21 percent of funds (BANTRAL 1987). Of the agricultural loans disseminated, only 2 percent were allocated for growing basic grains (corn, beans, sorghum, rice); the rest was allocated for production of export commodities (BANTRAL 1987). A similar pattern of capital disbursement is evident in the loans provided by the national agricultural development bank: between 1980 and 1982, only 5 percent of the loan funds went for the production of corn, beans, and sorghum with the rest going for livestock, cotton, and sugar—commodities produced by large farmers primarily for export (Stonich 1986, 124–127). Since then, the distribution of funds has changed somewhat reflecting government policies established in the early 1980s aimed at making Honduras more self-sufficient in the production of basic food grains. In 1986, 25 percent of all agricultural loans went for production of basic food crops. Most of the remaining funds were allocated for production of livestock, cotton, sugar, and various fruits and vegetables mainly intended for foreign markets (BANADESA 1987). During the 1982 to 1986 period, the amount of loan funds allotted to basic grains actually declined 12 percent, and livestock loans increased 216 percent (BANADESA 1987).

The combination of price ceilings and limited credit contributed to the stagnation of production by the small farms—the major suppliers for the national market. Nationally, per capita production of basic grains declined 31 percent between 1950 and 1985 (USDA 1985). As a result, Honduras has become a net importer of such basic staples as maize, beans, sorghum, and rice (FAO 1984, 103–104; Stonich 1986, 124–126). Between 1974 and 1986, cereal imports climbed from 52 MT (19.3 kg/cap) to 122 MT (27.1 kg/cap); food aid in cereals expanded from 31 MT (11.5 kg/cap) to 122 MT (30 kg/cap);[1] and the percentage of food aid in cereals to imports of cereals escalated from 60 percent to 111 percent (World Bank 1984–1988). Although between 1981 and 1986 the amount of corn imported into the country declined 17 percent (from 18,100 tons to 15,100 tons), this decrease was outstripped by a 73 percent boost in the amount of imported wheat flour and processed wheat products, from 75,000 tons in 1981 to 130,000 tons in 1986)—a shift that has resulted in greater consumption of wheat within the country (ADAI 1987).

Macroeconomic Factors Influencing Agricultural Development and Food Trade

Despite growing food deficits, the Honduran government continues to promote export agriculture (including food) in order to generate foreign exchange. Between 1980 and 1986, the average annual growth rate of agricultural production in Honduras was 2.2 percent (the highest of all Central American countries) (World Bank 1988). From 1981 to 1986, the total value of food exports compared to food imports climbed steadily from 253 percent to 573 percent (FAO-TY 1986, 45), with these earnings coming primarily from the export of fruits, vegetables, coffee, sugar, and meat (SALA 1988, 438).

Government efforts aimed at expanding export agriculture in order to generate foreign exchange are more understandable given Honduras's fiscal condition. Although the gross national product grew from 2 percent to 3 percent annually between 1983 and 1987, per capita GNP growth actually declined, with concomitant drops in wages, living conditions, and quality of life (ADAI 1987). Between 1980 and 1987 the annual consumer price index rose 146 percent for general goods and 127 percent for food (ECLAC 1987, table 222, 380–381). During the same period average annual per capita consumption dropped 1.7 percent (ECLAC 1987, table 27, 40–44). Demand for food, services, and semi-durable goods declined, reducing government tax revenues (ADAI 1987). In addition, between 1980 and 1987 the value of Honduran exports (at 1980 prices) fell by U.S. $55.7 million (ECLAC 1987, table 259, 458) and the index of purchasing power of exports declined by 12 percent (ECLAC 1987, table 258, 454–455). During the same period, Honduras's balance-of-payments deficit fluctuated between $100 million to $300 million annually, jeopardizing the country's international foreign currency reserve (which by 1985 had fallen to a one-month supply). Concomitantly, external debt rose 169 percent (to 73 percent of the GNP in 1986); external debt payments swelled from 19 percent to 27 percent of state revenues; and the percentage of earnings from exports that went toward servicing the external debt expanded from 10 percent to 20 percent (ADAI 1987). Despite efforts to lower the external debt, the ratio of the value of total external debt to exports of goods and services rose from 147 in 1980 to 324 in 1987, climbing 76 percent between 1980 and 1982, then increasing at an average annual rate of 5 percent from 1982 to 1987 (ECLAC 1987, table 14, 714). Given such macroeconomic conditions, it is unlikely that the national government will significantly reorient its agricultural policies away from attempting to expand export production. During the mid-1980s modifications in policies affecting agriculture did occur and were aimed at the diversification of agricultural production. But although an expanded array of commodities was encouraged, production was still aimed at the export market (ADAI 1987). In 1986, primary commodities contributed 83 percent of Honduran exports (World Bank 1988).

Ecological Transformations and Food Security in Southern Honduras

In the south, the expansion of capitalist agriculture affected the allocation of land and in the context of regional population growth exacerbated the concentration of landholdings (Stonich 1986, 139–143). At first, capitalist expansion was concentrated on large holdings located in the coastal lowlands but subsequently extended to include smaller holdings in foothill and highland areas (Boyer 1983, 1984; Stonich 1986). Regionally, the result was a reallocation of land from forest, fallow, or growing food crops to the production of export crops and livestock (Stonich 1986, 129–139). The change in land-use patterns was striking: between 1952 and 1974, the amount of land in forest dropped 44 percent and the area in fallow plunged 58 percent, while, simultaneously, the area in pasture rose 53 percent. By 1974, deciduous and pine forests covered only 13 percent of the region and pasture extended over 60 percent of the total land area. A more recent land-use classification by the Department of Choluteca (CRIES 1984) based on remote sensing data and field reconnaissance confirmed that pine and deciduous forests extended over less than 13 percent of the department in the early 1980s. Similar far-reaching transformations in land-use patterns occurred throughout Honduras: between 1952 and 1974 the amount of land in pasture increased from 41.9 percent to 61.1 percent and the amount of land in forest and in fallow declined accordingly. These far-reaching transformations in land use continue: between 1981 and 1986 forest loss in Honduras is estimated to have been 2.4 percent annually (LA Times 1987). These trends in land use were matched (or surpassed) in the other Central American countries during the same time period (Leonard 1987; Williams 1986) where annual deforestation rates were estimated to range from a high of 3.9 percent in Costa Rica to 2.9 percent in El Salvador and 2.7 percent in Nicaragua (SALA 1988).

A vivid display of the impacts of land-use changes in southern Honduras on food availability is presented in Figure 3.2. Since 1952, the number of farms, the area in food-crop production, and the total

FIGURE 3.2   Percent Changes in the Number of Farms, Area in Production, and Total Production of Corn, Beans, Sorghum, and Cattle in Southern Honduras: 1952–1974.

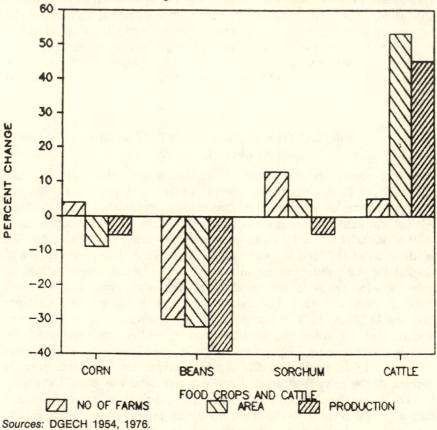

Sources: DGECH 1954, 1976.

production of corn, beans, and sorghum have stagnated or declined, but the area in pasture and the production of cattle has risen dramatically. At the same time, the number of farms raising cattle has increased only 5 percent—implying increased concentration of production in the hands of fewer farmers.

The augmentation of holdings for expanded commercial production, as well as population growth and in-migration, contributed to the further concentration of landholdings. This concentration especially excluded the small farmers, for whom land had become increasingly scarce. In general, greatest population densities and smallest landholdings were located in the highlands, the areas with least agricultural potential (Stonich 1986, 155–156). Nevertheless, farmers strove to enlarge production in these marginal areas by more intensively farming land already in cultivation and/or by farming previously uncultivated, steeper, and even more marginal areas (Stonich, 1986, chap. 6). Despite these efforts, per capita production of food crops in the region dropped drastically between mid-century and the 1980s; corn production fell 71 percent, sorghum 73 percent, and beans 81 percent (Stonich 1986: 137).

Although the regional expansion of export-oriented, capitalist agriculture initially resulted in the growth of wage-labor opportunities, jobs were limited in number and subject to the same "boom and bust" cycles as were the export commodities themselves (Boyer 1983; Stonich 1986). Declines in the prices of cotton and sugar led many large landowners to switch from these more labor-intensive crops to the much less labor-intensive but more land-extensive alternative—cattle raising. These decisions reduced the employment opportunities in the region and further aggravated the already unequal land-distribution pattern. Overall rural unemployment in 1980 based on the corresponding monthly supply of and demand for labor averaged 62 percent for the year, ranging from 16 percent in September to 95 percent in March. The increased amount of land in pasture and augmented livestock production did not lead to greater consumption of meat or an improvement of nutritional status: although the total production of beef increased more than 200 percent in Honduras between 1960 and 1980, per capita consumption of beef actually declined by 20 percent (DeWalt 1985).

After rising over 500 percent after 1950, beef exports reached their peak in 1981 and beef production topped in 1982 (USDA 1987). Between 1982 and 1986, beef exports declined 50 percent and beef production dropped 30 percent in response to reduced demand (primarily in the United States) and falling prices (USDA 1987). These national trends were apparent in the south where, by 1981, Honduran producers, unable to force up the prices paid for their beef in the United States, reintroduced on-the-hoof trade with El Salvador and Guatemala. By 1982, meat-packing plants frequently were shut down because of the lack of an adequate volume of cattle to operate efficiently (Stonich 1986, 117–118). Since 1982, national agricultural policy has been directed at diversifying agricultural production in the region; however, these efforts remain directed toward the expansion of export-oriented commodities rather than food crops (ADAI 1987).

The transformation of the agrarian structure in the south that included significant changes in land use, the radical fall in per capita production of basic grains, and restricted opportunities to earn cash for food aggravated widespread regional undernutrition. In 1979 the national planning agency concluded that 41 percent of all southern families did not have the purchasing power to meet subsistence levels (SAPLAN 1981). Analysis of the household/community–level data collected between

1981 and 1984 as part of the INTSORMIL (International Sorghum/ Millet Collaborative Research Support Program) study showed that approximately 37 percent of households in rural communities were unable to meet energy needs (Stonich 1986, chap. 7) and 65 percent of the children under 60 months of age were under 95 percent of the standard height-for-age ratio recommended by WHO (DeWalt and DeWalt 1987, 39). My regional breakdown of the results of the national nutrition study conducted in 1986 indicated that 36 percent of all first graders in the south were more than two standard deviations below the height-for-age ratio of the WHO reference population—indicating widespread moderate to severe degrees of undernutrition (SAEH/INCAP 1987).

Local-Level Responses to Capitalist Expansion

The development of capitalist agriculture led to socioeconomic differentiation of rural households and the subsequent requirement for many households to engage in a variety of off-farm activities in order to survive. This process of differentiation was dependent on a number of interrelated factors including diminished access to land, limited growth in wage-labor positions, and expanded opportunities for the investment of capital (Stonich 1986, 254–256). Diminished access to land made most farm households increasingly dependent on wage labor, migration, and remittances that came predominantly from family members living outside the household (Stonich 1991). Simultaneously, the evolution of a class of "rich" peasants depended on opportunities for realizing capital—particularly through cattle raising and through mercantile activities. As wage labor, cash earning activities, and short/long term migration became increasingly essential, the number of social and economic ties outside communities expanded and became more complex (Stonich 1991). Agricultural cooperatives, truckers acting as marketing brokers, and community members who traveled outside the community to take advantage of regional and national markets through the sale of their own produce, dairy products, and meat, all functioned as links in growing regional and national networks (Stonich 1986, chap. 6). Land-poor and landless peasants unable to produce enough for their own needs became integrated into the capitalist agricultural sector. Farmers with medium holdings who were able to produce enough for their families had little incentive to produce a surplus of basic grains. Instead, they and the large landholders continued to accumulate land, mechanized that part of their operations that they could, and turned more and more to export-oriented cattle production.[2] The regional trends discussed in previous sections were more extreme in the highlands where food-crop production fell drastically while the area in pasture rose 154 percent and the total number of cattle rose 68 percent between 1952 and 1974 (Stonich 1986, 170).

Food Security at the Local Level

Macrolevel external factors (such as economic dependence, foreign-owned debt, unfavorable terms of trade) as well as internal national forces (such as increased inequality in the distribution of land and wealth, export biases, government policies regarding access to credit and price controls on food items, demographic changes) fused to form a complex web of reinforcing pressures that affected food security at the local level. These factors linked to the socioeconomic differentiation and the environmental degradation that have occurred within many areas complicated the struggle of the rural poor against poverty and hunger. Earlier analysis has shown how the agricultural practices of each socioeconomically differentiated subgroup (that is, "rich," medium, and small farmers, and renters) resulted in mutually enhancing, deleterious effects on the biophysical system (Stonich 1989). To summarize, pasture is prevalent on most of the better lands that are owned by the larger farmers, but poor land-management practices result in much of this area being overgrazed. Poor farmers continue to clear steeper and more marginal lands on which to plant their subsistence crops and are also directly engaged by larger landowners in the forest-to-pasture conversion process. The result is enhanced deforestation and the concomitant genetic erosion of the faunal and floral species that inhabit the tropical dry forest environment. Soil quality deteriorates as fallow cycles are reduced or eliminated. Soil erosion is rampant with annual erosion rates of as much as 500 metric tons per hectare in areas already affected by thin topsoil layers (Leonard 1987). This rate is corroborated by extensive observation of severe gullying and frequent landslides. As a consequence, local agricultural production has been undermined and total yields and yields per hectare have declined despite increases in the total area put into production (Stonich 1986). Farmers realize all too well that they are working harder for a lower return. Based on aggregated community agricultural production and consumption data collected as part of this study, local farmers were contributing only approximately half the grains consumed by households in the villages (Stonich 1986, 271–273).

Contribution and Importance of Food Groups to Dietary Intake

Despite declines in per capita food grain production, rural highland families were highly dependent on such grains for both energy and

TABLE 3.2 Percentage Contribution of Food Groups to Diet in Honduras: National per Capita Supply Based on FAO-Food Balance Sheets (1979–81)[a]; INCAP Sample of Rural Areas in Honduras (1969)[b]; INTSORMIL Rural Highlands Sample (Dry season 1983 and rainy season 1983)[c]

Food Group	National per Capita Supply FAO-FBS 79–81	INCAP Rural Area 69	INTSORMIL Dry Season	INTSORMIL Rainy Season
Dairy products	4.5	7.0	1.2	1.3
Eggs	.5	1.0	.8	.6
Meat	2.4	5.0	3.5	2.4
Beef	(1.1)	–	(1.2)	(1.2)
Pork	(.4)	–	(1.7)	(.4)
Chicken	(.5)	–	(.6)	(.7)
Beans	4.3	11.0	1.4	1.0
Fruits/Veg.	8.8	5.0	7.3	6.5
Grains	54.8	50.0	75.3	77.1
Corn	(41.7)	–	(31.8)	(67.2)
Sorghum	(3.1)	–	(37.2)	(1.2)
Rice	(3.6)	–	(3.7)	(4.5)
Wheat	(6.2)	–	(2.6)	(4.2)
Fats	8.5	–	7.2	5.0
Sugar	15.2	8.0	5.5	5.8
Coffee	.2	–	.06	.0

[a]Data from FAO Food Balance Sheets (1979–1981 averages) 1984.
[b]Data from INCAP 1969.
[c]Data calculated from household surveys.

protein: grains constituted the majority of energy and protein intake and consumption of grains was highly correlated with the extent to which household energy needs were satisfied. Table 3.2 compares the *national* per capita supply of various food groups to diet as determined by FAO food balance sheets (FAO 1984, 103–104); the proportion of total energy intake represented by these same food groups as described by INCAP (1969) for *rural* areas of Honduras; and the percentage contribution of these foods as calculated for *rural highland* communities (once in the dry and again in the rainy season). It is noteworthy that according to the FAO food balance sheets and the INCAP study, grains contributed between 50 percent to 55 percent of energy intake. In the highland sample a much greater proportion of energy intake was provided by grains: from 75 percent in the dry season to 77 percent in the rainy season. Further, although the proportion of energy intake provided by grains remained similar in both seasons, the relative contributions of maize and sorghum differed significantly depending on the season. Consumption of sorghum was greatest in the dry season immediately after the sorghum harvest, although some families reported using sorghum as the tortilla grain for up to nine months of the year. Sorghum use was greater in the highlands, especially among tenant farmers, share-croppers, and those with less access to land. During drought years when the maize crop was lost, sorghum use for human food increased in both the highland and lowland areas. In general, sorghum is consumed by the neediest individuals in the population and by the entire population during times of economic stress.

Foods of animal origin (dairy products, eggs, and meat) provided 13 percent of energy intake (32 percent of protein intake) in the INCAP study and 7.4 percent according to the FAO food balance sheets, but only 5.5 percent of energy intake during the dry season and 4.3 percent during the rainy season according to the highland sample. Although for rural households beef constituted only 1.2 percent of energy intake and 3.4 percent of protein intake, consumption of beef significantly correlated with the amount of land owned ($R = .302$; $p <= .001$), the total access to land both owned and rented ($R = .299$; $p <= .001$), the number of cattle owned ($r = .654$; $p <= .001$), and other measures of wealth (Stonich 1986, chap. 7). These data provide evidence that the penetration of commercial cattle production into highland areas was having the most direct positive nutritional effect on wealthier farmers who also tend to be the livestock owners (Stonich 1989). Analysis of the relationship between the use of particular foods and the degree to which energy and protein needs were met or exceeded by each household shows that the use of grains ($R = .912$; $p <= .001$) and the use of animal products ($R = .53$; $p <= .001$) highly correlated with meeting energy needs in all villages studied.

Dietary Adequacy

According to the INCAP survey, which was based on data collected between 1965 and 1967, the average daily per capita energy intake in rural Honduras was only 89 percent of requirements although average protein intake met or exceeded 100 percent of requisites (1969). In the highland sample of families from which data were collected between 1982 and 1984, the range of household dietary adequacy in terms of energy and protein was considerable. For example, based on a one-week period during the rainy season, the mean intake for the entire sample was 114 percent of energy needs and 216 percent of protein requirements. These average figures, however, mask the diversity that existed among and within communities. The mean percent of energy needs met ranged from 100 percent to 128 percent depending on the community, and 34–57 percent of households in specific communities did not meet energy requirements. In terms of protein requirements, the average intake for all communities was 216 percent, but the mean for individual communities ranged from 181 percent to 250 percent. In contrast to the relatively high percentages of households that were unable to meet energy requirements, the percentage of households that did not meet protein requirements ranged from only 1–5 percent.[3]

Factors Influencing Dietary Adequacy and Food Security

In this study a number of factors that may have affected diet and dietary adequacy were considered. A number of variables have been identified by other researchers as potentially influencing diet and dietary adequacy including: occupation, income, land tenure, family structure, and commitment to subsistence agriculture (Valverde and Rawson 1976; Valverde et al. 1977, 1980, 1981; DeWalt, Kelly, and Pelto 1980). This analysis has included these and other factors affecting dietary adequacy.

Household Economic Well-Being. Here economic well-being was measured in terms of several indicators other than cash income. These indicators included a Guttman scale of household goods called the Material Style of Life Scale (MSL), the amount of land owned, total access to land (that is, the amount of land owned plus the amount of land rented), the amount of land planted, the amount of land planted per person living in the household, the number of large animals owned, the amount earned from the sale of animals, the percentage of wage earners to the number of people living in the household, and the estimated amount of money spent on food each week. The relationships of these variables to dietary adequacy are summarized in Table 3.3.[4] As shown, the degree to which families met energy/protein requirements was significantly related to the amount of land that the family owned, the total amount of land to which families had access (the amount owned plus the amount rented), the amount of land that the household had in cultivation, the amount of land in cultivation per person residing in the household, and the amount earned from the sale of animals. A similar relationship existed between this set of variables and certain dietary patterns; these variables were positively (and significantly) related to the percentage of dairy products, eggs, and meat (especially beef) in the household diet and negatively related to the percentage of grains (see Stonich 1986, chap. 7). In all villages, the estimated average amount of money spent on food each week was related to satisfaction of protein needs and to increased consumption of animal products. It is noteworthy that the percentage of wage earners to the total number of people living in the household was associated with meeting household energy needs more significantly than any of the other variables, highlighting the importance of off-farm generated income in enhancing the purchasing power of rural households (Stonich 1986, 1991).

TABLE 3.3   Zero Order Correlations Between Dietary Adequacy, Economic Well-being, Economic Strategies, and Household Structure Variables

	Energy Adequacy	Protein Adequacy
Amount of land owned	.210[a]	.178[a]
Total access to land (owned + rented)	.211[a]	.179[a]
Amount of land planted	.241[b]	.244[b]
Amount of land planted per person	.321[c]	.284[c]
% of wage earners to no. of people in household	.392[c]	.154
Weekly budget for food	.149	.149
Number of people in household	−.305[c]	−.193[a]
Household dependency ratio	−.242[b]	−.212[a]

[a]$p \leq .05$.
[b]$p \leq .01$.
[c]$p \leq .001$.

Source: Compiled by author from survey data.

Land Tenure. In an earlier analysis (DeWalt, Fordham, and Thompson, 1982), it was found that there were differences in the dietary patterns of landowners and renters in terms of their use of alternative grains. Sixty-eight percent of households owning land used maize exclusively (rather than using sorghum); only 44 percent of households renting land used maize exclusively throughout the year, reflecting the more limited resource base for nonowners of land. A comparison of household land tenure in highland communities with a number of variables related to dietary adequacy showed that in both the dry and the rainy season the mean percentage of energy needs met by landowning households surpassed that of renter households. Moreover, over time, the degree to which owners met energy requirements remained virtually the same (113 percent), but the mean percentage of energy needs met by renters fell by more than 10 percent (from 108 percent to 97 percent). This is particularly significant because this was a period of steadily worsening drought conditions. The fact that owners were better able to maintain their energy requirements suggests greater food security on their parts and also points out the vulnerability of renters to extended drought conditions.

Family Structure. Family structure is another factor often found to be related to nutritional patterns (Valverde and Rawson 1976). The ways in which this component was related to diet are also summarized in Table 3.3. Family structure was analyzed in terms of the total number of people living in a household and in terms of the "dependency ratio" (the number of children in the household divided by the number of adults). For the total sample, the average number of people in the household was 6.5 persons. For the total sample, the number of people in a household was negatively related both to meeting energy needs and protein needs, and the dependence ratio was significantly (negatively) related only to satisfying energy requirements (although the strength of this relationship varied among communities). It appears that the more people (and in some villages the greater proportion of children to adults) in the family, the lower the ability of the household to meet its nutrient requirements. This is not to say that large families could not meet their energy and protein needs, however; the patterns varied a great deal among villages. For example, depending on the community, from 47–71 percent of households with more than the average number of people were unable to meet 100 percent of their energy needs.

Coping with Drought: Households Under Stress

The steep slopes, erosive soils, and irregular precipitation patterns in southern Honduras make agriculture risky for rural highland farmers, who expect to lose every third maize crop to drought. The drought conditions that occurred during the period of field research persisted longer than usual, however, and provided an opportunity to study how households coped with continuing drought. Because dietary data were collected twice, a comparison of the extent to which households met energy requirements at both points in time was used as a measure of the food security of households. At both times data were collected, 48 percent of households were unable to meet their energy requirements and 52 percent of households were capable of satisfying their energy needs. The extent to which the *same* households were meeting or not meeting needs is suggested by the Pearson correlation coefficient comparing the percentage of energy needs met in the dry season with the percentage of energy needs met in the rainy season. For highland households this association was positive and significant ($R = .283$; $p <= .01$), although there was a great deal of variation among communities, that is, from $R = .114$ to $R = .421$ ($p <= .001$). For the households that were unable to meet their energy requirements at the time the first data were collected, 54 percent remained unable to meet needs, and 46 percent achieved minimum requirements by the time of the second data collection. In contrast, of the households that had satisfied their energy essentials at the time data were first collected, 41 percent failed to achieve requirements at the time of the second collection and 59 percent continued to meet energy needs. In sum, for all households sampled,

27 percent remained unable to satisfy their energy needs, 30 percent sustained energy requirements, and 43 percent fluctuated either from satisfying needs to not satisfying requirements, or the reverse—thereby demonstrating the dietary vulnerability of the majority of households. Households that had the greatest dietary security (that is, those that continued to meet energy needs) had access to significantly more land, cultivated more land and had more land per person, had a higher percentage of wage earners, and spent more money per week on food than did any other groups. In addition, this subgroup had the lowest number of people in the household and the lowest dependency ratio. Conversely, households that remained unable to satisfy energy requirements had the lowest mean values for all variables that measured well-being, the greatest mean number of people, and the highest household-dependency ratio. In between were the households that fluctuated between meeting and not meeting needs: those households were remarkably alike in terms of the variables considered. Altogether these findings point to the complexity of household characteristics and economic strategies that influenced food security and also demonstrate the dietary vulnerability of the majority of families in highland villages.

Summary

Data from the research communities indicated several relationships between development and the availability and the distribution of food. Socioeconomic differentiation associated with capitalist agrarian expansion left the large majority of families as (or more) dependent on off-farm employment, wages, and transfer payments for their subsistence than on their own agricultural production. Given the local social and ecological constraints, local agricultural production could provide, at best, 50 percent of the necessary corn, sorghum, and beans—that is, if harvested crops were distributed equally to all households in the communities, which they were not.

Although aggregated statistics suggest that nutritional needs were being adequately met (114 percent energy needs; 216 percent protein needs), energy and protein were not equally distributed among the families in the different villages. The uneven distribution of households satisfying energy requirements was related to a number of socioeconomic and equally important household structural variables. However, even if nutritional risk were minimally defined to include those households not meeting, or marginally meeting, energy requirements, it would be extremely difficult to devise a functional classification scheme that could be used to identify the households at risk. A scheme based on economic indicators would most effectively separate out only the most affluent households. Given the multiplicity of economic options exercised in the communities, a scheme based on *income* or *occupations,* likewise, would be inadequate. Given the overall lack of an adequate land base for most households throughout the highlands, access to land would not discriminate among the majority of households. Moreover, the size of a family and the ratio of the number of children to the number of adults were important predictors of adequacy, with larger, younger families at a disadvantage. However, generally those families who *owned* land were better able to satisfy nutrient requirements than were families who rented land. On the whole, however, comparison of the diets of households in these communities with national surveys shows that these villages are worse off nutritionally than the national average. As in many recent surveys, energy intake was found to be more limited than protein intake.

Conclusions

Since the end of World War II, an intricate network of external and internal factors have affected food security in Honduras. External elements (including economic dependence, terms of trade, and foreign debt) have combined with national forces (such as unequal distribution of wealth and land, export biases, and government policies) to influence food security at all levels. National strategies of economic development aimed at augmenting export-oriented agriculture (and other schemes designed to exploit natural resources) resulted in widespread environmental destruction and increasing poverty and hunger.

Southern Honduras was affected by this national strategy and underwent the growth of capitalist social relations that transformed the agrarian structure. The agrarian structure that existed at the time of this study includes a complex web of interest groups and classes that control various amounts of social power. Those groups that maintain stations of prestige and wealth also have a greater say in the realm of public policy. As a result, the ways in which natural resources have been utilized have been determined by the mandates of capitalist accumulation, and international and national forces have combined to affect the economic options of families in the south.

Although not specific targets of "development" schemes, the communities reported on in this chapter were affected by the attempts to develop the region. The concentration of landholdings made land scarce for small farmers. The spatial patterning of commercial agriculture contributed to densely populated highland communities, where shifting cultivation predominated and where export production dominated more sparsely settled and more fertile lowlands. Wage labor availability declined both within the communities and throughout the region (and the nation).

All of these effects of development schemes impacted people in rural villages. Despite the existence of a complex mix of household economic survival strategies, large segments of people in all communities did not have the purchasing power to satisfy their minimum energy requirements. Such households have been compelled to adopt agricultural strategies that have accelerated environmental decline. Resource-poor farmers often directly cause environmental destruction because they are forced to do so by existing social relations. They are under such urgency to provide a livelihood that the short-term costs of conservation efforts are prohibitive. For them, decisions that appear to be "adaptive" in the short term become maladaptive in the long term when multiplied by thousands of other households making the same decisions.

It is essential, however, to examine the systemic interrelationships among different power-holding groups before determining the causes and solutions of environmental problems. Although the agricultural practices of the smallest landholders appear to be the most destructive, such farmers have little alternative and, in fact, act as agents of the more powerful, larger landowners in the forest-to-pasture conversion process. In southern Honduras environmental destruction emanates from the structure of society and is intricately linked to problems of poverty.

The interrelated processes identified in this chapter that lead to destructive ecological change and food insecurity in Honduras are widespread throughout Central America (Williams 1986; Leonard 1987). The transformation of substantial amounts of land from forest or from growing food crops to pasture arose from the development efforts that were promoted after World War II. These efforts were intensified during the 1960s as part of the Alliance for Progress and continued to the present as shown by the Kissinger Commission report of 1984.

The result for rural areas was that large landowners expanded their holdings, in many cases driving small farmers off the land and thereby exacerbating the already skewed distribution of land. In the search for maximum profits, landowners invested in machinery, techniques, and commodities that reduced their need for labor. The result was that the percentage of labor force in agriculture declined and migration from rural to urban areas increased. Conversion of cropland to pasture and increases in livestock production were the most insidious parts of these processes. Livestock could be handled with very little expenditure for labor, and increasing the production of cattle depended on expanding landholdings because of the land-extensive nature of livestock raising in Central America. The increased inequalities generated by the Alliance for Progress and continued in present policies may thus have made revolutions in Central America "inevitable" (LaFeber 1982, 1983). The danger of the present course is that policies being implemented in the

United States, the multilateral lending institutions, and the Central American countries will lead to additional destruction of the remaining tropical forests, augment economic inequality, promote already unacceptable levels of undernutrition, and heighten the conflicts within and among the countries.

It is beyond the scope of this chapter to make specific recommendations concerning measures that could be taken to accomplish positive development in the region. In contrast to export-dominated development policy, assistance efforts must concentrate more directly on achieving fundamental changes in the social and economic structure of the region through meaningful land reform and equitable access to credit and technical assistance. In order to promote food security and reverse the serious social problems that are dominant in all Central American countries, development objectives for the region should entail: (1) attaining greater total production of basic foods, many of which now must be imported in order to compensate for the export of agricultural commodities such as coffee, fruits, sugar, cotton, and meat; (2) increasing the agricultural productivity of resource-poor farm families who presently constitute the majority of the population and who grow the bulk of the basic foodstuffs; (3) stressing the prerequisite of enhanced employment opportunities, including rural nonfarm jobs. These measures would boost the purchasing power of rural families, provide them the means to satisfy their nutritional requirements, ensure a productive workforce, and promote stable social conditions.

None of these goals can be accomplished unless international development-assistance agencies and Central American governments dedicate much greater efforts to the management and rehabilitation of the natural-resource base upon which all economic development in the region essentially rests. The economic and physical well-being of the majority of the people of Central America is fundamentally dependent upon production from the region's natural-resource base. The economic contribution of natural resources accounts for significant shares of national employment, export revenues, and income in every Central American country. Yet, throughout the isthmus, natural resources are being extracted, wasted, poorly administered, and steadily degraded. The destructive consequences of "development" are obvious in many parts of the region. Without the political and economic will to make the critical changes, Central America may be destroyed by development.

Notes

The research reported here was supported by the International Sorghum/ Millet Collaborative Research Support Program (INTSORMIL) through contract

#AID/DSAN-G-0149 and by two University of Kentucky summer research fellowships.

1. MT = metric tons; kg/cap = kilograms per capita.

2. Why landowners are more interested in growing pasture to feed livestock rather than growing basic grains or some other crop for export is made clear by comparing the potential returns on investment. Given the economic and environmental constraints in southern Honduras, there is a good chance that a farmer will not make any profit from growing grain (SRN 1980, 63). Estimates based on the "best-case" scenario (that is, where the market price is highest and the inputs lowest), a farmer would be able to make a profit of only about $75.00. This potential profit is not enough to entice most large landowners to produce grain beyond what they require for their own consumption. Those farmers with small holdings or those who are landless do have an incentive to produce their own grain. Grain production requires intensive labor and only minimal cash outlays, whereas significant cash outlays are required to purchase grains at retail prices (DeWalt 1985, 177–188).

3. Analysis of diets showed that the limiting nutrient in inadequate diets was energy. Although a large percentage of families, more than 50 percent in some communities, failed to meet their calculated requirements for energy, almost all exceeded their requirement for protein, even when the lower protein quality of grain-based diets was taken into consideration. (For thorough discussions of both energy and protein intakes as well as dietary patterns in the research communities see Thompson, DeWalt, and DeWalt 1985; and Stonich 1986).

4. No relationship was found between MSL and the degree to which families met energy and protein requirements. MSL was related, however, to the contribution of certain food groups to diet: It was negatively related to energy intake from grains and positively related to protein intake from meats. In other words, families who were higher on the MSL scale got less of their energy from grains and more of their energy from meats than did families who scored lower on the scale.

References and Bibliography

ADAI (Ateneo de la Agroindustria)
  1987   "Lineamientos para un Mejor Aprovechamiento de la Ayuda Ali-
          mentaria." Informe del Semenario del 26 al 29 de Octubre, 1987.
          Doc. no. 42/87. Tegucigalpa: ADAI.
BANADESA
  1987   *Prestamos Otorgados por Sistema BANADESA.* Boletin Estadistica. Te-
          gucigalpa: BANADESA. Mimeo.
BANTRAL
  1987   *Prestamos por Sistema BANCARIO.* Boletin Estadistica preliminar. Te-
          gucigalpa: BANTRAL. Mimeo.
Blaikie, Piers
  1984   *The Political Economy of Soil Erosion in Developing Countries.* London:
          Longman.

Boyer, Jefferson
1983   *Agrarian Capitalism and Peasant Praxis in Southern Honduras.* Unpublished Ph.D. dissertation, University of Michigan. Microfilm.
1984   "From Peasant Economia to Capitalist Social Relations in Southern Honduras." *Southeastern Latin Americanist* 27:1–22.

CEPAL (Proyecto de Necesidades Basicas en el Istmo Centroamericano a base de informacion de los paises y CELADE)
1982   *Boletin Demografico.* Year 14, no. 28. Santiago: CEPAL.

CRIES (Comprehensive Resource and Inventory and Evaluation System)
1984   *Resource Assessment of the Choluteca Department.* East Lansing: Michigan State University and the U.S. Department of Agriculture.

Crouch, Luis, and Alain de Janvry
1980   "The Class Basis of Agricultural Growth." *Food Policy* (Feb.): 3–13.

CSPE/OEA (Secretaria Tecnica del Consejo Superior de Planification Economico y Secretaria General de la Organizacion de Estados Americanos)
1982   *Proyecto de Desarrollo Local del Sur de Honduras.* Secretaria Tecnica del Consejo Superior de Planificacion Economico y Secretaria General de la Organizacion de Estadoes Americanos. Tegucigalpa: CSPE/OEA.

de Janvry, Alain
1975   "The Political Economy of Rural Development in Latin America: An Interpretation." *American Journal of Agricultural Economics* 57:490–499.

DeWalt, Billie R.
1983   "The Cattle Are Eating the Forest." *Bulletin of the Atomic Scientist* 39(1):18–23.
1985   "Microcosmic and Macrocosmic Processes of Agrarian Change in Southern Honduras: The Cattle Are Eating the Forest." In *Micro and Macro Levels of Analysis in Anthropology: Issues in Theory and Research,* edited by B.R. DeWalt and P.J. Pelto. Boulder: Westview Press, 165–186.

DeWalt, Billie R., and Kathleen M. DeWalt
1982   *Socioeconomic Constraints in the Production, Distribution, and Consumption of Sorghum in Southern Honduras.* INTSORMIL Farming Systems Research in Southern Honduras Report no. 1. Lexington: University of Kentucky Department of Anthropology.
1987   "Nutrition and Agricultural Change in Southern Honduras." *Food and Nutrition Bulletin* 9(3):36–45.

DeWalt, Kathleen M., M. Fordham, and K. Thompson
1982   "Sorghum as Human Food in Southern Honduras." Paper presented at the Annual Meeting of the Society for Applied Anthropology, March, Lexington, Kentucky.

DeWalt, K.M., P.B. Kelly, and G.H. Pelto
1980   "Nutritional Correlates of Economic Microdifferentiation in a Highland Mexican Community." In *Nutritional Anthropology: Contemporary Approaches to Diet and Culture,* edited by N.W. Jerome, R.F. Kandel, and G.H. Pelto. New York: Redgrave Publishing, 205–211.

DGECH (Direccion General de Estadistica y Censos)
  1954   *Censo Nacional Agropecuario 1952.* Tegucigalpa: DGECH.
  1968   *Censo Nacional Agropecuario 1965.* Tegucigalpa: DGECH.
  1976   *Censo Nacional Agropecuario 1974.* Tegucigalpa: DGECH.
Durham, William
  1979   *Scarcity and Survival in Central America: The Ecological Origins of the Soccer War.* Stanford: Stanford University Press.
ECLAC (Economic Commission for Latin America and the Caribbean)
  1987   *Statistical Yearbook for Latin America and the Caribbean.* New York: United Nations Publications: ECLAC.
FAO (Food and Agricultural Organization of the United Nations)
  1984   *Food Balance Sheets: 1979–81 Average.* Rome: FAO, 103–104.
FAO-PY (Food and Agricultural Organization Production Yearbook)
  1986   *Food and Agricultural Organization, Production Yearbook: 1986.* Rome: FAO, various tables.
FAO-TY (Food and Agricultural Organization Trade Yearbook)
  1982– *Food and Agricultural Organization, Trade Yearbook: 1982–86.* Rome:
  1986   FAO, various tables.
Horowitz, Michael, and Muneera Salem-Murdock
  1987   "The Political Economy of Desertification in White Nile Province, Sudan." In *Lands at Risk in the Third World: Local Level Perspectives,* edited by Little and M. Horowitz. Boulder: Westview Press, 95–114.
IHMA (Instituto Hondureno de Mercadeo Agricola)
  1987   *Analsis y Propuestas para el Establecimiento de los Precios de Garantia para Granos Basicos.* Tegucigalpa: IHMA.
INCAP (Instituto de Nutricion de Centro America y Panama)
  1969   *Evaluacion Nutricional de la Poblacion de Centro America y Panama: Honduras.* Guatemala City: INCAP.
Kissinger Commission
  1984   *Report of the National Bipartisan Commission on Central America.* Washington, D.C.: U.S. Government Printing Office.
LaFeber, Walter
  1982   "Inevitable Revolutions." *Atlantic Monthly* 249:74–83.
  1983   *Inevitable Revolutions: The United States in Central America.* New York: W.W. Norton.
Larson, Donald
  1982   *The Problems and Effects of Price Controls on Honduran Agriculture.* Minneapolis: Experience Incorporated. Mimeo.
LA Times (Los Angeles Times)
  1987   "World Ranking of Annual Loss of Tropical Soils 1981–1986." June 14, 1987.
Leonard, H. Jeffrey
  1987   *Natural Resources and Economic Development in Central America.* New Brunswick, N.J.: Transaction Books.

Little, Peter.
   1987   "Land Use Conflicts in the Agricultural/Pastoral Borderlands: The
             Case of Kenya." In *Lands at Risk in the Third World: Local Level
             Perspectives*, edited by P. Little and M. Horowitz. Boulder: Westview
             Press, 195–212.
OAS (Organization of American States)
   1962   *Informe Oficial de la mision 105 de asistencia directa a Honduras sobre
             reforma agraria y desarrolla agricola*. Vol. 1. Washington, D.C.: OAS.
O'Brien Fonck, Carlos
   1972   *Modernity and Public Policies in the Context of the Peasant Sector:
             Honduras as a Case Study*. Latin American Studies Program Dissertation
             Series. Ithaca, N.Y.: Cornell University.
Painter, Michael
   1987   "Unequal Exchange: The Dynamics of Settler Impoverishment and
             Environmental Destruction in Lowland Bolivia." In *Lands at Risk in
             the Third World: Local Level Perspectives*, edited by P. Little and M.
             Horowitz. Boulder: Westview Press, 169–192.
Perez Brignoli, Hector
   1982   "Growth and Crisis in the Central American Economies." *Journal of
             Latin American Studies* 15:365–398.
Posas, Mario, and Rafael del Cid
   1981   "La construccion del sector publico y del Estado Nacional en Honduras,
             1876–1979." *Revista de Estudios Sociales Centroamericanos* 15:86–88.
SAEH/INCAP (Secretaria de Educacion Publica Direccion General de Educacion
Primaria Servicio de Alimentacion Escolar de Honduras/Instituto de Nutricion
de Centro America y Panama)
   1987   *Primer Censo Nacional de Talla en Escolares de Primer Grado de Educacion
             Primaria de la Reppublica de Honduras, 1986*. Tegucigalpa: SAEH/
             INCAP.
SALA (Statistical Abstract of Latin America)
   1988   *Statistical Abstract of Latin America*. Vol. 26, edited by J. Wilkie, D.E.
             Lorey, and E. Ochoa. Los Angeles: UCLA Latin American Center
             Publications, University of California.
SAPLAN (Sistema de Analisis y Planificacion de Alimentacion y Nutricion)
   1981   *Analysis de la Situacion Nutricional durante el Periodo 1972–1979*. Te-
             gucigalpa, Honduras: Consejo Superior de Planificacion Economico
             (CONSUPLANE). Mimeo.
Schmink, Marianne, and Charles Wood
   1987   The Political Ecology of Amazonia. In *Lands at Risk in the Third World:
             Local Level Perspectives*, edited by P. Little and M. Horowitz. Boulder:
             Westview Press, 38–57.
Spooner, Brian, and H.S. Mann (eds.)
   1982   *Desertification and Development: Dryland Ecology in Social Perspective*.
             London: Academic Press.
SRN Secretaria de Recursos Naturales
   1980   *Los Granos Basicos en su Aspecto Economico*. Tegucigalpa: SRC.

Stares, Rodney
1972   *La Economia Campesina en la zona Sur de Honduras: 1950–1970.* Prepared
       for the Bishop of Choluteca, Choluteca, Honduras. Mimeo.

Stonich (Duda), Susan
1986   *Development and Destruction: Interrelated Ecological, Socioeconomic, and
       Nutritional Change in Southern Honduras.* Unpublished Ph.D. disser-
       tation, University of Michigan. Microfilm.
1988   "Integrated Socioeconomic, Remote Sensing, and Information Man-
       agement Procedures for Rural Development and Agricultural Policy
       Design." Paper presented at the Annual Meeting of the Society for
       Applied Anthropology, Tampa, April. Mimeo.
1989   "Society and Land Degradation: A Central American Case Study."
       Population and Development Review 15(2) (June): 269–296.
1991   "Rural Families and Income from Migration: Honduran Households
       in the World Economy." *Journal of Latin American Studies* 23(1):131–
       161.

Thompson, Karen S., K.M. DeWalt, and B.R. DeWalt
1985   *Household Food Use in Three Rural Communities.* Farming Systems
       Research in Southern Honduras Report No. 2, Department of Sociology
       and Department of Anthropology. Lexington: University of Kentucky.

United States Agency for International Development (USAID)
1981   *Environmental Profile of Honduras.* Tucson: Arid Lands Information
       Center.
1982   *Country Environmental Profile.* Virginia: JRB Associates.

USDA (United States Department of Agriculture)
1959– *World Indices of Agricultural and Food Production, 1950–84.* Washington,
1979, D.C.: USDA.
1985
1987   *Livestock and Meat.* Foreign Agriculture Circulars (cited in Leonard
       1987, 216–217). Washington, D.C.: USDA.

Valverde, Victor
1986   "Nutritional Status in Central America and Panama." Paper presented
       at the conference, Health and Nutrition in the Americas, University
       of Kentucky, Lexington, April.

Valverde, Victor, and Ian Rawson
1976   "Dietetic and Anthropomorphic Differences Between Children from
       the Center and Surrounding Villages of a Rural Region of Costa
       Rica." *Ecology of Food and Nutrition* 5:197–203.

Valverde V., et al.
1977   "Relationship Between Family Land Availability and Nutritional Sta-
       tus." *Ecology of Food and Nutrition* 6:1–7.
1980   "Lifestyles and Nutritional Status of Children from Different Ecological
       Areas of El Salvador." *Ecology of Food and Nutrition* 9:167–177.
1981   "Income and Growth Retardation in Poor Families with Similar Living
       Conditions in Rural Guatemala." *Ecology of Food and Nutrition* 10:241–
       248.

Warren, John P.
   1984   *The Natural Resources Management Project: A Status Summary.* Tegu-
           cigalpa: OET/AID/Honduras. Draft copy.
White, Robert
   1977   *Structural Factors in Rural Development: The Church and the Peasant
           in Honduras.* Unpublished Ph.D. dissertation, Cornell University.
Williams, Robert
   1986   *Export Agriculture and the Crisis in Central America.* Chapel Hill:
           University of North Carolina Press.
World Bank
   1984–   *World Development Report.* Various editions. New York: Oxford Uni-
   1988   versity Press.

4

Land, Malnutrition, and Health: The Dilemmas of Development in Guatemala

Kjell I. Enge and Pilar Martinez-Enge

Investigators with a variety of disciplinary viewpoints have tried to relate hunger and disease, especially in children, to inadequate access to agricultural land, falling incomes, and rising unemployment levels. As a region, Central America has been the object of much of this kind of research and commentary. Using the case of Guatemala, we explore the relationships between resource availability, land tenure, rising costs of living, malnutrition, health, and population growth. Our analysis is framed in the context of a recent history of extreme violence; a present plagued with mounting violence, poverty, and hardships; and grave concerns for the future. We will examine why so many Guatemalans, especially the Mayan population, find it increasingly difficult to feed their families and why they see no signs of any improvement or meaningful change.

Ironically, when compared to the other Central American republics, Guatemala is by far the leader in agricultural resources, petroleum reserves, and mineral deposits. The potentials for equitable economic growth for the ethnically diverse population was taken into consideration and incorporated into the development plans made by the Cerezo government. To help the government achieve its goals, the United States, the European Economic Community, and Japan gave unprecedented financial support.[1] But Guatemala, like so many of its neighbors, continues to suffer the effects of the economic stagnation from 1980 to 1990 reflected by high rates of malnutrition for adults and children of all ages. In this chapter, we examine the underlying causes for the downward spiral in the quality of life for most Guatemalans. In our approach we integrate disparate findings from other studies to create a realistic picture of what happens when access to productive resources is severely limited. The goal is to achieve a synthesis of a history of periodic violence, periods of economic growth and stagnation, and the majority's continual struggle to provide the barest of essentials for existence.

Economy, Land, Employment, and Income

Guatemala occupies 22 percent of Central America and has 26 percent of the region's most fertile soils. Within Guatemala's 131,800 square kilometers, nearly 42 percent of the land can be cultivated to produce high to moderate yields of most crops native to the region. The central and western highlands are mountainous and rugged, but the valleys have an abundance of fertile soils that are cultivated using labor-intensive technologies; these lands are best suited for traditional food crops such as corn, beans, and squash; the population density is high with a characteristic *minifundia* pattern of very small landholdings.

The middle altitudes of the Pacific escarpment to the south and the Verapaces to the northeast are areas currently used for large-scale commercial coffee cultivation for export, and some of the best and most productive land is located in the Pacific lowlands called the Costa Sur. This fertile strip of some 15,000 square kilometers stretches 255 kilometers from El Salvador in the southeast to Chiapas in the northwest and corresponds to 11 percent of the country's total land area. It is a lush and verdant tropical carpet. Landholdings are large and mechanized, producing cotton, rubber, bananas, sugar cane, and cattle. Because of the good climate and abundant precipitation, the agricultural yields are some of the highest in Central America. To the north of the central highlands, across the majestic Cuchamatanes mountains, the terrain drops through a series of rugged slopes to the Petén, a great expanse of lowlands stretching to the Mexican border. This area covers 40 percent of the country and has abundant rainfall, but the soils are thin and acidic, requiring skillful management for sustained agriculture. As of 1990 a lack of roads and other infrastructures has, to a large extent, left the region underdeveloped (Universidad Rafael Landívar 1984). A notable exception, however, has been large-scale logging of tropical hardwoods for the export market.

Although the wealth of agricultural resources in Guatemala is striking, the poverty affecting most of the population is beyond the expectations of even the most experienced observers of Third World problems and development. A look at two extended periods of violence, the first during the 1960s and the second during the early 1980s, provides many answers to questions about developments in Guatemala since the 1960s. The insurgency during the middle 1960s was organized by the Fuerzas

Armadas Rebeldes (FAR), a rebellious faction of the army. Most of the armed confrontations took place in the eastern lowlands and were repressed by the end of the decade. In the 1970s and after the 1976 earthquake, the Guatemalan economy experienced unprecedented growth during the same time that the military consolidated its grip on the government with increased oppression in rural areas.

Although the economy expanded during the 1970s as evidenced by an extraordinary growth in the GNP,[2] the poor received few, if any, benefits. This was also a time of reorganization and expansion of rebel movements that had retreated to the northern highlands and the Petén. The remnants of the FAR and two new movements, the EGP and ORPA,[3] worked extensively to gather support among the rural population. The major difference, however, was that this time the involvement of the indigenous population was considered essential for the success of the revolutionary movements. Numerous rural communities gave their support to the guerrillas, especially after the 1976 earthquake. Most of the casualties from this natural disaster were indigenous peoples who saw government efforts to provide aid and to finance reconstruction as inadequate. In areas where the government did not, for whatever reason, provide sufficient aid, the void was partially filled by development assistance from abroad, and to a very significant degree, by the guerrillas who were rapidly gaining strength in terms of numbers, financial resources, and arms.

In the years after the earthquake, the guerrilla movements became more visible with sporadic attacks on large plantations, especially on the south coast. After Lucas Garcia became president, the military was increasingly concerned with the mounting "communist" influence and threats in rural areas. Increasingly, the policy became one of immediate and violent suppression of any movement that could possibly be linked in any way to the insurgents. The consequences of these policies became painfully evident by the end of the decade as exemplified by the massacre at Panzós and the occupation of the Spanish Embassy in Guatemala City. Adams provided a lucid summary of what ensued:

> The growth of guerrilla activities led the government to intensify counterinsurgency. Suspicious about possible "left wing" or guerrilla affiliation led to increased terrorist killing of civilians, and lists of future targets were often published by paramilitary groups. In the early 1980s the threat of insurgent success in mobilizing Indian support led the military to wipe out—at a conservative estimate—over two hundred Indian villages and fifty thousand Indians. Perhaps as many as five hundred thousand Indians fled to Mexico and to the United States—where there are currently between one and two hundred thousand—or went into hiding in Guatemala. One

day before the inauguration of Guatemala's new civilian president in January 1986, the retiring military regime granted general amnesty to those who had engaged in these activities, so there is no way the truth will readily come to light (Adams 1987, 4).

This period of protracted violence lasted from the latter part of 1979 and was generally thought to have ended by the beginning of 1983. "End" in this case did not mean that the insurgencies had been wiped out but merely that the frequency and intensity of armed confrontation had been significantly reduced. This state of relative calm remained constant up to the inauguration of Venicio Cerezo in 1986 when a real feeling of change came over the country; people began to see new hope and chances for prosperity. Unfortunately, these feelings were not real signs of economic and political improvements leading to greater equity in Guatemalan society.

In 1983, after nearly four years of violence and conflict, Guatemala continued to have the highest per capita GDP in Central America, but by any measure its population was and continues to be among the most ill fed, uneducated, and unhealthy in the region, or in all of Latin America for that matter. In 1980 adult literacy was 48 percent—14 percent below that of El Salvador, the poorest country in Central America, and only about half that of Costa Rica. The incidence of malnutrition in preschoolers was over twice that of Costa Rica, and the infant mortality rate among the indigenous population in the central highlands in 1980 was estimated at 160 per 1,000 live births, a rate twice the average for Latin America and comparable to rates in Haiti, Bolivia, and Zaire (World Bank 1986). As we will show, the situation has not improved but may, in fact, be worse, especially for young mothers and their children.

The explanation for the high illiteracy rates, poor health conditions, and desperate poverty is, without a doubt, the tremendous inequality in the distribution of income. Overall, Guatemala had the worst income distribution in Central America. As early as 1970, the bottom 50 percent of the population earned only 13 percent of the total income and the wealthiest 5 percent earned the greatest share of the total GDP. Figures from 1987 show that the lowest 40 percent of households earned 14 percent of private income and that 74 percent of the rural and 66 percent of the urban population lived below absolute poverty income levels. In comparison, in Honduras, long thought to be the poorest country in Central America, the percent of the rural and urban population below absolute poverty was 55 and 14, respectively, and for Nicaragua, it was 19 percent for rural residents and 21 for urban (World Bank 1987a).

To understand the lopsided distribution of wealth in Guatemala is to account for the very reasons or actual roots of such massive poverty. Although real per capita GDP increased at a rate of 2 to 3 percent per year in the period from 1960 to 1978, the benefits of this growth did not reach much of the population. Because Guatemala is primarily agricultural and rural, it does not have the industrial base and labor markets that have to some extent redistributed wealth in the Western industrialized nations, and furthermore, Guatemala has not had the commitment nor concern to invest in activities to benefit the poor in terms of rural infrastructure and access to resources. An important indicator of this lack of commitment is the percentage of GDP spent on education. In 1985, that figure was 2 percent, less than what was spent by El Salvador and Honduras and a fraction of what was spent by Costa Rica (Academy for Educational Development 1985).

Because Guatemala is an agricultural country, a discussion of poverty would not be complete without a more detailed look at the most important economic resource, land. In 1982, Guatemala had the most unequal land distribution in Central America, even more so than El Salvador and prerevolutionary Nicaragua. Using the GINI index to represent degree of inequality, where 100 is maximum inequality and 0 is perfect equality, Guatemala was 85; El Salvador, 80.1; and Nicaragua, before the revolution, 82.7 (Hough et al. 1982).

In 1982 the number of farms in Guatemala with a land area of less than 1.4 hectares, or about 3.4 acres, was 288,083, representing 54.2 percent of the total number of farms. These farms, however, occupied only 4.1 percent of the arable land. The number of farms with over 450 hectares was 1,362, or 0.26 percent of the total number; but they had 34 percent of the land. Furthermore, in 1982 there were 185,000 families without any land, representing about 1 million rural residents. A large percentage of the landless, perhaps 75 to 80 percent, were Indians in the central and western highlands (Hough et al. 1982).

A recent study shows that on a sector-by-sector basis rural households had incomes that were one-tenth to one-half those of the corresponding urban households in Guatemala City. In 1981, there were 303,943 rural households with incomes below 1,200 quetzales per year,[4] and of these, 233,849 were agricultural wage laborers and farmers. In addition, the study showed that the risk of being extremely poor was at least 3.5 times higher in rural areas than in Guatemala City. In some of the highland departments such as Sololá, Totonicapán, and El Quiché, the risks were several times higher. Poverty, although widespread, appears to affect certain segments of the population more, namely the indigenous peoples of the central highlands (Franklin et al. 1987).

TABLE 4.1   Fluctuations in the Prices of Corn, Beans, and Rice from 1980 to 1987 (prices are in quetzales per pound)

Year	Corn	Beans	Rice
1980	.11	.37	.29
1981	.12	.37	.33
1982	.11	.28	.35
1983	.13	.29	.34
1984	.11	.32	.31
1985	.13	.41	.31
1986	.22	.56	.68
1987	.25	.60	.83

Source: Banco de Guatemala 1987.

Because of large numbers of low-paid urban and rural wage laborers, it is of no surprise that most families, both rural and urban, had to purchase most of their basic foods for survival. In Guatemala, this meant the consumption of three basic staples: corn, beans, and rice. The prices for beef, pork, and chicken rose to such an extent that they were generally beyond the means of the poor. A look at the changing prices of basic grains during the 1980s shows that inflation of food prices was gravely aggravating an already desperate situation for many. Figures released by the Bank of Guatemala show the average annual consumer prices per pound in Guatemala City for corn, beans, and rice (see Table 4.1).

It is important to keep in mind that salaries remained relatively constant and for many actually decreased. There were also considerable fluctuations in prices from month to month, reflecting variation in supply as a function of the agricultural cycles in diverse parts of the country. The results of a more than doubling in the price of corn and rice are clear indicators of the increased strain placed on families trying to cope and meet daily food requirements.

To further complicate the economic picture, unemployment and underemployment continued to increase significantly. The Guatemalan Social Security Institute estimated that between 1981 and 1985 220,000 jobs were lost and that during each year some 62,000 individuals were added to the economically active population. In 1986, according to the government planning office (SEGEPLAN), the unemployment rate was 47 percent of the economically active population, which was divided into 12 percent for people without any form of employment and 35 percent who were underemployed (INFORPRESS 1987, 26).

As we have shown above, prices continued to rise dramatically during the 1980s with the Consumer Price Index (CPI) averaging an annual increase of about 25 percent. Although the price increases were across the board in all parts of the country, food prices increased much more than prices of most other products. It is difficult to pinpoint the precise cause of inflation except to say that all the Central American republics had large government budget deficits and that governments responded by printing excessive amounts of currency; Guatemala was no exception. This situation was exacerbated by monopolistic production and marketing practices, excessive balance of trade deficits leading to dollar shortages, and the steady deterioration of the international quetzal exchange rate (INFORPRESS 1987). As of the end of 1990 there were no signs that this high rate of inflation would decrease anytime in the near future. In all probability, inflation would continue unabated.

Nutrition

In 1984, the estimated median income per capita in rural areas was $400, and 35 percent of Guatemalan households had incomes that were inadequate to cover the costs of the minimum food basket. Per capita protein intake in rural areas declined from 68 grams in 1965 to 51.2 grams in 1976, and energy intake declined from 2,117 kilocalories to 1,637 kilocalories during the same period. Corn, sugar, and beans supplied more than two-thirds of energy requirements (World Bank 1986).

National nutrition surveys done in 1965, 1976, 1978, and 1985 by INCAP identified protein-energy malnutrition, hypovitaminosis A, iodine deficiency, and iron deficiency as the most serious nutritional problems. The trends that emerged from these studies showed that some conditions were, in fact, getting worse. There is overwhelming agreement on the fact that generalized malnutrition has a particularly severe impact on the physical condition of infants and young children.

As of 1985 Guatemala had the highest (30.5) percentage of children under five years of age weighing below 75 percent of the standard weight for age in tropical Latin America; as compared to Honduras's 29.5 percent, Brazil's 20 percent, and Nicaragua's and Venezuela's 14 percent. Children below 75 percent have been classified as Gomez type II (60 to 74 percent of normal weight for age) and type III (under 60 percent) malnutrition, and are usually called moderate and severe, respectively. Type II and III child malnutrition are more prevalent in rural areas all over Guatemala (World Bank 1986).

The 1978 INCAP survey showed very clearly that weight for age retardation was associated with relative economic standing. The data showed that children in two- to three-children households with access to 3.5 or more hectares or in households where the head was a skilled worker had an average weight retardation of 17.5 percent. Forty-three percent of children in households with access to one manzana (1.4 hectares or 3.45 acres) or less had moderate to severe malnutrition as

TABLE 4.2 Socioeconomic Profile of Families Most Affected by Malnutrition

Region and Occupation	# of Families	Percent of Families			
		Without Latrines	Earth Floors	Illiterate Adults	Children Underweight
Central dry region agricultural laborers	71	61.2	87.8	61.2	43.7
Highland farmers with less than 0.7 ha	200	73.8	87.6	54.9	43.0
Northern farmers with 0.7–1.4 ha	26	76.5	94.1	76.5	42.3
Pacific Coast agricultural wage laborers	429	74.2	65.2	57.1	39.2

Source: INCAP 1980.

shown in Table 4.2 (INCAP 1980). This study was done in six regions and included the following departments:

Metropolitan	Guatemala City and surrounding countryside
South Coast	Escuintla and Suchitepéquez
Central Dry	El Progreso and Baja Verapaz
Western Highlands	Huehuetenango and Sololá
East	Chiquimula and Jalapa
North	Alta Verapaz

Table 4.3 summarizes the results of the 1986 Maternal Child Health and Nutrition Survey, which also included the weights of children classified for age using Z scores, clearly demonstrating the relative geographic distribution and degree of malnutrition.

According to Franklin et al., who examined much of the same data cited above and in addition looked at a 1986 height-for-age survey done by the Investigative Unit (USIPE) of the Ministry of Education and INCAP,

Guatemala has a longstanding problem of chronic malnutrition, and large segments of its population are currently severely underweight. Evidence of this is given by the fact that in 1978 approximately 60 percent of the children living in the rural areas fell below 2 standard deviations from the median height for their respective ages to cause them to be classified as chronically malnourished. The most recent data from USIPE/INCAP (1986) indicate that seven highland departments have at least 10 percent of the population that attends school (six to ten years of age) with severe retardation in height for age. These seven departments have from 28 to

TABLE 4.3 Percentage of Children Under 36 Months with Low Weight for Age (Z scores by department)

Department	< −2.0	−1.99 to −1	−0.99 to 0.00
Region I			
Escuintla	34.8	33.1	21.0
Suchitepéquez	28.5	33.4	20.3
Retalhuleu	28.2	31.1	19.8
Santa Rosa	29.0	35.1	23.4
Jutiapa	24.4	28.6	26.5
Jalapa	46.6	28.9	15.6
Region II			
Quetzaltenango	39.6	32.2	15.7
Totonicapán	37.5	28.8	19.6
El Quiché	48.6	28.6	13.9
Sololá	44.4	30.0	16.9
San Marcos	49.3	28.4	13.8
Huehuetenango	40.4	33.4	16.7
Region III			
Zacapa	16.0	22.5	30.9
Izabal	19.0	32.5	25.9
Chiquimula	33.3	31.4	19.6
Alta Verapaz	32.6	31.5	22.6
Baja Verapaz	40.6	30.7	15.6
El Progreso	34.8	30.4	22.2
Region IV			
Amatitlán	34.4	26.5	22.8
Sacatepéquez	28.0	37.2	20.9
Chimaltenango	32.9	31.9	18.6
Region V			
Guatemala Sur	26.5	33.7	22.3
Guatemala Norte	26.0	36.7	20.4
Region VI			
El Petén	23.3	31.5	26.0
National	33.6	31.3	20.3

Source: INCAP 1986.

49 percent of their pre-school aged (five years and younger) children classified as severely underweight for their ages (MSPAS/INCAP, 1986). The USIPE/INCAP height census of the primary schools may understate the prevalence of chronic malnutrition in the school-aged population, because more than 60 percent of the school-aged population does not attend school. The weight for age data from the Ministry of Health's *"Centros Centinelas"* may, perhaps, reveal a selectivity bias in that it represents pre-school-aged children being served by health centers. If both sets of data are correct, they jointly suggest a very serious problem and possibly indicate that in the last five years the nutritional situation has worsened from that of the previous five years (Franklin 1987).

The seven departments referred to above are (in order of severity of malnutrition in the cohort attending school) Sololá, Totonicapán, El Quiché, Huehuetenango, Chimaltenango, Suchitepequéz, and San Marcos. There is very close correspondence between these and the departments with high prevalence of severely underweight preschoolers. The obvious conclusion from the data is that these are the places where most of the indigenous population lives and where the landholdings are the smallest. Because there has, at best, been no improvement in the situation since the last nutritional survey in 1985 and no significant change in land-tenure patterns, the results from the earlier (1979) INCAP survey must be taken even more seriously.

Demography

In view of the distribution of land and the steady increase in malnutrition, the situation is even more alarming when population dynamics are examined. A very reasonable question would be to ask, what will life have to offer the average Guatemalan in the year 2010? Given the distribution of resources and barring any radical change, the answer would be a quality of life significantly worse than what existed at the end of 1989.

Estimates projected from counts taken in the 1981 census indicate that the Guatemalan population will number 12 million by 2000, 20 million by 2025, and making certain assumptions about decreasing growth rates, the population should stabilize at 32 million by 2030 (World Bank 1989, 214). About 60 percent of the population in 1989 could be considered rural, and the density varied from 12 people per square kilometer in the Petén to 620 for the department of Guatemala, where two-thirds of the urban population lived. Three-fourths of the rural population lived in the central and western highlands, with a population density of about 300 people per square kilometer. Furthermore, the population was very young; in 1983, 18 percent were under five years of age and 28 percent were between five and fourteen years (World Bank 1986).

Census data have also shown that Guatemala's growth rate increased by 81 percent, from less than 1.6 percent per year in 1943 to 2.9 percent in 1963, primarily due to a decline in the crude death rate; later estimates ranged from 3.2 to 3.5 percent per year (World Bank 1986). There were also important and marked differences in fertility among population groups. For example, the number of children per family was consistently higher among rural families than urban ones. Parity was also consistently higher among indigenous women, especially among the fifteen to nineteen year age group—40 percent higher than among nonindigenous women (World Bank 1986; Westinghouse Health Systems 1987).

For the purposes of the 1981 census, "rural" was defined as those who live in a population center with less than 1,000 inhabitants or in any other town with dispersed settlement patterns. Ethnicity, for the census, was based on the individual's own identification. The use of self-classification as a method for identifying indigenous people probably contributed to an underestimation of the size of the Indian population. Another reason to believe the figures may be low is that the 1981 census was taken during the height of guerrilla activities and the government's counter-insurgency campaign; many regions were not visited, and large segments of the population were displaced and homeless.[5]

If the estimated birth rates are correct and do not decrease, Guatemala's population will double in less than twenty years—by the year 2010, there will be almost 18 million people competing for the same limited resources. Food insecurity and consequent malnutrition will most certainly be even more extreme for the urban and rural poor, both indigenous and Ladino. The essence of the problem is the poor distribution of resources, but in light of high estimates for rates of population growth, the absolute availability of resources will be a limiting factor. As will be shown below, this limit has already been reached for arable land.

The Indigenous Population

Estimated in 1988 to be at least 3.5 million of a total population of 8.5 million, the indigenous population has undergone numerous changes since the Spanish Conquest. At the time of the conquest, there were at least 1 million Mayans divided into many ethnic groups. The two largest were the Quiché and Cakchiquel, who were organized into complex states, complete with nobility, priesthood, armies, artisans, merchants, and commoners. During the 450 years that followed, each sector of the different ethnic groups interacted with the myriad of European influences in distinct ways. In other words, the indigenous people were not homogeneous at the time of the conquest, and they are not today (Enge 1985).

Indian ethnicity is difficult to define because of the tremendous amount of cultural, linguistic, and economic variation that divides the indigenous people in Guatemala. A number of different criteria have been used and include religious beliefs, self-image or self-identification, rituals, economic activities, dress, food, and, of course, language. Problems appear when an attempt is made to establish uniform criteria for each of these variables; it simply is not possible. Indians can be conservative Catholics, progressive Catholics, Evangelical Protestants, or *costumbristas*;[6]

or they can proclaim no religious belief at all. Their economic activities vary from farmer to factory worker and their residence from rural to urban. Dress can be traditional for both men and women, or both may have adopted European dress. Many speak only one of twenty-three Mayan languages and their multitude of dialects, and some speak many tongues; others claim to speak only Spanish but still consider themselves indigenous. To further complicate the picture, some declare themselves to be Ladinos in the urban context and promptly deny any Indian characteristics, including language. These same individuals will consider themselves completely indigenous when visiting relatives in the countryside (Enge 1985).

Our definition of "indigenous" is both cultural and economic, taking into consideration location of residence as well as ethnic identification, making the Guatemalan indigenous population highly stratified, with a small wealthy elite, a middle range of moderate income, and a large majority of the very poor who live primarily in rural areas (Enge 1985). This latter group are what development experts call "the poorest of the poor."

Since 1954 the history of indigenous people and land tenure has been one of extreme violence and conflict. During the 1960s and 1970s, the Guatemalan economy was expanding due, in a large part, to the growth of export agriculture. A result of this relative prosperity was increased competition over land in the form of title disputes, land invasions, and armed confrontations. The Indians were most often the losers as commercial coffee, sugar, cotton, and vegetable production continued to expand and enrich the Ladino landholders; the Indians found it increasingly more difficult to survive as their children fell victim to malnutrition and disease. As the indigenous population became increasingly involved in armed conflicts against the government in the late 1970s, they became the victims of repression and violence on a scale unprecedented in Central America. As many as a million people were displaced and over one hundred thousand sought refuge in Mexico, the United States, Belize, Honduras, and elsewhere (Arias 1985; Cultural Survival 1987; Krueger and Enge 1985; Manz 1988; Washington Office on Latin America 1989).

Although the intensity of the guerrilla war subsided after 1983, there is now an increasing number of confrontations, especially in Chimaltenango, San Marcos, Sololá, and the Petén. Using the aura of peace as a justification, the Cerezo government has been actively attempting to convince the refugees in Mexico to return to their villages in Guatemala. As of the middle of 1990 relatively few have returned. But if most did return, chaos would certainly follow in their home municipalities. The reason is that lands owned by refugees have been redistributed to others, and government policies and actions designed for short-sighted political gain have complicated an already difficult and tense land-tenure situation (Cultural Survival 1987; Manz 1988; Washington Office on Latin America 1988, 1989).

Although all sectors of the Guatemalan population have been affected by political violence and continuous economic deterioration, the indigenous peoples have borne the brunt of brutality and suffering in terms of rapidly deteriorating quality of life. Making ends meet in the past was a struggle, but today the ability of many families to put the barest of meals on their tables is very much in question. We now examine the consequences of this dire situation in terms of health.

Health

According to UNICEF, the best indicator of the physical well-being of a population is the health of its children. The ability of children to develop and thrive depends on their families being able to adequately feed and clothe them. Chronic malnutrition and poor health can, therefore, adversely affect an entire generation and severely impede physical and psychological development.

Nearly one-half of the Guatemalan population were under the age of fifteen in 1985 and more than one-half of the total reported deaths occurred among infants and children. In 1985, 58 percent of the total deaths were children under five years of age, and the official infant mortality rate in 1986 was 79.8 per 1,000 live births (MSPAS 1986; Bossert and del Cid Peralta 1987). Many investigators we interviewed felt this is an underestimate and that in some rural areas and poor urban neighborhoods, the real infant mortality rate was three to four times higher.

The leading causes of death in children under five, in descending order, were: diarrhea, respiratory infections, perinatal problems, immunopreventable diseases, and malnutrition (MSPAS 1986). The fact that highly contagious diseases such as diarrhea and respiratory infections were on top of the list as the principal causes of death for both children and adults is an indication of poor hygiene, substandard living conditions, and abject poverty of a large percentage of the population; the resultant low health status was an obvious product of the combined long-term effects of these conditions.

It is disturbing that most of the deaths in both infants and children under five were caused by preventable diseases. Deaths from diarrhea, measles, polio, whooping cough, tuberculosis, and tetanus are all preventable with early and timely vaccinations. Achieving sufficient vaccination coverage of 80 percent to prevent large-scale outbreaks eluded the government.[7]

The provision of health care for 80 percent of Guatemala's population is primarily the responsibility of the Ministry of Health and Social Welfare (Ministerio de Salud y Asistencia Social—MSPAS). The other major public health institution is the Guatemalan Social Security Institute (Instituto Guatemalteco de Seguridad Social—IGGS), which serves part of the working class and salaried workers located for the most part in the cities; in 1985 IGSS covered 8 percent of the population. Private sector physicians and practitioners tended to approximately 6 percent of the population, mostly in the higher income brackets; the military served about an equal number. Nongovernment groups, religious and secular, provided services to less than 1 percent (World Bank 1986). A 1985 survey of some 9,000 households showed that most Guatemalans looked to pharmacies and local stores that sold a large variety of "prescription" medicines for most of their medical care (Harrison and Enge 1988).

According to its own statistics (1986), the Ministry of Health provided some form of health care and related services to a little more than 2 million people, only about 30 percent of the total nominally covered. Of the remaining 4.7 million, nearly half lived in remote communities with difficult access to Ministry facilities. The other half did not use available services for a variety of reasons that included: limited hours of service, lack of medicines, personnel who did not speak the local indigenous languages, perceived low quality of service, and little or no supplemental food available for distribution.[8]

In the early 1980s allocations from the national budget provided 85 percent of the Ministry of Health's financial resources; loans and user fees made up the rest. The budget represented less than 1 percent of the gross domestic product (GDP), which is less than one-half of the allocations made by other Latin American countries in a similar situation. According to the World Bank (1986), the main reason was the small share of GDP captured by government revenues.

The allocation of funds by the Ministry of Health during the 1980s affected the extension of delivery and quality of health care at the primary Health Post and community level. Three-quarters of the Ministry's operating expenses were for hospital operation and Ministry administration, leaving only 14 percent for maternal-child health, environmental sanitation, and health education. A World Bank (1986) analysis showed that of the $15 per capita available to the MSPAS, $12 was spent on hospital care and only $1 on high priority primary health care activities. To provide appropriate services in family planning, growth monitoring to identify malnutrition, maternal-child health, and immunization would require an expenditure of at least $10–$15 per capita.

Although most statistics on health and nutrition indicate that the well-being of the population is declining, numerous attempts have been made to ameliorate the symptoms, but not the underlying structural causes. In the next section, we examine rural development and a number of projects designed to improve the quality of life and the economic well-being of the rural population.

Development Initiatives

Guatemala has a long history of large-scale development projects in agriculture, commerce, health, family planning, and education involving numerous Guatemalan and international donor agencies. The first peak of activity was reached after the 1976 earthquake, which measured 7.5 on the Richter scale and killed 25,000. Most of the victims were Indians and low-income urban residents who made up the majority of the nearly 1 million left homeless. In the aftermath of the disaster, the relief effort was the responsibility of the National Reconstruction Committee (*Comité Nacional de Reconstrucción*), which had to administer and coordinate local and international efforts to provide both immediate relief and long-term rebuilding.

Development efforts continued until the end of the 1970s when the level of political violence escalated, culminating in three years of conflict bordering on open warfare. Virtually all development efforts came to an abrupt stop. In 1979 there were over 200 private voluntary organizations working in the highlands; by 1983, only a handful remained. With the decrease of military activity and the return to what some call normalcy, development projects and the involvement of international donors again reached unprecedented high levels, especially after the return of civilian rule in January 1986. As a result, the influx of money placed considerable strain on the Guatemalan institutional structure to absorb, make plans for, and appropriately spend large sums from the United States, the European Economic Community, and Japan.

We believe that it is not unreasonable to say that unequal access to land is one of the root causes of violence and the deplorable nutritional status of large segments of the population. Estimates have put the total landless population at 500,000 with another 3.5 million who need more land just to reach production for a meager subsistence (Dewart and Eckersley 1988). However, the idea or mere suggestion of agrarian reform in Guatemala evokes passionate responses leading to conflict and death.

An examination of available land that includes a combination of land that is for sale and government-owned holdings, however, indicates severe limitations. Hough et al. used three options to calculate how many rural landless families could be settled on land that was potentially available for distribution—land in the public domain (*terrenos baldios*) and idle land (*tierras ociosas*). "If one includes only first class, second class, and multiple use land then the potentially arable area is 2.95 million hectares. The area currently under cultivation in annuals, perennials, and pasture is 2.9 million hectares; it is evident that under this option there is only a minimal amount of arable land that is not already in use" (1982, 12).

If karst forest land is included, the amount of potentially arable land increases to 4.8 million hectares. A large percentage of this land is in the Franja Transversal and the Petén. Karst soils are acidic, thin, and very subject to erosion once the forest cover has been removed and would not sustain traditional agriculture for very long. In view of these findings, Guatemala simply does not have enough to provide a family-size plot to everyone who needs it. "Any quantification of land available based on soil conditions and the current size of the population shows that in the worst case, Guatemala can accommodate only 31 percent of its landless; in the best case it can provide sufficient land to only 64 percent" (Hough et al. 1982, 15).

We have not encountered any estimates of how many farmers could be accommodated if an all-out land reform were to take place, complete with expropriation and maximum limits on farm size. Using AID estimates that 3.5 hectares of prime quality land or 7 hectares of poor quality are needed for a family to subsist, and assuming that about 3 million hectares of "good" land exists regardless of ownership, we can conclude that a little less than 1 million people can be accommodated at subsistence levels. It quickly becomes obvious that given demographic trends, there are no easy solutions to land scarcity in Guatemala either within the prevailing system of tenure or under restructured revolutionary conditions.

With the support and cooperation of the United States Agency for International Development (USAID), Cerezo's government made possible the creation of a private land market where individuals and groups can purchase land with government subsidized credit, and he promised to redistribute some government-owned land. At the same time Father Andres Girón, an activist priest from the Department of Escuintla, organized the National Association of Peasants for Land (ANC) with a membership in 1987 of at least 130,000 (Dewart and Eckersley 1988). Under Girón's leadership, the ANC made several marches on the capital in attempts to pressure Cerezo to accelerate the distribution of government-owned land. Girón succeeded in keeping land scarcity and the need for reform in the national limelight. But Cerezo, under constant scrutiny by the military, was in no position to even hint at upsetting the system of private land ownership. He had, however, provided a limited amount of government land to peasant groups as a symbolic gesture that his government was doing what it could to alleviate the plight of the landless.

International agencies also attempted to address the problem of land scarcity. In August 1984, USAID provided the Penny Foundation (*Fundación del Centavo*) with $1 million in grant funds to do a Pilot Commercial Land Market Project. The Penny Foundation was charged with the responsibility of providing a mechanism to permit small farmers to purchase arable land and also to provide them production credit and technical assistance. This effort, like that of the government, was done on a small scale in the Department of Sololá and did not pose a threat to established landowners or the system of tenure.[9] Although the project has been considered a success, it has had a negligible impact.

The provision of land alone, however, is not enough. It has been commonly recognized by both Guatemalan and international planners that in order to achieve integrated rural development, other important factors must be included. Among the many problems that confront rural residents are lack of schools, health services, and social workers to tie residents into existing and new services systems. Links with the Ministries of Education, Development, and Health should be created, so they can provide appropriate facilities and services. Family planning, as part of an integrated effort in public health, has become a top priority for international development organizations working in Guatemala.[10] It is our hope that appropriate birth control devices will be made available to all who want them at nominal prices for those who can pay and free of charge for those who cannot.

The Ministry of Urban and Rural Development (*Ministerio de Desarrollo Urbano y Rural*) was created by the Cerezo government for the purposes of determining development priorities, implementing the government's own projects, and coordinating efforts by international organizations. A 1987 study by this ministry showed that the benefits of development projects have been concentrated in certain parts of the country. The three departments with the highest per capita investments were Guatemala, Escuintla, and El Petén, which was included because of its large area and very small population. In terms of actual financial investment by the government, Guatemala, Sacatepéquez, and Zacapa received, and by 1987 were still receiving, the most. The three departments that received the least were Totonicapán, Huehuetenango, and El Quiché, and these were also the departments with the largest number of indigenous residents (von Hoegen 1988). With the exception of Totonicapán, these were also the departments that suffered the most, in both the loss of human life and material destruction, during the 1979–1983 period of political violence.

The Ministry of Development has been characterized by political favoritism, scandals, and an extremely low budget, making it essentially ineffective and relatively powerless to implement meaningful projects or coordinate large-scale international efforts. Based on our many years of experience in Guatemala and Latin America, we feel that international organizations such as the World Bank, UNICEF, FAO, the Inter-American Development Bank, the European Economic Community, USAID, and others essentially set their own agenda in relation to what is believed to have been successful elsewhere and what represents the current trends and fashions in the international development community. As a consequence, there is a lack of coordination between organizations combined with a dearth of local personnel to design and guide efforts to benefit those who have the greatest need.

One of the oldest continuous programs that has addressed acute and chronic hunger in Guatemala has been United States food aid under Public Law 480, a part of U.S. foreign assistance since 1954. PL480 provides for the transfer of surplus foods such as corn, evaporated milk, cooking oil, wheat, soya, and other products to Third World countries. In 1966 the program was amended to shift from a simple disposal of surplus agricultural commodities to more specific humanitarian and development objectives. The program funds are appropriated annually with a budget of about $1.5 billion serving more than seventy countries for the purchase of agricultural commodities. PL480 is administered by the U.S. Department of Agriculture and the Agency for International Development, in Cooperation with the Departments of State and Commerce, and the Office of Management and Budget (Wing 1987).

PL480 consisted of two very different forms of food transfer. Title I, consisting of about two-thirds of the entire budget, was a direct concessional sale to a country and was paid for in a mix of local currency and U.S. dollars.[11] Title I commodities were introduced into the marketing system of a developing country by commercial banks, export/import firms, and private retail traders. The rationale was that an overall increase in supply would have the effect of decreasing retail prices for low-income consumers. Title I Guatemalan imports for fiscal 1986 totaled 113,000 metric tons of food at a cost of $16.4 million; in 1987 imports were increased to 147,000 metric tons at a cost of $24 million.

Title II was designed to provide free food to those who were unable to produce or purchase adequate food to meet minimal nutritional needs. These food donations were part of agreements with private voluntary organizations and Guatemalan government agencies. Because the cost of direct food donations was high, the U.S. government supplied the food commodities and the cooperating agencies were responsible for administration, proper storage, and distribution.

According to the Agency for International Development:

> Agricultural commodities made available under Title II may be provided on behalf of the people of the United States to meet famine or other urgent or extraordinary relief requirements; to combat malnutrition, especially in children; to promote economic and community development in friendly developing areas; and for needy persons and non-profit school lunch and preschool feeding programs outside the United States. This assistance to needy persons shall, insofar as practicable, be directed toward community and other self-help activities designed to alleviate the causes of the need for such assistance. Title II programs are to supplement and reinforce other developmental and nutritional activities and are to be conducted within a framework of increasing local participation in management and funding. USAID views Title II donations assistance to projects as interim assistance to reach specific objectives (Wing 1987).

During fiscal 1984 and 1985, some 30,192 metric tons were imported through Title II and included soy-fortified bulgur, cornmeal, nonfat dry milk, vegetable oil, whole-grain corn, and wheat flour; the increase from 1984 to 1985 was about 3,000 metric tons. The total value in 1985 was a little under $4 million as compared to $19.6 million for Title I during the same year (Wing 1987).

The constant increases in the prices of basic foods and the deteriorating economic situation during 1980 to 1988 brought the levels of poverty, malnutrition, and disease to unacceptably high levels; we feel that the food injected into the national market under Title I has been and will continue to be out of reach for those who really need it. Food transfers under Title II have a much greater potential for immediate impact on malnutrition, but Title II is a minuscule effort in relation to the magnitude of problems. Clearly, the maximum impact in the short-run would be accomplished by converting all Title I to Title II commodities; the mechanism for accomplishing this end is provided for in Title III of PL480.

More recently, development initiatives by USAID and the World Bank are strongly urging Guatemalan small farmers to switch to the cultivation of nontraditional exports such as brussels sprouts, snow peas, and broccoli. These exports were never intended for sale in local or regional markets as a means to improve nutrition and food security, but rather as a means to improve conditions in rural areas and to provide an opportunity for new U.S. investment (Barry 1987, 85). It can be argued that increased local incomes will enable rural families to improve their standard of living, but in view of the unpredictable and often drastic shifts in international commodity prices, farmers run the risk of having less than they did before.

The Guatemalan government has long recognized the effectiveness and tenacity of local organizations, which accounts for why many local leaders were killed or forced to flee during the violence. In the aftermath of the 1979–1983 conflict, the government imposed a hierarchically structured Inter-Institutional Coordination System designed to link local community organizations with the municipality, the departmental and national governments, and the army, with the stated objective that local communities form the basis of "integrated" development. This highly centralized structure was abandoned by the Cerezo administration, but communities were still encouraged to organize local development committees (*Comites Pro-Mejoramiento; Comites de Desarrollo Comunal*). The new committees, like the old, however, included the assistant mayor, military commissioners, and civil patrol leaders. Project activities were limited to building schools, roads, or water systems (Washington Office on Latin America 1988, 39). Such projects did nothing to improve local food production or generate disposable income.

In contrast to government and international development programs, independent local indigenous organizations were formed in increasing numbers or, in some cases, were reorganized in the aftermath of the violence. Typically, such organizations have a philosophy of grassroots participatory development and work in education, agriculture, community health, and in microenterprises with limited financial support from outside agencies and foreign governments. Such local initiatives are quite different in membership and purpose from those described previously.

According to comments made in May 1988 by the director of one such nongovernmental development organization (NGO) in Sololá, there are still relatively few indigenous NGOs in the highlands, and the most plausible reason is that as a result of the political violence at the beginning of the 1980s, people are still very timid and afraid to form "development" organizations. After 1986 movements grew and became stronger, but religious division between catholics and evangelicals was splitting many communities. Community residents insisted that the new NGOs coordinate their activities with civil and military authorities to make sure that their projects could in no way be considered subversive.

The spending of more money on health care, agricultural technology, export crops, food processing, and education will not alter the underlying basis of poverty and malnutrition: the lack of adequate farmland for the majority of rural residents. In a pastoral letter issued by the Catholic church in Guatemala, this relatively conservative clergy claimed that the socioeconomic situation and violence were consequences of unequal land distribution and that the disparity between the rich and poor, large landowners and small farmers, was accelerating. The letter called for a land reform combined with integrated rural development and an emphasis on poor rural residents, particularly Indians; without reform, the clergy claimed, new waves of violence worse than ever were inevitable (Episcopado Guatemalteco 1988).

Prospects for the Future

As of 1990 Guatemala's predicament forebodes a reactionary and violent repetition of the recent past. Ten years have ensued since the last time a threshold was reached when some believed that real change was a possibility. Instead, countless thousands have died or disappeared and the underlying causes for injustice, poverty, and disease remain unchanged. Now, as before, the most pressing problem for both the rural and urban poor is meeting the basic requirements for daily survival under conditions that are growing worse. There are no encouraging signs that the economy is about to recuperate and that more jobs will be available. Even if employment were to improve, the wage structure and inflationary prices would continue to restrict purchasing power, leading to persistent malnutrition and poor health for the majority of the population.

Some hopeful signs can be found in a limited number of local initiatives that are having some success in generating income, but these efforts are not sufficient to make an impact on a broader national scale. Nevertheless, many development experts agree that grassroots initiatives are one of the few ways that significant change can come about in ways that bypass government inefficiencies and abuses. Our feeling is that nongovernmental efforts by private voluntary organizations, both Guatemalan and international, can make a difference, providing local residents have a part in planning and project implementation.

In our opinion, development efforts need to be sufficiently well financed and designed to benefit the people who have the greatest need. As we have discussed in this chapter, Guatemala is receiving unprecedented amounts of funding from international agencies, but funds are not being spent on activities and commodities to directly ameliorate the plight of the poor. We find it difficult to believe that sufficient political will could not reprogram efforts to address immediate needs and provide for a more secure future. Furthermore, it is not a theoretical impossibility to redirect a portion of Guatemala's own resources, such as the military budget.

Events in Guatemala during the summer and fall of 1989, however, indicated that political violence was increasing at rates approaching the late 1970s. The civilian government was virtually powerless to take any effective measures to reduce assassinations and disappearances of politicians, students, and labor leaders; public confidence in the Cerezo government was at an all-time low by the end of his term in January 1991. In effect, recent coup attempts and threats of more have, for the time being, paralyzed the government.

President Jorge Serrano, a conservative businessman and evangelical protestant, was inaugurated on January 14, 1991, amid promises to impose law and order, negotiate a peace with the guerrillas, and reverse the economic decline. But if the past is any measure of the future, the prospects for change do not bode well for most Guatemalans, least of all for the indigenous population.

Notes

1. Levels of development assistance to Guatemala in 1987 from all sources were at least three times higher than during the years following the 1976 earthquake, which killed 25,000 and left 1 million homeless. The following shows the sharp increases in expenditures from 1979 to 1987 (in millions of dollars):

1979	67	1984	65
1980	73	1985	83
1981	75	1986	135
1982	64	1987	241
1983	76		

(World Bank 1987, 1988, 1989)

2. Per capita GNP went from $300 in 1965 to $430 in 1973 and continued to rise to a high of $1,250 in 1985. In 1986, the GNP dropped to $930, and in 1987, it rose slightly to $950. Overall economic production grew by an average annual rate of 5.9% from 1965 to 1980, but from 1980 to 1987, there was an average annual decline of 0.7% (World Bank 1987b, 1988, 1989).

3. The country was essentially divided up between the three guerrilla movements. The FAR continued to work in the Petén and parts of Alta Verapaz; the EGP (Ejercito Guerillero de los Pobres) extended its influence in the western and northern highlands of Huehuetenango and El Quiché, primarily north of the Pan-American Highway. ORPA (Organización Revolucionaria del Pueblo en Armas), however, concentrated its efforts south of the Pan-American Highway in San Marcos, Quetzaltenango, Suchitepéquez, and Sololá. Furthermore, ORPA made a concentrated effort to control the rich coffee-growing region known as the Boca Costa, the middle altitudes of the escarpment between the central highlands and the South Coast.

4. In 1981, the Guatemalan quetzal was equal to $1.00 U.S.; by mid-1989, the quetzal had fallen to about 2.7 quetzals to $1 U.S.

5. A more in-depth view of demographic trends and their underlying causes can be obtained from the examination (1983) of the 1978 and 1983 Contraceptive

Prevalance Surveys conducted by the Centers for Disease Control (CDC) and APROFAM (Asociación Pro Familia Guatemalteca) and by Westinghouse Health Systems and INCAP (Instituto de Nutrición de Centro América y Panama) in 1987. Both the current findings and trends shown by the successive surveys are general cause for not just concern but alarm; finding more effective means for promoting and providing family-planning information and methods is imperative. If population growth cannot be decreased, other development efforts will be of little practical utility.

When comparing the results of the 1987, 1983, and 1978 surveys, we see that contraceptive use among married women increased by 6 percent, from 19 percent in 1978 to 25 percent in 1983. Over the next four years, however, use dropped to 23 percent. The 23 percent current-users percentage at the time of the survey included all methods, both modern and traditional; only 18 percent of married women used modern methods. The contraceptive prevalence for all 5,122 women in the 1987 sample was 16 percent for all methods and 13 percent for modern methods. The greatest part of the increase in the five years between 1978 and 1983 was in the department of Guatemala, followed by Ladinos resident in other parts of the country (Westinghouse and INCAP 1987).

For the Indian population, the 1983 survey showed a prevalence of 4.6 percent, which was virtually unchanged from 1978. The 1987 data show that 5.5 percent of indigenous women in the sample were using some form of contraception; the most frequently used method by indigenous women was female sterilization (2.8 percent) followed by traditional methods (1 percent) and the pill (1 percent). Traditional methods include periodic abstinence (rhythm, or Billings method), withdrawal, and other traditional methods (Westinghouse and INCAP 1987).

6. Indians who still practice elements of pre-Hispanic ritual; both ritual and ideology are mixed to varying degrees with catholicism.

7. Despite numerous national vaccination campaigns and extended immunization programs, the coverage remained extremely low. This was especially the case for measles and BCG immunizations (Westinghouse and INCAP 1987). Dehydration caused by diarrhea, the principal cause of child deaths, can be prevented by timely administration of homemade solutions or by using a prepared mixture of oral rehydration salts. The high rates of respiratory diseases resulted from poor housing, overcrowding, and malnutrition. Depending on severity, most of the respiratory infections can be treated in the home with analgesics and inexpensive antibiotics.

8. Structurally, in 1987 the Ministry of Health and Social Welfare was a three-tiered pyramid. At the bottom there were some 590 health posts located in communities of 500 to 1,000 inhabitants and serving a population of about 5 million. Each was staffed by an auxiliary nurse, a rural health technician, and occasionally a last-year medical student doing his or her obligatory six-month rural service. The services provided by the health posts included immunizations, pre- and postnatal care, child growth monitoring, family planning, first aid, administration of supplementary feeding programs, and treatment of all illnesses in the area. Supervised, trained midwives and volunteer health promoters

participated in outreach activities involving home visits. Services were to be provided to an average population of 8,000 per facility, which was above and beyond the capacity of the staff under the best of conditions. Furthermore, the health posts were not evenly distributed. In five departments the average population served was under 5,000, and in seven it was 10,000 to 26,000 per health post. The worst distribution was in the highland departments with a high percentage of indigenous residents (Bossert and del Cid Peralta 1987).

9. In August 1985, a second grant was signed with the Penny Foundation to provide additional funds to conduct the Land Market Project and also to establish an off-shore bank to support mortgage certificates and mortgage bonds issued by the foundation in local private capital markets. As of the end of fiscal 1986, USAID had funded the project with a total of $3 million.

The Penny Foundation has been active in supporting rural development since the 1960s. Their philosophy has been to assist rural people in improving living standards and raising incomes through loans for productive projects and improved housing. The beneficiaries receive loans that must be paid back; bad debts have been minimal in past projects managed by the Foundation. Foundation staff have acted as both promoters and loan-payment collectors (Planning and Human Systems 1987).

Evaluations in 1987 claimed that the Pilot Commercial Land Market Project had been effective and successful and expressed surprise that there had been no strong reaction, positive or negative, among the politically conservative, land-owning elite. Large landowners sold to the Penny Foundation despite opposition by landholders' organizations. As a result, the project expanded slowly, and several cooperative federations will be participating in the program (Planning and Human Systems 1987).

It is important to note that this was a private-sector project; no one was coerced into doing anything. Large landholders who owned land that was not being used productively had been seeking buyers. The poor wanted to own farmland but lacked money for the down payment and could not obtain mortgages. What was needed was an intermediary organization and mechanisms for bringing this demand and supply together. The characteristics of the intermediary organization were crucial. The Penny Foundation has a good, long-term reputation among all sectors of the population in the field of agrarian and rural development. Being a Guatemalan organization, it was not subject to questions about ulterior motives, and it understands the culture in which it operates. Because of its experience, it knows what will work and what will not work and has operational procedures in place and functioning (Planning and Human Systems 1987).

10. One of the largest projects financed by AID was the Immunization and Oral Rehydration Services for Child Survival, which provided a major portion of the Ministry of Health's financial resources for virtually all maternal and child health activities; additional support was provided by the European Economic Community through UNICEF. Project goals, background, and methodologies were essentially a reflection of previous experience in Guatemala.

The project is designed to use a community-based approach using local volunteers and public health personnel, especially the Rural Health Technician

(Técnico de Salud Rural—TSR). The TSRs have received two years of training using an innovative curriculum mixing curative, preventive, and community-development activities, with an emphasis on the latter two. The TSRs were intended to work in local communities outside of health centers and posts, and a major task was to help select and train community volunteers or health promoters. The TSR's efforts since the 1970s have resulted in an extensive network of promoters who have served and who continue to provide primary care in their communities.

11. The sales to any one country are based on annually negotiated agreements with the local governments where interest rates, repayment and grace periods, and the currencies accepted for payment are decided; ideally, the agreements may include needed reforms of food-production policies in the recipient country.

References and Bibliography

Academy for Educational Development
  1985   *Guatemala: Education Sector Assessment*. Washington, D.C.: AED.
Adams, Richard N.
  1987   "The Conquest Tradition of Mesoamerica." Prepublication Working Papers of the Institute of Latin American Studies. Austin: University of Texas at Austin.
APROFAM/CDC
  1983   Guatemala Family Planning and Maternal and Child Health Survey. Guatemala City: APROFAM.
Arias, Arturo
  1985   "El Movimiento Indígena en Guatemala: 1970–1980." In *Movimientos Populares en Centroamérica*, edited by Daniel Camacho and Rafael Menjívar. San José: EDUCA.
Banco de Guatemala. Departamento de Investigaciones Agropecuarias e Industriales
  1987   *Estadísticas de Productos Agropecuarios: 1972–1988*. Guatemala City: Banco de Guatemala.
Barry, Tom
  1987   *Roots of Rebellion: Land and Hunger in Central America*. Boston: South End Press.
Bossert, Thomas J., and Eusebio del Cid Peralta
  1987   *Guatemala: Health Sector Assessment*. Guatemala City: Agency for International Development.
Cultural Survival
  1987   *Counter-Insurgency and the Development Pole Strategy in the Ixil Region of Guatemala*. Unpublished manuscript.
Dewart, Tracey, and Michel Eckersley
  1988   "Guatemala's Giroón: Good Shepherd or Pied Piper?" *NACLA Report on the Americas* 22(2): 6–8.

Enge, Kjell
  1985   "The Indigenous Population: Access to Secondary/Technical and Higher Education." In *Guatemala Education Sector Assessment*. Washington, D.C.: The Academy for Educational Development.
Episcopado Guatemalteco
  1988   *El Clamor Por La Tierra*. Carta Pastoral Colectiva. Guatemala City: EG.
Franklin, David L., Marielouise Harrel, and Ralph L. Franklin
  1987   *A Nutrition Strategy for USAID/Guatemala*. Raleigh: Sigma One Corporation.
Harrison, Polly, and Kjell Enge
  1988   *Community Survey of Maternal-Child Health in Guatemala: Knowledge, Attitudes and Practices—Immunization and Control of Diarrheal Disease*. USAID/Guatemala and the Primary Health Care Technologies Project (PRITECH) of Management Sciences for Health. Washington, D.C.: PRITECH.
Hough, Richard et al.
  1982   *Tierra y Trabajo en Guatemala: Una Evaluación*. Washington, D.C.: Agency for International Development and Development Associates.
INCAP (Instituto de Nutrición de Centro América y Panama)
  1980   *Proyecto: Regionalización de la Problemática Nutricional en Guatemala y Sus Posibles Soluciones*. Guatemala City: INCAP.
  1986   *Informe Final: Encuesta Nacional Simplificada de Salud y Nutrición Materno Infantil*. Guatemala City: Ministerio de Salud Pública y Asistencia Social.
INFORPRESS
  1987   *Guatemala 1986: The Year of Promises*. Guatemala City: INFORPRESS Centroamericana.
Krueger, Chris, and Kjell Enge
  1985   *Security and Development Conditions in the Guatemalan Highlands*. Washington, D.C.: The Washington Office on Latin America.
Manz, Beatriz
  1988   *Refugees of a Hidden War: The Aftermath of Counterinsurgency in Guatemala*. Albany: State University of New York Press.
MSPAS (Ministerio de Salud Publica y Asistencia Social)
  1986   *Plan Nacional de Salud Materno-Infantil*. Guatemala City: MSPAS.
Planning and Human Systems, Inc.
  1987   *Final Report: Evaluation of the Pilot Land Market Project*. Guatemala City: Agency for International Development.
Simon, Jean-Marie
  1987   *Guatemala: Eternal Spring, Eternal Tyranny*. New York: Van Nostrand.
Universidad Rafael Landívar, Instituto de Ciencias Ambientales y Tecnologia Agrícola (ICATA)
  1984   *Perfil Amniental de la República de Guatemala*. 3 vols. Guatemala City: Talleres Gráficos de la Universidad Rafael Landívar.

USIPE/INCAP
  1986   Primer Censo Nacional de Talla. Guatemala City: Ministry of Education.
Washington Office on Latin America
  1988   *Who Pays the Price: The Cost of War in the Guatemalan Highlands.* Washington, D.C.: Washington Office on Latin America.
  1989   *Uncertain Return: Refugees and Reconciliation in Guatemala.* Washington, D.C.: Washington Office on Latin America.
Westinghouse Health Systems and Instituto de Nutrición de Centro América y Panama (INCAP)
  1987   *Guatemala Encuesta Nacional de Salud Materno Infantil.* Guatemala City: Ministerio de Salud Publica y Asistencia Social.
Wing, Harry
  1987   *U.S. Food Aid Programs and the Guatemalan Experience.* Guatemala City: The Agency for International Development.
World Bank
  1986   *Guatemala: Population, Nutrition, and Health Sector Review.* Washington, D.C.: World Bank.
  1987a   *Social Indicators of Development.* Washington, D.C.: World Bank.
  1987b   *World Development Report.* Washington, D.C.: World Bank.
  1988   *World Development Report.* Washington, D.C.: World Bank.
  1989   *World Development Report.* Washington, D.C.: World Bank.
von Hoegen, Miguel
  1988   *La Concentración Geográfica del Desarrollo en Guatemala.* Guatemala City: Asociación de Investigación y Estudios Sociales.

5

Lack of Access to Land and Food in El Salvador

Martin Diskin

Few circumstances reveal national priorities or values of governance more clearly than the distribution among a national population of the most basic form of national wealth, food. If food security means the promise that all citizens of a country will be guaranteed a basic diet, then virtually no country in the world lacks the means to accomplish this. Measured by food produced per capita, and by the financial means to make up production shortfalls, almost all countries in the world still qualify.[1] Yet, in 1991 endemic malnutrition and systematic deficiencies in nutritional intake still plague much of the world. Although these deficiencies are most obvious in the Third World, developed countries such as the United States contain pockets of undernutrition and hunger as well.[2]

There is no single route to food security. But we may generally distinguish two paths by which governments claim to achieve this universally accepted goal. First is the idea that food security can only be achieved as a by-product of a successful economic system. That is, high national output and profits will lead to more absolute wealth that will in turn achieve better distribution of this wealth, and the population will have greater access to food. This can occur either through an employment effect (higher wages, fringe benefits) or through government spending made possible by higher tax revenues from the productive system. This is the "trickle-down," or the "rising-tide-floats-all-boats," idea.

The other general approach states that the government's primary obligation to its population is to feed it, whatever the costs and whatever the measures that need be taken. This is sometimes characterized as a "basic-needs" approach (Weeks & Dore 1982) or as a human right

(Catholic Institute for International Relations 1987, 2–3). The basic-needs approach usually envisions serious state intervention to marshal and direct the necessary resources, to control the distribution system, to enact the necessary legislation, and to carry out the required research (Barraclough 1982). Such a policy is independent of the gross domestic product, balance of payments, or other measures of the economic health of the government. It has been called "the logic of the majority" in the Nicaraguan case.

The trickle-down school focuses on strengthening the climate for capital accumulation. It is usually associated with capitalist systems, where market forces constitute the major means of ordering the economy. It tends to see the state as legitimate only if it facilitates the activities of the private sector and limits its own regulatory power. It regards its solution to food problems as ultimately more efficient because it focuses on production efficiency, although it may entail some possible short-term discomfort or even suffering of those most in need. A corollary of this vision is that those who cannot feed themselves are usually deficient in some respect, that is they don't have the necessary drive, intelligence, education, or "culture," to enter the market and provide for themselves.

Trickle-down approaches founder because the control for the downward evolution of benefits is often in the hands of those who profit. As individuals they do not feel responsible for reducing hunger and claim that the market is the final arbiter, the invisible hand that decides who benefits and who languishes in poverty. One difficulty with this view is that it typically ignores distribution factors. That is, if national aggregate outputs are high, that does not guarantee that food security exists. Further, it is unclear at what point the national wealth begins to trickle down or what the mechanisms are to ensure this outcome. These are matters for visible hands (for an analysis of how government policy helped achieve more equitable income distribution in Taiwan, see Kuo, Ranis, and Fei 1981).

In capitalist Third World countries, the state often acts in agreement with the private sector. As a result, policies that increase taxes, raise wages, guarantee welfare through health care, social security and other redistribution measures are absent. With a state that does not advocate for the poor, a private sector that does not acknowledge the need for improving welfare, and a military that shores up the status quo, the system may be called a "reactionary despotism" as Baloyra terms it for the Salvadoran case (1982), or, in Jeane Kirkpatrick's formulation, an autocracy where traditional autocrats leave in place existing allocations of wealth, power, status, and other resources, which in most traditional societies favor an affluent few and maintain masses in poverty. But they worship traditional gods and observe traditional taboos. They do not disturb the habitual patterns of family and personal relations. Because the miseries of traditional life are familiar, they are bearable to ordinary people who, growing up in the society, learn to cope, as children born to untouchables in India acquire the skills and attitudes necessary for survival in the miserable roles they are destined to fill (Kirkpatrick 1982, 49–50).

Thus, security is achieved, not by providing enough, but rather through the "tradition" and "habit" of favoring an affluent few. And, of course, this is not food security. For redistributive measures to be carried out, something more than ordinary rationality, or common decency, must provide the stimulus. In El Salvador the "traditional autocracy" has developed its own momentum and maintained inequality even where the population's poverty is a source of economic and political instability.

The autocratic system is able to claim stability through the imposition of violently sanctioned order. This order contributes to efficiency through the suppression of the wage rate and curtailment of workers' rights (Cambranes 1985). In Central America, the highly profitable cotton industry yielded wealth for the planters at the cost of substandard wages for harvest workers and unacceptably high use of chemical inputs that increased yields and costs, injured workers, and poisoned the environment (Williams, 1986, chap. 3; Leonard 1987, 144–159). This vaunted efficiency is achieved through control over other aspects of the social and economic system (taxes, exchange rates, credit, suppression of dissent) that increase profit (White 1973, 121–127). It does not reflect real competitiveness or market pressure. Investment in research, plant breeding, cultivation practices, and technology are not the basis of this efficiency (Pino Cáceres 1988).

The logic of the majority regards the state as the agent of the masses, often in opposition to an elite, and as associated with socialist governments. Concerned with mass problems such as large-scale food deficits, the state often proposes collective solutions, such as communes, state farms, and agricultural cooperatives. It may invest national resources in research to stabilize food production and increase yields (such as drought-resistant seed strains, open-field pollination practices to allow farmers to experiment themselves) and to train the rural poor in agronomy and farm management. It may intervene in the price structure of food to subsidize urban populations with cheap food. The logic of the majority is a moral commitment, but at the same time it shores up political support for the government.

However, popular support for such governments may in turn disguise inefficiency. The inefficiencies observable in socialist food-security planning are often cited as evidence for the lack of feasibility of socialism itself (Colburn 1986 writing about Nicaragua; Powelson 1987, chap. 1). Inefficiency may co-exist with steady progress in providing more food to the poor. Moving toward food security sometimes creates difficulties because of the increased demand and consumption (Utting 1987).

Not all situations are so black and white. No government is openly supportive of widespread hunger and starvation. Nor does any country devote its resources exclusively to the eradication of hunger. In all cases, national policy is a blend of pragmatic considerations, political party or interest group competition, the economic condition of the country, and foreign policy. These dynamics determine who the most significant clientele of the state is (Barraclough 1970). The returns to this clientele help define political will, that is, the level of priority a government assigns to the food-security question.

In each case, the various priorities are ordered differently, and this ordering gives us a glimpse into the national political will. Although the trickle-downers may correctly speak about the efficiency of their system, success in accomplishing higher aggregate output is no guarantee of greater food security. Likewise, those who propose collective solutions may have to live with lower efficiency but may, through state intervention, make this output travel farther. However, insuring that the GDP is equitably distributed to the population is no guarantee that the system is self-sustaining. So, it may be that productive efficiency and effective distribution (or redistribution) are either independent of each other or are inversely related, that is, low efficiency is related to equitable food distribution and high efficiency to stratification and inequity.

An example of the latter would be Cuba, where, although yields of sugar and other crops have not been high under a collective productive regime, none doubt that basic needs, particularly food security, are provided to all. In fact, by way of dramatic contrast, the yields per surface area of sugar on the northeast coast of Brazil are higher than in Cuba, even though sugar is produced there on small holdings. But Northeast Brazil is an area of endemic hunger, even starvation (Gross and Underwood 1971). Cuba, in the words of the 1982 report of the Joint Economic Committee of the U.S. Congress, guarantees food security to its people through a "highly egalitarian redistribution of income that has eliminated almost all malnutrition, particularly among young children" (quoted in Benjamin, Collins, and Scott 1984, 90).

Recent research on the quality of life suggests that high GDP and equity of distribution are probably unrelated (UNDP 1990). Studies such as these suggest that political will alone is necessary to resolve problems of inequitable distribution of national wealth.

Food Security and Social Change

In this chapter, I treat the case of El Salvador, where the distribution of food reflects the distribution of other national resources. That is, a large percentage of the population lives in a constant state of deprivation. That same sector earns the lowest incomes, has access to the least amount of land or is landless, and has virtually no opportunity to express itself in an organized fashion in defense of its interests. Since a military coup in October 1979, a series of reform measures have been designed to change this situation and to benefit the lowest socioeconomic sector. The Military Proclamation of October 15, 1979, found that the social inequities were "the result of the antiquated economic, social and political structures that have traditionally prevailed in the country, structures that do not offer the majority of the inhabitants the minimum conditions essential for their human self-fulfillment" (quoted in Americas Watch and American Civil Liberties Union 1982, 260.) This proclamation was an abrupt rupture with an ancien régime and expressed goals that went far beyond the food question; in this chapter I analyze the government's activities and successes in achieving that specific goal.

The Pre-Coup Food Situation

During the 1970s, El Salvador was a country composed of two worlds. A small elite, numerically inconsequential, controlled most of the land, and the majority of the population (including almost all the rural population) lived at a level below what was necessary to survive. 40.9 percent of the rural population was landless in 1971, up from 11.8 percent in 1961 (Deere and Diskin 1984, 18), and 70.9 percent of all farms were below 2 hectares in size (compare Table 5.1). Agricultural production patterns also reflected the duality. 77.9 percent of maize, 78.3 percent of beans, and 82.3 percent of sorghum (grown for human consumption in El Salvador) were produced on farms 10 hectares or less (Deere and Diskin 1984, 21). In contrast, 74 percent of coffee and 89.3 percent of sugar was produced on farms over 20 hectares in size (Deere and Diskin 1984, 21). Basic grains constituted only 10.1 percent of the market value of all crops; coffee, cotton, and sugar accounted for 83.6 percent of the market value of all crops (Deere and Diskin 1984, 22).

The landless and land-poor (numbering more than 350,00 families) survived through a combination of cultivation and wage work that

TABLE 5.1 Changes in Land Distribution, El Salvador, 1950–1971

Farm Size (hectares)	1950				1961				1971			
	No. Farms	%	Area (hectares)	%	No. Farms	%	Area (hectares)	%	No. Farms	%	Area (hectares)	%
–.99	70,416	40.4	35,203	2.3	107,054	47.2	61,366	3.9	132,464	49.0	70,287	4.8
–1.99	35,189	20.2	48,013	3.1	48,501	21.4	68,542	4.3	59,063	21.9	81,039	5.6
–4.99	34,868	20.0	106,973	7.0	37,743	16.6	117,470	7.4	43,414	16.0	131,985	9.1
–9.90	14,064	8.1	99,446	6.5	14,001	6.2	98,791	6.2	15,598	5.8	110,472	7.6
10–19.99	8,875	5.1	122,477	8.0	8,524	3.8	117,426	7.4	9,164	3.4	126,974	8.7
20–49.99	6,660	3.8	206,334	13.5	6,711	3.0	208,628	13.2	6,986	2.6	215,455	14.8
50–99.99	2,107	1.2	147,640	9.6	2,214	1.0	154,704	9.8	2,238	0.8	154,164	10.6
100–999.99	1,881	1.1	459,119	30.0	2,023	0.9	505,582	32.0	1,878	0.7	437,939	30.2
1000 or more	145	0.1	305,118	19.9	125	0.1	248,919	15.7	63	0.0	123,579	8.5
Total	174,204	100	1,530,323	99.9	226,896	100.2	1,581,428	99.9	270,868	100.3	1,451,894	99.9

Source: Dirección General de Estadísticas y Censos (DGEC): Censo Agropecuario 1950, 1961, and 1971 (El Salvador, 1950, 1961, and 1971).

TABLE 5.2   Composition of Annual Net Income by Source, El Salvador, 1975 (percentages)

Farm Size (hectares)	Farm Income				Nonfarm Income				Total
	Crops	Fruits	Animal	Subtotal	Wage Work	Trade	Other[a]	Subtotal	
Landless	—	20	8	28	52	14	6	72	100
Less than 1	25	26	8	59	31	7	3	41	100
1.0–1.9	34	28	13	75	19	5	1	25	100
2.0–4.9	64	18	10	92	6	2	0	8	100
5.0–9.9	74	12	7	93	2	4	1	7	100
10.0–50.0	74	9	11	97	2	2	2	6	100

[a]Other includes artisan production income, remittances, and rental payments.

Source: United Nations Development Programme (UNDP). *Realidad campesina y desarrollo nacional,* Project ELS/73/003, vol. 7. San Salvador, 1976, p. 83.

generally deepened their poverty each year. The vast bulk of the poor depended to a considerable degree upon wages to complete family income. The rural poor, those working less than 2 hectares of land, or the landless, earned only a portion of their income from farm work on their own land. Those working one hectare or less earned 60 percent of family income on their own land. The landless earned 72 percent of their income through wage labor on others' farms. In 1975, 75 percent of rural households fell below a threshold that would enable them to buy the minimal diet (Deere and Diskin 1984, 7, table 3). In February 1968, when the minimum wage was 2.25 colones/day for agricultural work, many campesinos preferred the old, lower wage of 1.50 colones/day because they customarily received three meals. The sad conclusion is that they could not feed themselves adequately on .75 colones/day. At .75/day virtually all the landless and land-poor population would have earned too little to meet basic food requirements (CIDA 1968, 78).

In general, 1975 incomes for the rural poor represent a real decline compared to 1961 (see Table 5.3). The income of landless families fell 16 percent in that period, and the income of families who worked one hectare or less dropped by 20 percent (Deere and Diskin 1984, 7). This drop in real income was also accompanied by shifts in land tenure. For farms of one hectare or less, ownership fell from 43 percent in 1950 to 28.5 percent in 1971 (see Table 5.4). Ownership of farms from 1–2 hectares fell from 52.7 percent in 1950 to 31.4 percent in 1971 (Deere and Diskin 1984, 19). Thus, with smaller farms, even smaller income shares were staying with those who worked the land.

Although farms one hectare and less in size accounted for 49 percent of all farms, they received only .8 percent of total agricultural credit. Farms in the 1–10 hectare category, accounting for 43.7 percent of all

TABLE 5.3 Average Rural Household Income, El Salvador, 1961–1975 (1975 colones)

Farm Size	1961			1975		
(hectares)	No. of Households	%	Average Income	No. of Households	%	Average Income
Landless	30,451	12	940	166,922	41	792
Less than 1	107,054	42	1,252	138,838	34	1,003
1–9.9	100,245	39	1,752	94,330	23	2,287
10–50	19,957	7	6,010	7,927	2	6,342
Total	257,707	100		407,387	100	

Source: UNDP. Realidad campesina y desarrollo nacional, Project ELS/73/003, vol. 7. San Salvador, 1976, p. 75.

TABLE 5.4 Changes in Land Tenure by Farm Size, El Salvador, 1950–1971

	Ownership	Nonownership[a]	Total
1950			
Farm size (hectares)			
1 and less	43.0	57.0	100.0
1–2	52.7	47.3	100.0
all farms	61.9	38.1	100.0
1971			
Farm size (hectares)			
1 and less	28.5	71.5	100.0
1–2	31.4	68.6	100.0
all farms	39.9	60.1	100.0

[a]Includes, primarily, arrendamiento simple and colonia.

Source: Dirección General de Estadísticas y Censos (DGEC), 1950 and 1971.

farms, received only 12.5 percent of credit (Deere and Diskin 1984, 23). Wages increased during the previous decade by 78.1 percent for coffee harvesters (the maximum) and fell 18.2 percent for permanent farm workers (the minimum); the general cost of living went up by 95.2 percent (Deere and Diskin 1984, 34, table 18).

The consequences of this poverty were reflected in the most sensitive indicator of welfare: the nutritional status of children. In a study conducted by INCAP (Instituto de Nutrición de Centro América y Panamá) in 1965–1967, 78 percent of Salvadoran children were undernourished, of whom 25 percent were "moderately" undernourished, and 3.2 percent "severely" affected. Survey data for 1976–1978 indicate improvements, although the situation was still far from acceptable. Sixty-four percent of children tested were malnourished, 12 percent moderately and .9 percent severely[3] (USAID 1985, 80–92).

A carefully controlled study in the mid-1970s that looked at malnutrition among children according to their precise economic niche indicated that permanent residents on coffee plantations suffered from the greatest degree of malnutrition. They differed from the land-poor and landless in the greater frequency of third degree malnutrition, 2.2 percent (Valverde et al., 1980).

These measures of malnutrition have their counterparts in the poor state of rural health, education, housing, and life expectancy. The slight improvements in nutritional status in 1976–1978 reported in the INCAP study probably reflected the greater number of urban workers who benefited from a certain amount of industrialization, but the rural situation remained critical. Perhaps the worst aspect of this was that, with no institutional change, the global situation was headed for explosion. Efforts to promote change, whether government-inspired or through participation from below, were consistently met with repression.

During the late 1970s, food-production levels were higher in El Salvador than in any other Central American country (Leonard 1987, 213, table A.23). El Salvador's economy was also growing at a vigorous rate (5.9 percent in 1960–1970) (de Janvry 1981, 36), but the rural income distribution worsened, with the Gini coefficient of income distribution changing from .52 in 1961 to .68 in the early 1970s (Deere and Diskin 1984, 7). High rates of economic growth and production levels, coupled with profound human misery, cast the trickle-down theory in real doubt. When presented with the previous details, members of the Salvadoran private sector argued that even higher levels of growth were needed before the trickle-down effect could begin. The president of the private-sector assocation ANEP (Asociación Nacional de la Empresa Privada) told me in 1984 that general benefits would flow when the private sector made a sustained annual growth of 35 percent. The following year he amended this to a mere 19 percent, citing Taiwan as the relevant precedent. The logic of this argument is hermetic, because the preconditions to achieve this end would give such total control over the society to the private sector that whether trickle-down would occur at that time or not would not matter.

During this period of growth in production, population was growing at a vigorous rate, 3.1 percent between 1950 and 1971, with a 3.5 percent rural rate and a 2.9 percent urban rate (Banco Mundial 1979, 11). Although the numbers may suggest that poverty is the inexorable outcome of high population growth, Durham's research clearly shows that land-use patterns contribute much more to rural impoverishment than population growth (Durham 1979). In the 1960s and 1970s, agricultural employment opportunity was higher than the growth rate of the rural labor force. "Between 1961 and 1971, the rural labor force increased by 2.2 percent, i.e., 0.4 percent less than the growth rate of agricultural employment" (Deere and Diskin 1984, 31). Per capita cereal production was decreasing in the period 1975–1981, as was general per capita food production in 1974–1982 (Leonard 1987, 214). At the same time, El Salvador had a positive balance of food trade in the 1981–1983 period of $330.3 million. This meant that the deficit in cereals, meat, dairy products, fruits, vegetables, and animal and vegetable oils of $103.9 million was counterbalanced by revenues of $434.2 million, of which coffee revenues accounted for $419.3 million (Leonard 1987, table A.26 215). In macroeconomic terms, this process may be called development, that is, the value of the shortfall in food production is more than compensated for by coffee revenues. But that positive balance was not used to benefit the rural poor.

Agrarian Reform—A Way to Food Security?

The military coup of 1979 specifically sought to redress the social injustice that the agro-export system ("the majority") had wrought. The junior officers who seized power felt that by eliminating the repression, corruption, and arbitrary anti-democratic behavior, they could increase yields, better distribute farmland, and therefore increase family incomes. The most important means to accomplish this was an agrarian reform.

The kind of agrarian reform envisioned was the product of considerable debate during the 1970s. It would have had rather severe acreage limitations on landholdings (about 50 hectares), would have offered technical and financial support to the new beneficiaries, and would have encouraged the formation of peasant-run cooperatives (Alvarenga 1977, 139–140). In late 1979 and early 1980, there was widespread support for establishing agricultural cooperatives as well as for titling small holdings. At least, the members of the civilian-military junta supported such measures. They were joined in this by the Ministry of Agriculture and Cattle (MAG), members of labor and church organizations, and academics. Had the reformist tone of the junior officers who accomplished the coup prevailed, that tone would likely have shaped the agrarian reform decree. In fact, the American Embassy believed, just days before the decree was issued, that the document would reflect such intentions.[4]

But between the formation of the junta on October 15, 1979, and the emission of Decree 153 (the Basic Law of Agrarian Reform, March 6, 1980) the political complexion of the government changed drastically (Dunkerley 1982; Armstrong and Schenk 1982; Montgomery 1982; Baloyra 1982). Behind-the-scenes negotiations were going on between the junta, the MAG, ISTA (Instituto Salvadoreño de Transformación Agraria), UCS (Unión Comunal Salvadoreña), the American Embassy, the Salvadoran military, and the rural oligarchy. The reformers seemed to be losing ground as the military old guard assumed more prominent positions in the government. The military stamp was seen in the intensification of repression against all forms of government opposition activity. The installation of then Col. García to the junta and the Ministry of Defense and the retention of Gen. Jaime Abdul Gutiérrez meant a decline in power for the original reformist officers such as Col. Majano. Demonstrators were shot down in the streets, while the junta was seeking a negotiated accommodation with them through the implementation of reforms.

Because of these events, the decree was different than expected. It placed the upper limit on land ownership at 100 hectares and ordered the confiscated lands to be made into peasant cooperatives. The next day an implementing decree made it clear that only properties over 500 hectares would be "intervened" immediately, confiscation of the remainder would be indefinitely postponed. At that time, an emergency suspension of civil liberties was also decreed, giving near total power to the military, something it had held in any event, without benefit of decrees.

On April 26 of the same year, decree 207 was passed by the junta. This stated that small-holding tenants, that is, renters, sharecroppers, and other nonowning cultivators, would become owners of the lands they worked, up to a limit of 17 acres. Although the authors of this decree intended that its effect would be immediate, it became the slowest and most problematical part of the land-reform program. Instantly dubbed the "most sweeping land reform in the history of Latin America" by its United States supporters (Prosterman and Temple 1980), it was supposed to lead to increased family-farm production of basic grains. That would, in turn, help fuel industrial development that would feed back into increased agricultural production through improved technology. This spiral of economic development and recovery would involve so many of the rural poor[5] that the pool of recruits for the FMLN (Farabundo Martí National Liberation Front) guerrilla force would dry up and the country would "escape the threat of a civil war" (Prosterman and Temple 1980, 4). This was not to be.

Any effort at agrarian reform was fiercely opposed by the landowners and their military allies. The confiscation of lands over 500 hectares, Phase I, was done very soon after decree 153 was issued.[6] The military saw to it that landowners did not resist, but at the same time, it unleashed a wave of terror in the countryside. This double message meant that the new or potential beneficiaries of reform should not become too exuberant in seeking to use their new status to promote more changes. It was a message stating that reformism would be limited and that it would not threaten the power of the military or the rural elite that still maintained holdings. Not only was this form of "implementation" of the reform a hardship, but the economic burdens of the new cooperative

TABLE 5.5   Estimated Benefits at Beginning of Agrarian Reform (1981)

	Area		Beneficiaries	
	# of Hectares	% of Total Land in Farms	# of Families	% of Rural Population
Phase I	223,000	15.4	50,000	11.9
Phase II	343,000	23.6	50,000	11.9
Phase III	175,000	12.1	150,000	35.7
Total	741,000	51.1	250,000	59.5

Source: Diskin 1988.

TABLE 5.6   Agrarian Reform Outcome vs. Original Estimated Goals

	Area (ha.)	% of Goal	% of Farmland	# Families Benefited	% of Goal	% of Rural Families
Phase I	218,566	98	15.1	31,259	68	7.5
Phase II			N E V E R I M P L E M E N T E D			
Phase III	96,566	55	6.7	37,500	25	8
Total	315,132	42	21.8	68,759	28	15.5

Source: Diskin 1989.

members of these properties were overwhelming. Overcompensation of former landowners (an informal bribe) and the systematic decapitalization of properties left new cooperatives with an agrarian debt too large to pay.[7] Added to that were difficulties in obtaining credit and technical assistance: The new cooperatives were left to sink or swim, with the former landowners hoping for failure.

Decree 207 hardly sparked an instant transfer of land; it took almost a year before anything was done at all. When new financial and bureaucratic machinery was finally put in place, eligible peasants were faced with an impenetrable thicket of rules, procedures, and paperwork that had to be initiated by each campesino, all in an environment of increasing lethal violence.

Those who benefited from either measure, that is, Phase I and decree 207, moved from a status of technical landlessness to one of only technical landownership. This was so for different reasons. Phase I beneficiaries were severely circumscribed by regulations that prevented the full exercise of ownership and did not grant them the assistance needed to run the new properties. Many new cooperatives were run by the more highly skilled staff of the previous landowner, so for the field hands it meant only a change in bosses. There was no increase in wages because returns from harvests were controlled by the agrarian agency and the bank. There was almost never enough of a surplus to improve the status of the rural poor beneficiaries. If there was a surplus, the government agrarian reform agency (ISTA) placed that money in restricted noninterest bearing accounts to keep against payments on the agrarian debt. The technical support needed to manage complex activities such as cotton production was very difficult to obtain, especially if the cooperative leadership was composed of former peasant field hands rather than the previous skilled managers associated with the previous landowners. A peasant I interviewed in May 1988 told me that the difference between his condition now and before the reform was only that he now had more days of work each year but not an increase in the wage rate or a dividend from profits on sales.

For 207 beneficiaries, there was a constant diet of violence and intimidation. Instead of upward of 150,000 beneficiary families as originally stated, as of June 16, 1988, only about 37,500 families actually received land (FINATA 1988). Although there is some indication that these beneficiaries have taken their ownership seriously, improved their lands, invested in improvements, and experienced a slight increase in family income (MAG-OSPA-PERA 1985, 105–110), their numbers are so few as to not have any impact on the rural sector in general.

Impact of Reform, the War, and U.S. Aid on Food Security

The agrarian reform of 1980 was an effort to redistribute land among an impoverished rural mass. The institutional tension between landowners, the private sector, the military, labor unions, peasant organizations, and church groups, did not change significantly. The only real change was in the intensification of the conflict into a full-blown civil war.

The data available show that the condition of the rural poor has since deteriorated. The most recent report of the congressional Arms Control and Foreign Policy Caucus entitled "Bankrolling Failure" describes some of this situation. For FY 1988, U.S. Aid to El Salvador exceeded El Salvador's own contribution to its budget. The United States contributed $608 million compared to the $582 million national budget (Hatfield, Leach, and Miller 1987, 1–2). This enormous subsidy to El Salvador, if consistent with the publicly stated U.S. foreign policy goals, should be used primarily to implement reforms, improve welfare, and contribute to the Salvadoran military's effort to defeat the insurgency. President Reagan and his secretary of state often said that the military portion of the aid served as a "shield" behind which reforms could be carried out.[8] However, a close examination of the real destination of this aid convinced the caucus that *"Three dollars of U.S. aid were devoted to the war and its effects in 1987 for every one dollar used to address its root causes"* (Hatfield, Leach, and Miller 1987, 2, emphasis theirs). The U.S.

government acknowledged that its highest priority was given to the war by calling this pattern of aid transitional to assistance for reform and development (USAID 1985, 63). Worse still, a significant portion of this aid was administered directly by the Salvadoran military, although this is in contravention of U.S. law that prevents the use of food aid for "military or paramilitary purposes" (Hatfield, Leach, and Miller 1987, 9). This skewed pattern of U.S. aid accompanied a sharp deterioration in living standards, a worsening economic system, and a "collapse of political will" (Hatfield, Leach, and Miller 1987, 20).

In 1991, after eight years of a stalemated war, the social changes that have occurred may best be described as a rebirth of the political power of the rural oligarchy and the private sector. The enormous growth in the military budget has greatly increased the political influence of the military. In opposition to this was the growth of peasant organizations (some within the agrarian reform and others outside its structure), a renewed militancy of the labor movement, and an increased military capability of the guerrilla forces.

U.S. support for rural development has focused more and more on private agricultural development. USAID has advocated a process of rural privatization during the past few years. For campesinos who will be relocated on presently abandoned agrarian reform properties, for new beneficiaries who will be placed on Phase I properties, and for new beneficiaries who will be placed on land to be bought by the government—all of these groups would be given titles for small, privately owned plots. Rather than consider that the lack of social change, that is, the failure to break the power of the rural oligarchy, has impeded healthy agrarian change, AID has come to think that the reasons for stagnation in production, the continuing low levels of rural welfare (New York Times, Oct. 16, 1988), and the continued oppression of rural organizations lie in the existence of cooperative forms of production. Little attention is given to the continuing institutionalized violence, the difficulties of obtaining credit for small producers, or the domination of rural affairs by the large growers' associations. About all that is agreed upon is that the conditions of campesinos in El Salvador remain abysmal.

It should be noted that of the two general strategies to achieve food security, U.S. spending strongly favors the trickle-down approach. It justified the military portion of the aid package as a necessary measure to create the conditions for development. "AID spends over 40 percent of the local currencies generated by U.S. aid on guarantees and lending programs for business, rather than on basic needs and long-term development projects" (Hatfield, Leach, and Miller 1987, 19).

Under the Reagan administration there was a spate of new, semi-governmental agencies such as the Bureau of Private Enterprise, the

Trade Credit Insurance Corporation, and the Center for International Private Enterprise, which was created expressly to stimulate and aid the private sector throughout Central America and in other countries. These groups in conjunction with other U.S. government institutions such as the Overseas Private Investment Corporation (OPIC), the Export-Import Bank (EXIMBANK), the National Endowment for Democracy (NED), in turn spawned many local business groups and think tanks for the private sector (Barry and Preusch 1988, chap. 3). Through the use of portions of the U.S. assistance budget such as Economic Support Funds, PL480 (Title I) food assistance, roughly 75 percent of USAID spending in Central America was destined for "stabilization," that is, support for the financial structure of the recipient country (direct aid to the private sector). Very little USAID spending has addressed the social causes of the conflict (Barry and Preusch 1988, 21).

Outcome and Update

The economic devastation created by the war and the depopulation of certain areas caused by military actions left the country in disastrous financial condition. Now, in 1991, roughly half a million Salvadorans live outside their country because of the war and government repression. Many people living in displaced persons camps in El Salvador or in United Nations–supervised camps in Honduras have returned to their home villages. Under and unemployment rose to 50 percent (Hatfield, Leach, and Miller 1987, 19). Consumption declined 30 percent in the first four years of the war (Hatfield, Leach, and Miller 1987, 19). A 23 percent drop in purchasing power coupled with a 32 percent inflationary rise in 1986 pushed many of the rural poor into a desperate situation (Hatfield, Leach, and Miller 1987, 19). A 1985 study of the nutritional status of children of displaced families showed that among this stressed portion of the population, conditions were worse than ever previously recorded. Only 28.8 percent of these children were normal and 28.1 percent were in grades 2 and 3 (moderate and severe malnutrition) with 5.9 percent in grade 3 (USAID 1985, 83, table 8-1). The highest rate of grade 3 malnutrition (7 percent) was found among children living in the marginal urban sections of San Salvador (USAID 1985, 86–87, table 8-3). These figures contradict the usual idea that the urban environment offers the most economic opportunity and reflect the fact that displaced people in camps were probably eating better because of international assistance and the efforts of different institutions, including religious agencies, that care for these people. The disastrous outcome for urban displaced children reflects the extreme downturn of the national economy.

Agricultural production has diminished considerably. This downturn was caused in part by low market prices for the principal export crops and also reflects the private sector's efforts to withhold production in order to obtain concessions from the government. This has been especially true in the case of cotton production.

The disastrous condition of the rural poor would be worse yet were it not for the high level of subsidy that U.S. aid represents and the generosity of numerous PVOs (private voluntary organizations) that maintain a presence there (Arias 1989, 79, 93). Government data from 1985 show that about 3 million people fall below a level of absolute poverty, that is, below what is required for their physical reproduction, even if they spend 100 percent of their income on food (CENITEC 1989, 11). This situation has worsened since then. The cost of food has risen about 400 percent since 1978, with most of the increase occurring during the past two years (Centro Universitario 1990); the increase in 1989 was about 33 percent (Instituto de Investigaciones 1990). By 1989 real wages had fallen to between 32 and 43 percent of 1978 levels (Instituto de Investigaciones 1990).

If the setbacks were merely momentary reverses in a well-conceived reformist plan, the continued application of more of the same should bear fruit for the population as conditions stabilize. However, should the war end tomorrow, the underlying problems of rural poverty, food insecurity, and inequity of land ownership would still be present. That is, the underlying institutional obstacles to fair distribution of national wealth would remain to be attacked. The continuation and ferocity of war is an indication of the resistance to change by the private sector and military.

The conditions described developed under the Christian Democratic administration of President Duarte, a lifelong reformer. Duarte failed to realize the thorough implementation of the agrarian reform because of corruption within his administration and his inability to challenge the continuing veto exercised by the traditional right-wing alliance of the military and the oligarchy. When the government passed into the hands of the ARENA (Alianza Republicana Nacionalista) party in 1988 (municipal and legislative elections) and 1989 (presidential elections), a very different developmental philosophy took over.

ARENA's view of private-sector-driven development (ECA 1989; Universidad Centroamericana 1988) dovetailed nicely with USAID free-market guidelines (Lievano and Norton 1988; Norton 1990). In the macroeconomic sphere it signaled the end of price supports to consumers, devaluation of the currency as a stimulus to agro-export production, and elimination of protective tariffs. In effect, wage controls and the suppression of union activity continued apace, ostensibly to prevent an inflationary spiral. It also meant privatization of government-owned assets, private marketing arrangements (including foreign trade of coffee), the return of banks to private hands, and the attempted breakup of agrarian reform cooperatives by issuing individual titles to each member of the cooperative.

What the future also holds is a probable reduction of the U.S. subsidy because congress is beginning to question the efficacy of continued aid. Hence, the resolution to these severe problems is yet to materialize. USAID seeks to return to a "free market" situation that might grant slightly more access to rural private property. But there is no reason to believe that now the invisible hand will successfully order Salvadoran society where it has failed in the past.

Conclusion

The two forms of political will (trickle-down and logic of the majority) seem to present clear tradeoffs and challenges. Trickle-down has a capacity to benefit the population, but the question remains regarding the location of the trigger point in national income formation. Must the Salvadoran economy await a steady 19 percent annual growth rate as the private sector advocates? That would place the economy in the realm of phantasy. All we know is that in El Salvador, high rates of growth in the GDP are possible with declines in the general level of welfare.

The logic-of-the-majority approach permits rapid changes in production patterns and distribution of food and therefore the elimination of hunger. But can this approach lead to significant enough levels of growth in the GDP to consolidate these immediately obtainable benefits? It can guarantee the protection of the population from the worst effects of hunger, but can it overcome inherent inefficiency and frequent bureaucratic torpor?

For both cases there is another significant aspect. Each system requires social order and support, or at least quiescence and lack of active opposition. El Salvador has pursued a policy, through war and peace, of emphasizing a leading sector, the private agrarian and industrial producers, as the engine of development. The welfare of the bulk of the population is left to a loaded market environment. For two decades, more and more people have experienced declining real incomes and standards of living. Order and legitimacy have been obtained through intimidation by military and paramilitary means from the 1880s to the present. But with changes in church leadership, the rise of rural or- ganizations, new political parties, and an active guerrilla insurgency, the legitimacy of the Salvadoran state and government is itself in jeopardy. In no other way can the success of the FMLN be explained (Bacevich et al., 1988). U.S. policy, guided by a "low-intensity conflict" strategy has advocated reform to win "hearts and minds" but has not offered adequate financial and political support to accomplish the original goals of agrarian reform.

The 1980s have seen some efforts and much talk about reforms. These efforts have been carried out in order to moderate the disenchantment of the rural population, to create "small-scale capitalists" who would increase production by means of "an agricultural sector someday as conservative and efficient as south Korea, Taiwan, and Japan" (U.S. Embassy Cable, March 4, 1980b). But, as we have seen, this has not been the outcome of policy. What the "reactionary despots" (Baloyra 1982) seem unable to see is that the way to end the war is to end the historic injustice the oligarchs and much of the military are fighting to preserve. Preservation of this injustice is a formula for disaster, and this is what we are presently seeing.

El Salvador in the 1980s shows that the primary goal for the Salvadoran government and the United States is to win a counter-insurgency war rather than to benefit the vast bulk of the population and thereby erase the fundamental sources of the conflict. The near future will clarify whether this war can be won without the support of a population that has been repeatedly abused in the name of this policy. If the U.S.-supported project triumphs, then trickle-down will have the opportunity to demonstrate that it can improve the welfare of the majority. If not, the conflict will continue to needlessly claim innocent lives.

Notes

1. In cases such as famines in the horn of Africa, adequate food supplies, although not derived from local production, could be given to those in need were it not for political and military factors.

2. Although the United States enjoys the highest per capita income in the world, there was a measurable and growing amount of hunger in 1991. The significance, indeed the existence of this phenomenon, was the subject of intense debate and polemics. The Reagan administration said at various times that its programs were adequate for the problem, there was more welfare fraud than genuine hunger, and some of the hungry preferred food handouts to work. Opponents of the administration accused it of callousness and indifference to human suffering.

3. (The categories "mild," "moderate," and "severe" are terms referring to weight-for-age data measured against the Iowa reference scale for acceptable child growth.) Children are called normal if they are within 90 percent of the Iowa range for their age, mildly malnourished if they are within 75–89.9 percent, moderately malnourished if they are within 60–74.9 percent, and severely malnourished if they are under 60 percent on the Iowa scale. This so-called

Gomez classification is normally presented as grades 1 (mild), 2 (moderate), and 3 (severe) (USAID 1985, 81–82).

4. Three days before decree 153 was issued, Professor Roy Prosterman, described by Ambassador White as a "prominent land-reform expert," briefed the embassy staff about the law to be issued. Prosterman had enjoyed privileged access to all the participants in the agrarian reform negotiation. He spoke about a 35-hectare limit on the best lands. He called this sort of reform "good" and "not radical," referring to the much lower retention limits of the Taiwanese and Japanese reforms (U.S. Embassy Cable, March 3, 1980a).

5. In Alexander Haig's 1984 book, *Caveat,* he remembers it this way, "In March 1980, this junta headed by Duarte, announced a land reform program that expropriated all estates larger than 1,250 acres and promised to grant 90 percent of all other arable land to peasant cooperatives or sharecroppers" (Haig 1984, 126).

6. Phase I, the only well-implemented part of the reform, was carried out in the reformist euphoria of early 1980. The Christian Democrats entered into a pact with the military whereby they would enter the governing junta and grant it a certain legitimacy in return for the military's promise to implement the agrarian reform.

7. This was because decree 153 specified in article 30 that the agrarian debt, i.e., the amount given to ex-landlords, was to be repaid to ISTA (Instituto Salvadoreño de Transformacion Agraria) (MAG 1980, 35–36).

8. Before Secretary of State Schultz, Secretary of State Alexander Haig put it this way, "The Salvadoran armed forces needed equipment and training so they could guarantee the safety of their government while the process of land redistribution and social and economic reform was completed" (Haig 1984, 124).

References and Bibliography

Alvarenga, Ivo P.
   1977   *Temas de Derecho Agrario y Reforma Agraria.* San Jose: Editorial Universitaria Centro Americana (EDUCA).
Americas Watch Committee and the American Civil Liberties Union
   1982   *Report on Human Rights in El Salvador, January 26, 1982.* New York: Vintage Books.
Arias, Salvador
   1989   *Seguridad o Inseguridad Alimentaria: Un Reto Para la Región Centroamericana. Perspectives Para el Año 2000.* San Salvador: UCA Editores.
Armstrong, Robert, and Janet Shenk
   1982   *El Salvador: The Face of Revolution.* Boston: South End Press.
Bacevich, A.J., J.D. Hallums, R.H. White, and Thomas F. Young
   1988   *American Military Policy in Small Wars: The Case of El Salvador.* Working Group Study. Cambridge: The John F. Kennedy School of Government.
Baloyra, Enrique
   1982   *El Salvador in Transition.* Chapel Hill and London: The University of North Carolina Press.

Banco Mundial (World Bank)
  1979   *El Salvador: Cuestiones y Perspectivas Demograficas.* Washington, D.C.:
          Banco Mundial.
Barraclough, Solon
  1970   "Agricultural Policy and Strategies of Land Reform." In *Masses in*
          Latin America, edited by Irving Louis Horowitz. New York: Oxford
          University Press, 95–171.
  1982   *A Preliminary Analysis of the Nicaraguan Food System.* United Nations
          Institute for Social Development, Food Systems and Society Series.
          Geneva: United Nations.
Barry, Tom, and Deb Preusch
  1988   *The Soft War: The Uses and Abuses of U.S. Economic Aid in Central*
          America. New York: Grove Press.
Benjamin, M., J. Collins, and M. Scott
  1984   *No Free Lunch: Food and Revolution in Cuba Today.* San Francisco:
          Institute for Food and Development Policy.
Cambranes, J.D.
  1985   *Coffee and Peasants in Guatemala.* CIRMA/Plumsock Mesoamerican
          Studies. South Woodstock, Vermont: CIRMA.
Catholic Institute for International Relations
  1987   *Right to Survive: Human Rights in Nicaragua.* London: Catholic Institute
          for International Relations.
CENITEC (Centro de Investigaciones Tecnológicas y Científicas)
  1989   "Las Dimensiones de la Pobreza Extrema en El Salvador." *Cuadernos*
          de Investigación, no. 1 (Feb.). San Salvador: CENITEC Dirección de
          Investigaciones Económicas y Sociales.
Centro Universitario de Documentación e Información
  1990   "Consideraciones Macroéconomicas en Torno al Problema de la Ex-
          trema Pobreza." *Proceso* 445 (Sept. 26). San Salvador: Universidad
          Centroaméricana "José Simeón Cañas."
CIDA (Comité Interamericano de Desarrollo Integral
  1968   *El Salvador: Características Generales de la Utilización y Distribución de*
          la Tierra. Mexico City: CIDA.
Colburn, Forrest D.
  1986   *Post-Revolutionary Nicaragua: State, Class, and the Dilemmas of Agrarian*
          Policy. Berkeley, Los Angeles, London: University of California Press.
Deere, C.D., and M. Diskin
  1984   "Rural Poverty in El Salvador: Dimensions, Trends, and Causes."
          World Employment Program Research Working Paper 10–6/WP64.
          Geneva: International Labor Organization.
de Janvry, Alain
  1981   *The Agrarian Question and Reformism in Latin America.* Baltimore:
          Johns Hopkins University Press.
DGEC (Dirección General de Estadísticas y Censos)
  1954   I Censo Agrario, 1950. San Salvador: DGEC.
  1967   II Censo agrario, 1961. San Salvador: DGEC.

1975   III Censo agrario, 1971. San Salvador: DGEC.

Diskin, Martin
1989   "El Salvador: Reform Prevents Change." In *Searching for Agrarian Structure and Agrarian Reform in Latin America,* edited by William C. Thiesenhusen. Boston: Unwin Hyman.

Dunkerly, James
1982   *The Long War: Dictatorship and Revolution in El Salvador.* London: Junction Books.

Durham, William H.
1979   *Scarcity and Survival in Central America: Ecological Origins of the Soccer War.* Stanford: Stanford University Press.

ECA (Estudios Centroamericanos)
1989   "La Política de Reforma Agraria de ARENA." *Estudios Centroamericanos,* no. 492 (Oct.). San Salvador Universidad Centroamericano "José Simeón Cañas," pp. 843–846.

FINATA (Financiera Nacional de Tierras Agricolas)
1988   *Decreto No. 207: Situacion del Proceso de Ejecucion.* June 16, 1988, San Salvador: FINATA.

Gross, Daniel R., and Barbara A. Underwood
1971   "Technological Change and Caloric Costs: Sisal Agriculture in N.E. Brazil." *American Anthropologist* 73: 725–740.

Haig, Alexander M.
1984   *Caveat: Realism, Reagan, and Foreign Policy.* New York: MacMillan.

Hatfield, Mark O., J. Leach, and G. Miller
1985   *U.S. Aid to El Salvador: An Evaluation of the Past, a Proposal for the Future.* February, U.S. Congress, Washington, D.C.: Arms Control and Policy Caucus.

1987   *Bankrolling Failure: United States Policy in El Salvador and the Urgent Need for Reform.* A Report to the Arms Control and Foreign Policy Caucus, U.S. Congress. Washington, D.C.: Arms Control and Policy Caucus.

Instituto de Investigaciones Economicas
1990   "Necesidades Básicas y Deterioro de las Condiciones de Vida." *Coyuntura Económica* Year 5, no. 28 (Jan.-Feb.): 17–19. San Salvador: Universidad de El Salvador.

Kirkpatrick, Jeane J.
1982   *Dictatorships and Double Standards: Rationalism and Reason in Politics.* New York: The American Enterprise Institute and Simon and Schuster.

Kuo, Shirley, Gustav W.Y. Ranis, and John C.H. Fei.
1981   *Taiwan Success Story: Rapid Growth with Improved Distribution in the Republic of China, 1952–1979.* Boulder: Westview Press.

Leonard, Jeffrey H.
1987   *Natural Resources and Economic Development in Central America: A Regional Environmental Profile.* New Brunswick and Oxford: Transaction Books.

Liévano, Mirna, and Roger Norton
  1988   "Food Imports, Agricultural Policies and Agricultural Development in El Salvador, 1960–1987." Washington, D.C.: Robert Nathan Associates.

MAG (Ministerio de Agricultura Y Ganaderia)
  1980   *Legislacion de la Junta Revolucionaria de Gobierno Aplicable al Proceso de Reforma Agraria.* Departamento de Informacion Agropecuaria. Santa Tecla, El Salvador: MAG.

MAG-OSPA-PERA
  1985   *Segundo Perfil de Beneficiarios del Decreto 207.* Document PERA-1-04-86. San Salvador: MAG-OSPA-PERA.

Mision Interagencial del Sistema de Naciones Unidas
  1986   "La Pobreza Rural en El Salvador: Elementos Basicos Para Una Politica Campesina." Informe de la Mision (Version Preliminar), January 1986. San Salvador: MISNU, 21–29.

Montgomery, Tommie Sue
  1982   *Revolution in El Salvador: Origins and Evolution.* Boulder: Westview Press.

Norton, Roger
  1990   *An Assessment of the Recent Agricultural Policy Reforms in El Salvador.* San Salvador: USAID.

PAHO (Pan American Health Organization)
  1986   *Health Conditions in the Americas, 1981–1984.* Vol. 2, Scientific Publication no. 500. Pan American Health Organization. Pan American Sanitary Bureau. Regional Office of the World Health Organization, Washington, D.C.: PAHO.

Pino Cáceres, Jose Eduardo
  1988   "Crisis Estructural de la Caficultura Salvadorena. Una Hipotesis Alarmante." *Presencia* Year 1, no. 1 (April–June), San Salvador.

Powelson, John P., and Richard Stock
  1987   *The Peasant Betrayed: Agriculture and Land Reform in the Third World.* Boston: Oelgeschlager, Gunn, and Hain in association with the Lincoln Institute of Land Policy.

Prosterman, Roy L., and Jeffrey M. Riedinger
  1987   *Land Reform and Democratic Development.* Baltimore and London: Johns Hopkins University Press.

Prosterman, Roy L., and Jeffrey M. Riedinger
  1987   *Land Reform and Democratic Development.* Baltimore and London: Johns Hopkins University Press.

Prosterman, Roy L., and Mary Temple
  1980   "Land Reform in El Salvador." *Free Trade Union News* 35, no. 6 (June). Published by the Department of International Affairs, AFL-CIO.

UNDP (United Nations Development Program)
  1976   "Realidad Campesina y Desarrollo Nacional." Project ELS/73/003, vols. 5 and 7. San Salvador: UNDP.
  1990   *Human Development Report 1990.* New York: Oxford University Press.

Universidad Centroamericana
1988   "Parcelación o Colectivación: Dilema de la Reforma Agraria en El Salvador." In *Realidad Economico-Social.* San Salvador: Universidad Centroamericana "José Siméon Cañas," 363–368.
USAID (United States Agency for International Development)
1985   *Baseline Survey of the Displaced Population.* Contracting Corporation of America. AID Project no. 519-0178-C-00-5237-00. San Salvador: USAID.
1986   *Congressional Presentation.* Fiscal Year 1987, Annex III. Latin America and the Caribbean. Washington, D.C.: USAID.
U.S. Embassy
1980a   "Analysis of El Salvador's Land Reform Law." Cable sent to Dept. of State, March 3. San Salvador: U.S. Embassy.
1980b   "Land Reform Decree Nears Final Version." Cable sent to Dept. of State, March 4. San Salvador: U.S. Embassy.
Utting, Peter
1987   "Domestic Supply and Food Shortages." In *The Political Economy of Revolutonary Nicaragua,* edited by Rose Spalding. Boston, London, Sydney: Allen and Unwin.
Valverde, V., et al.
1980   "Lifestyles and Nutritional Status of Children from Different Ecological Areas of El Salvador," in *Ecology of Food and Nutrition.* Vol. 9, 167–177.
Weeks, John F., and Elizabeth W. Dore
1982   "Basic Needs: Journey of a Concept." In *Human Rights and Basic Needs in the Americas,* edited by Margaret E. Crahan. Washington, D.C.: Georgetown University Press.
White, Alastair
1973   *El Salvador.* New York and Washington, D.C.: Praeger Publishers.
Williams, Robert G.
1986   *Export Agriculture and the Crisis in Central America.* Chapel Hill and London: University of North Carolina Press.
Wolfe, Marshall
1981   *Elusive Development.* United Nations Research Institute for Social Development and Economic Commission for Latin America. Budapest: Statistical Publishing House.

6

From *Gallo Pinto* to "Jack's Snacks": Observations on Dietary Change in a Rural Costa Rican Village[1]

Michael B. Whiteford

Recent decades have witnessed some impressive accomplishments in certain areas of international public health. This is particularly true in reductions in rates of infant mortality (Dyson 1977) and improvements in dietary well-being for specific segments of the population in selected areas of the world. Nevertheless, there is still well-founded concern that for much of the world's population quite the opposite trends are occurring. In fact, in some areas declines in nutritional status have taken place at an alarming rate (Linowitz 1979; Teller et al. 1979; Fleuret and Fleuret 1980). Although clearly the record varies from country to country and from region to region, in the developing world the overall record on dietary improvement is mixed (Whiteford 1989).

Of particular concern to many health practitioners are the effects of inadequate diet over an extended period on especially vulnerable segments of the population: pregnant and lactating women and pre- and primary-school-age children. In many countries, such as the one in which the research reported here took place, intervention efforts are directed at improving the nutritional status of these individuals through such actions as low-cost food supplementation and government-subsidized food outlets and lunch programs.

The present discussion focuses on the intertwined themes of social dynamics and changing nutritional status. Specifically, this chapter addresses two themes: (1) longitudinal information from two periods on nutritional status of preschool children in the rural Costa Rican community of Veintisiete de Abril (Figure 6.1); and (2) an examination of some of the factors that help explain the changes in dietary well-being between 1965 and 1980, specifically, changing land-use patterns, greater involve-

127

FIGURE 6.1   Location of Veintisiete de Abril

Source: Compiled by author.

ment in a cash economy, and the introduction and increasingly easy access to "new" foods from outside the community.

Costa Rica

The nutritional status of children in Costa Rica generally was thought to be better than in some neighboring countries (Teller et al. 1979). Nevertheless, in 1975 the Ministry of Health noted that between 43 percent and 73 percent of the country's preschoolers suffered from nutritional deficits (USAID 1975, 14), and the government declared that "childhood malnutrition constitutes the country's most severe social problems" (USAID 1975, 2). Surveys conducted in the late 1970s and early 1980s show that close to half of the children of preschool age are undernourished (Novygrodt and Diaz 1979, 2).

Veintisiete de Abril

The province of Guanacaste, on Costa Rica's Pacific coast, where the present study was conducted, comprises one of the nation's poorest regions (IFAM/AITEC 1976, 14). The area contains some of the country's loveliest beaches, an agreeable hot, dry climate, and possesses considerable potential for tourism, facts not lost on the development-oriented Costa Rican government. In the 1970s an agreement was signed between the Costa Rican Institute of Tourism and the Economic Integration Bank of Central America to carry out a feasibility study of the zone for its tourism potential. Later in that decade the region became part of a massive tourism project that, if those plans had come to fruition, would have resulted in such developments as the construction of a series of new hotels, nightclubs, and golf courses (Lange 1980; Andreatta and Whiteford 1986). By the late 1980s, although there were some tourist hotels dotting the coast line, much of the interior was used for rangeland cattle or for commercial agriculture. According to a survey conducted in the mid-1970s by the Instituto de Fomento y Asesoría Municipal and Acción Internacional Técnica, close to 80 percent of the land in the *cantón* of Santa Cruz, the political subdivision that includes Veintisiete de Abril, is used for grazing cattle. Furthermore, the shift in land use from essentially subsistence agriculture to beef production has produced some of the highest levels of underdevelopment in the country (IFAM/AITEC 1976, 14).

Located some four kilometers off the road connecting one of the resorts with the provincial capital is the hamlet of Veintisiete de Abril. A village of slightly less than 500 inhabitants in 1980, it was by residents' own descriptions an impoverished agricultural community. Two thirds of the adult males worked in agriculture and fully three quarters of these were *landless* day laborers, many of whom contracted as seasonal workers outside the area for portions of the year. Although cotton and sorghum were grown on a commercial basis, most of the land around Veintisiete de Abril was *latifundio*, used as pasture for grazing beef cattle.

In many respects, the community was typical of the area. Houses were constructed out of unfinished lumber; half the dwellings had electricity; less than 50 percent had running water. Cooking was done primarily with wood, although some of the more prosperous families used a combination of wood and kerosene, and some had propane in their kitchens. The community's few small stores prominently advertised their commercial wares. At the time of the study there was only one telephone in the community, located in one of the village's bars. In May 1979 a Social Security clinic opened. During the time of our study, it had a physician and a dentist on a full-time basis. Other medical personnel made weekly visits, coming from the cantonal capital of Santa Cruz.

Nutritional Status of Children

The Costa Rican government has embarked on an aggressive national campaign aimed at greatly reducing or eradicating malnutrition in the country. Programs directed at improving general health care have been carried out by several different governmental agencies, and as of 1980 one is hard pressed to find communities of over several thousand inhabitants without new clinics. In the 1970s Costa Rica's "Family Assistance" law was passed, a primary goal of which was to aid the most vulnerable segments of the population in the purchase of inexpensive and nutritious foods (Bogan and Orlich, 1979, 76).[2]

Several thousand lunchroom programs were established, directed at serving pre- and primary school children, and several other semi-autonomous governmental agencies continue to monitor the nutritional status of the population and to design education and intervention programs. These combined efforts undoubtedly resulted in a decrease noted by the Costa Rican Ministry of Health in the incidence of low birth weight from 18.8 to 6.8 percent of live births between 1976 and 1979 (Novygrodt and Diaz 1979, 2). The Ministry interpreted the decrease as a sign of improved diet among expectant mothers. Further, anthropometric surveys conducted during this period by the Centros de Educación y Nutrición (CEN) and the Centros Infantiles de Nutrición y Atención Integral (CINAI), as well as studies conducted by the Departamento de Salud, all indicated a general amelioration in levels of childhood malnutrition. Some health planners actually began to be concerned with problems related to *over*-nutrition. These changes in the nutritional status of preschool children between 1966, the period when the original INCAP study was conducted, and 1980, when this research took place, are summarized in Figure 6.2.

How do the data from Veintisiete de Abril fit the national pattern? Several observations can be made. When the anthropometric data are compared with the national surveys conducted between 1966[3] and 1980, the Veintisiete de Abril results more closely resemble the nutritional situation in 1965 than today's national norms (see Figure 6.3).

We also compared the anthropometric measurements from Veinisiete de Abril to growth standards developed by the U.S. National Center for Health Statistics (NCHS). Because these standards are based on a much larger sample than the earlier Jackson-Kelly Standards, they have lower means and consequently are more applicable for use in developing nations. Mata (1978, 422) and others (Vargas 1979) have suggested that Costa Rica shift to these standards for evaluation of nutritional well-being. Thus, any further remarks related to nutritional status will refer to either weight-for-age or height-for-age, using the fiftieth percentile

FIGURE 6.2   Changes in Nutritional Status: Costa Rican Preschool Children

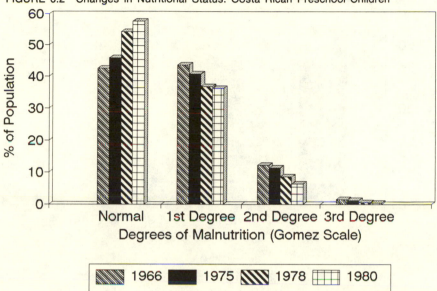

Source: 1966: INCAP/CDC (1972; 29); 1975, 1978: Éncuesta Nacionales de Nutrición, Ministerio de Salud, as cited in Novygrodt and Díaz (1979, 12); 1980: Informe Semestral del Departamento de Nutrición, as cited in Díaz and Novygrodt (1980, 27).

on the NCHS growth charts as reference points and corrected for sex and age to reflect the percent of standard obtained by individuals (see Table 6.1).

When we use the original anthropometric data collected by INCAP in Veintisiete de Abril[4] and compare these materials with information gathered in 1980, it appears that the nutritional status of children in that village declined during the period between the two studies.[5] In contrast to the national level, there does not appear to be improvement in the nutritional well-being of Veintisiete de Abril's preschool children.

There is other evidence to suggest that the nutritional status of children in Veintisiete de Abril was far from what it should have been. Twenty-four-hour dietary recalls were used to gather information on food intake (Whiteford and Hanrahan 1982) from a subsample of 67 individual items to total intake expressed as a percent of all items from the pooled intake records. The second column shows the average portion size, pooling all ages.

Table 6.2 presents data on dietary adequacy by age group using the INCAP recommended standards. For each age classification the mean value was compared to the standard. Reviewing these data we see deficits in all age groups for energy, retinol and niacin, and in younger

FIGURE 6.3   Changes in Nutrition Status: Gomez Classification Scale

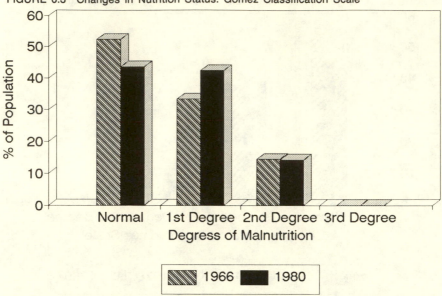

Source: Data from 1966 were graciously provided by Dr. Leonardo Mata. Figures for 1980 were based on weights and heights taken as part of this study.

TABLE 6.1   Classification of Children from Veintisiete de Abril on NCHS/WHO Standard Growth Charts (expressed in percentages)

Age	Mean Weight-for-Age		Mean Height-for-Age	
	1966	*1980*	*1966*	*1980*
0–11 months	102.5	94.4	99.8	98.3
12–23 months	95.3	91.8	104.0	96.2
24–35 months	99.5	89.3	99.0	96.1
36–47 months	92.0	84.2	99.0	97.4
48–59 months	88.2	90.8	96.0	97.8
60–72 months	82.1	86.5	96.3	97.0
Mean	90.7	89.5	98.0	97.1

Source: Data from 1966 were graciously provided by Dr. Leonardo Mata. Figures for 1980 were based on weights and heights taken as part of this study.

age groups for iron. Moreover, it is important to note that although the mean for many of the nutrients met the standard, individual children within each age group fell well below the standard.

In spite of access to outlets where low-cost government-subsidized foods were sold, in spite of nutrition education programs in the community, and even with the presence of a preschool lunch program, the

TABLE 6.2   Mean Nutrient Intakes in Relation to Standard Age (years)[a]

Nutrient	1 yr	1–1.9	2–2.9	3–3.9	4–6
Energy	no	no	no	no	no
Protein	yes	yes	yes	yes	yes
Calcium	yes	yes	yes	yes	yes
Iron	no	no	no	yes	yes
Retinol	no	no	no	no	no
Riboflavin	yes	yes	yes	yes	no
Thiamine	yes	yes	yes	yes	yes
Niacin	no	no	no	no	no
Ascorbic acid	yes	yes	yes	yes	yes

[a]"yes" indicates that the *mean* intake for the age group meets or exceeds the RDA; "no" indicates that mean value is below the RDA for nutrient.

Source: Compiled by author.

nutritional status of children in Veintisiete de Abril was out of line with national trends. Why did this occur?

Growth of the Beef Industry in Costa Rica

Since the late 1960s the growth of the Costa Rican cattle industry has been an important economic development.[6] Beef export represents one of the country's most important sources of hard currency. Raising beef, primarily for export, has been a lucrative business for ranchers all over the country. From 1960 to 1975 Costa Rica doubled its cattle production (Parsons 1976, 124). Where did the meat go? During the 1970s and 1980s, Costa Rica had an eager customer in the United States. A USDA report says: "Before 1957, nearly all of the beef produced in . . . Costa Rica went into domestic consumption; since that time, production gains have tended to move into export channels to . . . the USA" (USDA 1965, iii). In 1977 Costa Rican cattlemen exported $51.3 million dollars of beef to the United States (Solera-Ruiz, 1981, 1). In fact, Costa Rica became the third largest exporter of beef to the United States in the mid-1980s (Edelman 1987, 545). One paradoxical development accompanying this increase in cattle production was that although Costa Rican beef output grew by 90 percent between 1961 and 1970, this remarkable increase in volume was accompanied by a net decline of 26 percent in local per capita beef consumption (Berg 1973, 65–66).[7] As Lappé and Collins note, if the 60 million pounds of beef exported to the United States in 1975 had been eaten locally, per capita consumption would have doubled (1979, 289).

The growth of the cattle industry developed in conjunction with conversion of cropland pasture, a process simultaneously occurring in various parts of Costa Rica (Meehan and Whiteford 1985; Barlett 1982; Nations and Komer 1987). Between 1963 and 1973 land was converted to pasture for the cattle industry at the rate of 30,000 hectares per year, and by 1973, 50 percent of all farmland was allocated to pasture for cattle production (Solera-Ruiz 1981, 3).

In describing the situation in the Central Valley of the country, where the nation's capital is located, Barlett noted that between 1960 and 1980 in the region of Santiago de Puriscal, the amount of land taken out of subsistence production for grazing purposes doubled (1982, 87). For those with access to land, cattle is a good investment. "Compared to the cost of living, beef is the only land use option open to Pasanos that has greatly increased in value in spite of inflation" (Barlett 1982, 87). Yet, as Barlett points out, "Cattle as a land use option is low in labor and capital costs" (1982, 87). In other words, landless day laborers and small landowners find that the cattle industry has greatly reduced their economic options in the countryside. It is not surprising that the growth of the cattle industry often is accompanied by out-migration of agriculturally displaced persons (Meehan and Whiteford 1985; IFAM/AITEC 1976, 14).

Costa Rica has no monopoly on this type of agricultural production (DeWalt 1983; Partridge 1984; Williams 1986). "Compared with twenty years ago, Central America now has 80% more cattle and produces 170% more beef. This change in beef production has produced corresponding changes in land use as well" (DeWalt 1982, 3).

Land Use in Veintisiete de Abril

Perhaps the single most important explanation for changes in lifestyle and, specifically, in the nutritional well-being of children in Veintisiete de Abril is the dramatic increase in lands converted to pasture for raising beef cattle. In assessing the economic situation for the Cantón of Santa Cruz, the political unit that includes Veintisiete de Abril, investigators who compiled the IFAM/AITEC study made several important observations:

1. They noted an increased consolidation of lands in the Santa Cruz area over two intercensal periods (1953–1973), which was accompanied by increases in beef production and decreases in general agricultural output (IFAM/AITEC 1976, 39). They also developed a formula for computing the number of working days needed for a hectare of land used for particular agricultural production modes. According to this formula, permanent crops, such as bananas, plantains, pineapple, coffee, and sugar cane, need 118.2 working days per year. Annual crops, such as rice, corn, and beans require 42.2 working days per hectare per year,

and livestock management needs only 6 working days per hectare per year. Thus, the transformation of the region from an area of small farmers growing subsistence crops to one in which land was devoted to raising cattle led to appreciable unemployment and economic hardships (IFAM/AITEC 1976, 39).

2. They point out that farms of more than 100 hectares constitute two thirds of the cantón's land. Fully 77 percent of these lands are not in cultivation, but are used exclusively for pasture. The authors write: "small farms and medium-sized ones offer work to more people in comparison to the large farms, which are dedicated to more extensive cattle production and leave large amounts of land uncultivated" (IFAM/AITEC 1976, 26).

It is not possible from the census records alone to ascertain specific modifications in the size of landholdings during intercensal periods. However, for his analysis of changing land-use patterns in rural Costa Rica, Seligson (1980) was able to obtain copies of the 1963 and 1973 census tapes from the Costa Rica Bureau of Censuses. From his analysis of the data, he was able to identify changes in land-tenure systems. Among his conclusions were the following: (1) In spite of concerted and vigorous efforts by the government to give new lands to farmers, between 1963 and 1973 there was a disconcerting national trend toward *latifundization/minifundization*. That is, there was an increase both in the number and size of large farms, as well as an increase in the number of those holdings generally felt to be too small to support a family (Seligson 1980: 146). (2) For this period, in the Cantón of Santa Cruz there was a precipitous increase in inequality in size of landholdings (1980, 150). In other words, for much of the country there was a trend for large farms to grow at the expense of small landholders, and this process was exacerbated and greatly accentuated in the area around Veintisiete de Abril.

Discussion

What took place around Veintisiete de Abril appears to be yet another unfortunate example of a pattern that is developing in many areas of the world. Although rural residents have witnessed certain technological accomplishments, which have resulted in increases in certain commodities, ranging from beef cattle production to augmentations in rice and sorghum yields, relatively few people have benefited from these advances. On the contrary, from a nutritional perspective they frequently have not been able to maintain former levels. Certainly people in Veintisiete de Abril did not experience the dietary improvements that occurred in other parts of the country. Although nationally the percentage of preschool children classified as malnourished decreased by 15 percent between 1965 and 1980, during this same period the percentage of malnourished children in Veintisiete de Abril *increased* by 9 percent. Preschool children in the community were receiving an average of only 74 percent of the recommended caloric allowance.

It appears that the change in land-use patterns was the major cause of undernourishment. Families moved from subsistence farming to wage-laborer activities, working on commercial farms in the region. The shift from growing much of what one eats to purchasing most food is an expensive transformation. Further, in this case it probably resulted in a more restricted, less varied diet than was common during the previous decade. In spite of this, by the mid-1970s commercially packaged foods are found in Veintisiete de Abril that were not seen as late as 1980. Several times a day trucks pull into the community and unload foodstuffs of various kinds. For that minority who can afford them, tins of infant formulas, packaged white bread, commercially manufactured snack foods (many of which are sold under the brand name of "Jack's Snacks," a subsidiary of Frito Brands), plus a variety of canned fruits and vegetables are available in the several village stores.

What does the future hold? The Costa Rican government currently has no viable plans nor probably any desire to break up the landholding system in the region. In fact, former President Luis Alberto Monge's administration's theme of "Let us return to the land" was aimed at improving productivity of lands not currently in some mode of agricultural production. This means providing farmers with titles to lands in other parts of the country. Thus, as long as they remain in Veintisiete de Abril, they will not likely see an improvement in their situation in the short run. Many families left, and the region as a whole at the time of our study had the highest rate of out-migration of any area in the country (Dierckxsens et al. 1976; Schmidt de Rojas 1976). When we asked men what the opportunities for finding work around Veintisiete de Abril were, 90 percent responded that the economic situation was bleak; only a tenth of those questioned wanted to see their sons go into agriculture. Most anticipated their offspring would leave the area to find work elsewhere.

Apart from the direct effect of land-use patterns on food availability, economic organization affects children's nutritional status indirectly. Our data show that household composition is related to nutritional well-being: children from households where there is an intact conjugal unit—either married or in free union—appear to enjoy better nutritional status than do those preschoolers living in truncated households—those with only one parent (Chi square 2.98, p 0.1). Single-parent households, in part, are a reflection of the economic situation in which many individuals find themselves. Landless laborers, the poorest of the rural poor, leave the community seeking either seasonal agricultural employment elsewhere or work of other kinds in the Central Valley.

Conclusion

In examining the situation in Costa Rica, Seligson makes the poignant observation that "it has become clear that the development of export-oriented agrarian capitalist production has had a devastating impact on the peasant and his way of life" (1980, xxiv). In their now classic study, Gross and Underwood show that when rural Brazilians became employed in sisal production and moved (or were forced) away from subsistence agriculture, an accompanying reduction in the dietary status of their children occurred (1971). Similarly, the Fleurets note: "There is a limited amount of evidence that the worst nutritional experiences in rural areas happen when households are changing from subsistence to commercial production" (1980, 254). The data from Guanacaste join in the chorus. For families in Veintisiete de Abril, the lack of access to and control of land was a prima facie factor in explaining diminishing levels of nutritional well-being.

Notes

1. A shorter version of this chapter was presented at the 82d annual meeting of the American Anthropological Association, November 16–20, 1983, Chicago, Illinois. Research was conducted in Veintisiete de Abril between December 1979 and February 1980. Funding for the project came from a grant from the Rockefeller Foundation, whose assistance is gratefully acknowledged. Support for this research also came from the World Food Institute, the College of Sciences and Humanities, the Office of the Vice President for Research and the Anthropology Program at Iowa State University. In Costa Rica the project was aided greatly by its association with the Instituto de Investigaciones en Salud (INISA) and its director Leonardo Mata—whose friendship, procedural suggestions, loan of office space and equipment were appreciated.

2. Although several of these social-support systems were supposed to exist in Veintisiete de Abril, during the entire period of field research there were no provisions in the food commodities outlet and the pre- and primary school supplemental feeding programs had no supplies.

3. The original data were collected in 1965 as part of the Central American Nutrition Institute's (Instituto de Nutrición de Centro América y Panamá—INCAP) Costa Rican national survey and evaluation of nutritional status. In 1980 a research team from Iowa State University spent two-and-a-half months studying the same community. In addition to ethnographic materials, in-depth information on dietary consumption patterns, anthropometry, hematology, and

parasitology were gathered during this period on preschool children living in the district. These data constitute the basis for the comparisons of changing nutritional status.

4. The unpublished, raw data from the original INCAP survey were provided by Dr. Leonardo Mata and are used with his permission. Nutritional status evaluation is based on anthropometric data from all 78 preschool children in the district.

5. The primary method used to evaluate nutritional status in much of Central America, including Costa Rica, is still the Gomez Classification Scale of Malnutrition. Critics argue that the method should be abandoned as it does not differentiate chronic from acute malnutrition (Waterlow et al. 1977; Tripp 1978).

6. For an interesting review of the role of international lending institutions in the development of Costa Rica's beef industry, see Edelman (1987).

7. In discussing Central American beef exports to the United States, Nations and Komer make the rather apocryphal observation that "Despite slight declines in recent years of annual per capita beef consumption in the United States . . . an American house cat eats more beef in a year than the average Central American" (1987, 164).

References and Bibliography

Andreatta, S., and M. Whiteford
  1986   "The Plight of Playa Panamá: A Development Scheme Gone Haywire."
          Paper presented at the 46th Annual Meeting of the Society for Applied
          Anthropology, March 26–29, Reno, Nevada.
Barlett, P.
  1982   *Agricultural Choice and Change: Decision Making in a Costan Rican
          Community.* New Brunswick: Rutgers University Press.
Berg, A.
  1973   *The Nutrition Factor: Its Role in National Development.* Washington,
          D.C.: The Brookings Institution.
Bogan, M., and J. Orlich
  1979   "Salud y enfermedad." In *Costa Rica contemporanea*, vol. 2, edited by
          C. Zelaya. San José: Editorial Costa Rica.
DeWalt, B.
  1982   "The Big Macro Connection: Population, Grain, and Cattle in Southern
          Honduras." *Culture and Agriculture* Issue 14:1–12.
  1983   "The Cattle are Eating the Forest." *Bulletin of the Atomic Scientist*
          39(1): 18–23.
Diaz, C., and R. Novygrodt
  1980   *Programa nacional de nutrición.* Departamento de Nutrición. San José:
          Ministerio de Salud.
Dierckxsens, W., M. Fernández, S. Quevedo, and R. Vásquez
  1976   *La reproducción de la fuerza de trabajo.* Instituto de Investigaciones
          Sociales. San José: Universidad de Costa Rica.

Dyson, T.
   1977   "Levels, Trends, Differentials and Causes of Child Mortality—A
             Survey." *World Health Statistical Report:* 30(3): 282–311.
Edelman, M.
   1987   "From Costa Rican Pasture to North American Hamburger." In *Food
             and Evolution: Toward a Theory of Human Food Habits,* edited by M.
             Harris and E. Ross. Philadelphia: Temple University Press.
Fleuret, P., and A. Fleuret
   1980   "Nutrition, Consumption, and Agricultural Change." *Human Orga-
             nization* 39(3): 250–260.
Gross, D., and B. Underwood
   1971   "Technological Change and Caloric Costs: Sisal Agriculture in North-
             eastern Brazil." *American Anthropologist* 73(3): 725–740.
IFAM/AITEC (Instituto de Fomento y Asesoría Municipal/Acción Internacional
Técnica, División de Acción Internacional)
   1976   *Resumen Cantonal: Santa Cruz.* San José: Departamento de Planificación,
             Sección de Investigación.
INCAP (Instituto de Nutrición de Centro América y Panamá)
   1969   *Evaluación nutricional de la población de Centro América y Panamá:
             Costa Rica.* Guatemala City: INCAP.
INCAP/CDC
   1972   *Nutritional Evaluation of the Population of Central America and Panama.
             Regional Summary.* Institute of Nutrition of Central America and
             Panama. Washington, D.C.: HEW.
Lange, F.
   1980   "The Impact of Tourism on Cultural Patrimony: A Costa Rican
             Example." *Annals of Tourism Research* 7(1): 56–68.
Lappé, F.M., and J. Collins
   1979   *Food First: Beyond the Myth of Scarcity.* 2d ed. New York: Ballantine.
Linowitz, S.
   1979   *Preliminary Report of the Presidential Commission on World Hunger.*
             Washington, D.C.: Presidential Commission on World Hunger.
Mata, L.
   1978   *Criterios para evaluar el estado nutricional del niño en Costa Rica.* Revista
             Biologia Tropical 26(2): 415–430.
Meehan, P., and M. Whiteford
   1985   "Staple Theory and the Rise of Commercial Cattle Production in a
             Rural Costa Rican Community." In *Social Impact Analysis and De-
             velopment Planning in the Third World,* edited by W. Derman and S.
             Whiteford. Boulder: Westview Press.
Nations, J., and D. Komer
   1987   "Rainforest and the Hamburger Society." *The Ecologist* 17(4/5): 161–
             167.
Novygrodt, R., and C. Diaz
   1979   *Situación del estado nutricional en Costa Rica. Vigilancia epidemiologica
             nutricional y alimentaria.* San José: Ministerio de Salud.

Parsons, J.
1976   "Forest to Pasture: Development or Destruction?" *Revista de Biologia Tropical* 24 (Supplement 1): 121–138.
Partridge, W.
1984   "The Humid Tropics Cattle Ranching Complex: Cases from Panama Reviewed." *Human Organization* 43(1): 77–80.
Schmidt de Rojas, A.
1976   "Distribución espacial de la población y migraciones interiores." In *La población de Costa Rica*, edited by M.E. Fernandez, et al. San José: Editorial Universidad de Costa Rica.
Seligson, M.
1980   *Peasants of Costa Rica and the Development of Agrarian Capitalism.* Madison: University of Wisconsin Press.
Solera-Ruiz, C.
1981   "Assessment of the Goals and the Policies of the National Development Plan 1979–1982 for Beef Cattle in Costa Rica." Unpublished Ph.D. dissertation, Iowa State University.
Teller, C., R. Sibrian, C. Talavera, V. Bent, J. del Canto, and D. Saenz
1979   "Population and Nutrition: Implication of Sociodemographic Trends and Differentials for Food and Nutrition Policy in Central America and Panama." *Ecology of Food and Nutrition* 8:95–109.
Tripp, R.
1978   "Economic Strategies and Nutritional Status in a Compound Farming Settlement of Northern Ghana." Unpublished Ph.D. dissertation, Columbia University.
USAID
1975   *Nutritional Assessment for Costa Rica.* Washington, D.C.: USAID.
Vargas, W.
1979   *Clasificación del estado nutricional según diferentes criterios y estandares. Vigilancia epidemiological nutricional y alimentaria.* San José: Ministerio de Salud.
Waterlow, J., et al.
1977   "The Presentation and Use of Height and Weight Data for Comparing the Nutritional Status of Groups of Children Under the Age of 10 Years." *Bulletin of the World Health Organization* 55(1): 489–498.
Whiteford, M.
1989   "The Household Ecology of Malnutrition: The Case of El Ocotillo, Mexico." *Journal of Developing Societies* 5:82–96.
Whiteford, M., and K. Hanrahan
1982   "Dietary Factors and Nutritional Well-being: A Comparison of Two Costa Rican Villages." *Nutrition Reports International* 26:303–318.
Williams, R.G.
1986   *Export Agriculture and the Crisis in Central America.* Chapel Hill: University of North Carolina Press.

7

The Dilemmas of Food Security in a Revolutionary Context: Nicaragua

María Verónica Frenkel

As a result of economic policies that have promoted the extension and elaboration of the commercial agricultural export sector, the land and resources available for food production in Central America have decreased, and the food security of the region is being threatened. Despite the fact that agricultural export expansion initially fueled high rates of economic growth and increased the integration of the Central American economies into the world market, such economic "benefits" have come at a tragic human cost—increased levels of hunger and malnutrition and massive poverty for the majority of the region's population. These are inevitable results of a political-economic system whose structures have traditionally concentrated the benefits of development in a decreasing number of hands. In some instances, governments have attempted to alleviate the immediate food shortages by implementing agrarian reform laws. However, in the majority of cases, these reforms have focused solely on the limited redistribution of land and have left the political and economic power structures intact and the majority still hungry. Decisionmaking and economic planning have been in the hands of a political elite that has protected its interests in, but has not shared the benefits of, the traditional agro-export development model. Until this situation changes, more positive and long-lasting responses to the needs of the poor are not likely.

Apparently, any adjustment away from the traditional model of agricultural development in order to improve the lives of the peasantry and achieve food self-sufficiency must include not only moderate reform, but profound changes in the political, economic, and social structures of society. By radically transforming relationships between production,

income, and wealth, the Nicaraguan Revolution of 1979 represents the
first real effort in the Central American region to dismantle the traditionally exploitive social and economic structures that emerged from the
growth of export agriculture. Since 1979, the revolutionary government
has pioneered the development of new programs to increase the production
of food, particularly through a land-distribution program and through
credit and marketing policies designed to benefit the previously disen-
franchised small farmers and landless peasantry. However, from 1984
onward, food shortages have become one of the most difficult problems
for Nicaragua's economic planners, and the achievement of food security
has proven to be a seemingly elusive goal.

In an attempt to shed light upon this complex issue, this chapter
examines some of the particular obstacles that the revolutionary Sandinista
government faced in transforming agricultural institutions in order to
improve food self-sufficiency. An examination of the evolution of food
and agriculture in Nicaragua between 1979 and 1986 provides an
opportunity to more clearly identify and understand some of the contradictions that can emerge within a mixed economy that still relies on
agricultural export as the major source of much-needed foreign exchange
and as the center of capital accumulation. In order to maintain its political
commitment to the peasantry who supported it throughout the revolution,
the Sandinista government set as one of its primary objectives the
redirection and redistribution of the country's resources and productive
assets, particularly in the agrarian sector. In this way, it hoped to address
the needs of the poor majority, to eliminate the poverty, hunger, and
malnutrition that traditionally had characterized Nicaraguan life, and to
improve food security for the country as a whole. However, faced with
the inherited debt of the Somoza period, the destruction of industrial
and agricultural production as a result of the war, the social disruption
caused by the war, and the total collapse of the fiscal system, the new
government came to a difficult realization: for immediate economic
recovery, it would be essential to reactivate and maintain agricultural
export production, the traditional generator of much-needed foreign
exchange. This initial decision to maintain an external orientation in the
economy appeared in the eyes of many to be in direct contradiction to,
or at least a limitation on, the commitment of the revolution to the
rural poor and to the goals of redistribution of wealth and food self-
sufficiency.

An evaluation of the Nicaraguan case also highlights the particular
dilemmas of achieving food security in a political economy in the process
of transition. Between 1979 and 1985 numerous obstacles, tensions, and
contradictions emerged from the process of social, political, and economic
transformation, not only as a result of the preservation of an agricultural

export development focus, but also because of the complexities of the mixed economy and the disarticulation created by dismantling traditional structures. Since early 1985, many of the food and agricultural policies have undergone substantial reexamination and have been altered significantly. These adjustments reflect the government's efforts to confront some of the inadequacies and contradictions of its original policies and illustrate an important reorientation in the economic strategy of the revolution toward an inward, pro-peasant direction, with more emphasis on the domestic market than on agricultural export. The policy changes also mirror the government's overall policy shift toward a "survival economy" and the prioritization of production and defense, in the face of tremendous economic hardships and the contra war. The new direction in food and agricultural policy in Nicaragua illustrates one effort to deal with the complex dilemma that many revolutionary transformations have had to confront, that is, how to achieve economic viability through increased efficiency and productivity while simultaneously improving social and economic equity and food security through the redistribution of productive resources.

Prerevolutionary Agricultural Development

In analyzing contemporary Nicaraguan food policy, it is important first to briefly review the legacy of the prerevolutionary period, particularly the Somoza era, in order to understand what economic planners were confronted with following the revolution. As a result of the expansion of commercial agriculture throughout the nineteenth and early twentieth centuries, Nicaragua in 1979 had a dual agricultural system consisting of large farms producing for export and small farms producing primarily those commodities used for domestic consumption. However, the main focus of agricultural development in the century prior to the revolution was on the export sector rather than on food crops, a focus that occurred at the expense of peasant production, because the two most important basic food crops, beans and corn, were almost exclusively peasant produced (Weeks 1985, 103).

During the 1870s Nicaragua, like its neighbors, began to develop an economy based on coffee production, initiating a process whereby peasants were progressively separated from their land. During the first half of the twentieth century, coffee production increased even more dramatically, and coffee remained Nicaragua's most important crop, representing between one-half and two-thirds of the country's exports during the 1920s and 1930s (Vilas 1986, 50).

During the twentieth century, due to its limited industrial base, Nicaragua continued to follow an agricultural export development model and deepened its integration into the world market. Stagnant world demand for coffee during the Depression and World War II necessitated and encouraged the search for new export crops. In the 1950s, responding to increases in the world demand and market price for cotton, and as a result of the availability of pesticides after World War II, cotton cultivation expanded tremendously in Nicaragua, filling the vacuum created by the coffee decline. Between 1950 and 1965, production increased from 3,500 to 125,000 tons, and cotton's share of total exports went from 5 percent to 45 percent (Vilas 1986, 50).

When the price of cotton declined sharply in the mid-1960s, investments were diverted into beef exports, because a market for processed meats and fast foods was developing in the United States (Brockett 1984, 484; Warnken 1975, 16–19). Between 1960 and 1970, the relative share of beef tripled so that by the mid-1970s, beef production represented 25 percent of the value of food production (Vilas 1986, 51). Despite such rapid production increases, however, domestic consumption of beef was declining because of the increasing amounts being exported. Between 1964 and 1974, per capita beef consumption dropped 12.5 percent, a painful situation for a country already suffering from protein deficiency (Brockett 1984, 484).

Thus, throughout this period, the agricultural sector, geared toward production for export, assumed increasing importance to the economy. The government had some success at promoting industry and encouraging manufacturing, particularly through the formation of the Central American Common Market (CACM), but agricultural exports provided the bulk of Nicaragua's export earnings, with the five major agricultural products representing 66 percent of commodity exports between 1975 and 1979 (Weeks 1985, 77).[1] The burst in agricultural export production was accompanied by high rates of growth of the gross domestic product (GDP). Between 1945 and 1949, GDP grew at an average rate of 3.6 percent and reached a Central American high of 11.1 percent between 1960 and 1965 (Vilas 1986, 51; Weeks 1985, 62).

Agricultural exports were also indirectly linked to Nicaragua's manufacturing potential in that they provided the foreign exchange needed to import capital goods, spare parts, and raw materials for domestic industry. Such foreign exchange also enabled the country to import manufactured products and food for domestic consumption. In addition, the emerging domestic processing and textile industries relied directly on some of the export products as necessary raw materials and inputs (Reinhardt 1987, 3). Thus, rather than diminishing the importance of agricultural exports in the economy, the limited growth of industry and manufacturing during the 1960s and 1970s increased the dependence of the economy on these commodities (Bulmer-Thomas 1983, 271).

However, although the diversification and expansion of cash crops in Nicaragua did provide new sources of income and an impetus to economic growth, they had negative consequences for the rural and urban poor, threatened the country's food security, and created difficulties for the economy as a whole. More detailed analysis of the by-products of the agro-export model in Nicaragua are available elsewhere (see Enríquez 1985b; Frenkel 1987a; and Williams this volume). For the purposes of this chapter, I have summarized some of the more important consequences into four categories.

1. *Institutional Support and Overconcentration of Resources in Exports.* In prerevolutionary Nicaragua, with many of the larger export producers being either Somoza associates or family members, state economic policy interventions were designed to encourage export production. As a result, the private agricultural export sector controlled the provision of agri-production inputs, including credit, fertilizer, seed, and technological assistance. In addition, the direction of state investments in infrastructure (such as for roads, electricity, and agro-industrial projects) mirrored the government's goal of intensifying agricultural export production and facilitating the needs of the largest producers (PAN 1985, 1). The concentration of credit in exports is illustrated by the statistics for 1976, which show that coffee, cotton, and sugarcane, all controlled by large landowners, received 90 percent of agricultural credit, leaving the meager remainder for basic-grains production (Austin, Fox, and Kruger 1985, 20). Thus, staple crops produced for the internal market received less than 10 percent of agricultural credit, despite their being grown on over half the agricultural land (Austin et al. 1985, 20).[2]

2. *Increasing Land Concentration and Changes in Land Tenure Structures.* In prerevolutionary Nicaragua, the large commercial producers were able to make higher profits by producing export crops than the peasants made by producing food for the restricted internal market. As a result, increasing numbers of peasants were bought off their lands. Many were simply forced off; the political power of the large producers made it easy to incorporate peasant land into their operations and to restrict property rights. During the 1870s, coffee expansion began displacing peasants and creating a new class of landless laborers. Many of the former small holders lost only part of their land and became *minifundistas*. With insufficient land to meet subsistence requirements, these minifundistas were forced to supplement their income by working for wages on larger coffee farms. With the diversification of export production into cotton and beef in the twentieth century, the dispossession of basic-grains producers accelerated even more dramatically. Growth in cotton production was achieved through expansion onto new lands, rather than through increasing yields; thus thousands of peasants were displaced

from the fertile flatlands of the coastal region. Furthermore, the amount of land dedicated to pasture doubled between 1960 and 1975. As a result, more peasants—many of whom had been originally expelled because of expansion for cotton production—were pushed off onto marginal, unproductive lands of the frontier (Deere and Marchetti 1981, 44). The rapid process of land concentration is evident in the fact that in 1963, 5 percent of farms controlled 59 percent of farmland and 51 percent of farm families subsisted on 3.5 percent of farmland. Although the Gini index of land concentration was .74 in 1950, the lowest in Central America, by 1963 it had jumped to .81 (Vilas 1986, 51).

3. *Proletarianization, Unemployment, and Poverty.* For the increasing numbers of landless peasants, economic survival was very uncertain. For this displaced population, options were limited to wage employment, migration to frontier regions, or migration to the mushrooming urban areas. Irrespective of the chosen alternative, the fate of the dispossessed peasant prior to the revolution tended toward a life of unemployment and poverty. The process of proletarianization began with the creation of seasonal laborers, primarily minifundistas, who were forced into salary positions because of the size of their landholdings did not generate sufficient subsistence income. These minifundistas increasingly depended for their livelihood on part-time agricultural work on large commercial farms or in associated agricultural export activities (Barraclough 1982, 26). Lacking sufficient land and with primitive production conditions, low yields, and lack of access to financing or technology, they endured an accelerated process of explusion from their original properties toward the frontier at varying rates and stages during the two decades prior to the revolution. As a result, accurate measurement of the size of this group, as opposed to totally landless wage laborers, is difficult to obtain; however, most studies indicate that by 1978 at least two thirds of the rural economically active population (EAP) depended to some degree on wage labor and that between 32 and 40 percent had no access whatsoever to land for producing food and depended totally on wage work as permanent or seasonal laborers (Vilas 1986; Reinhardt 1987, 5). Their total dependence on wage labor was further aggravated by the increasing mechanization of export production, which eliminated many employment opportunities (Williams 1986).

Despite the urban migration that resulted from land concentration, in 1978 over 50 percent of the EAP was still involved in the agricultural sector, and the majority were impoverished. Estimates indicate that in 1987, 70 percent of the agricultural EAP earned less than required to meet minimum subsistence requirements (Deere and Marchetti 1981, 45). The United Nations Economic Commission for Latin America (CEPAL) stated that 62.5 percent of the prerevolutionary Nicaraguan population lived in a state of critical poverty, and that the poorest 50 percent of the total population received only 16 percent of the total income (Conroy 1985a, 48).

4. *Declining Food Security and Increasing Malnutrition.* Agricultural export expansion in prerevolutionary Nicaragua resulted in a dramatic decline in domestic food production and food security and an increase in hunger and malnutrition. In 1970, only 10.1 percent of Nicaraguan land was used for food, the lowest percentage in Central America (Weeks 1985, 102). Land in cotton production increased from 13,600 to 61,000 manzanas between 1952 and 1967; the area in basic grains decreased from 78,100 to 31,900 *manzanas* (Dorner and Quirós 1983, 229).[3] In the few instances when prime lands were planted in basic food crops, it was to produce corn and sorghum to feed cattle destined for the U.S. hamburger market (Collins 1985, 108). As a result, the government was forced to spend increasing amounts of scarce foreign exchange on food imports to meet domestic demand. The relationship between export expansion and food imports is evident when one notes that food imports increased 5 times between 1960 and 1977, the same rate as cotton exports (Barry and Preusch 1986, 153). Once an exporter of food, Nicaragua imported over 70,000 metric tons of grain between 1963 and 1967 (Dorner and Quirós 1983, 229).

Uneven performance in staples production had important nutritional consequences. A 1966 study by the Instituto de Nutrición de Centro-américa y Panamá (INCAP) showed that only 43 percent of Nicaraguan families consumed sufficient calories and that 57 percent of children under the age of 5 were malnourished (PAN 1985, 2). A 1976 USAID study indicated that 42 percent of children under the age of 4 suffered from first-degree malnutrition and that 57 percent of the rural population suffered from some degree of malnutrition (CIERA 1983b, 37).

Overall, the agricultural export system in prerevolutionary Nicaragua illustrates a process of capital accumulation and economic development that is "socially disarticulated" in the sense described by de Janvry (1978). Following de Janvry's conceptualization, due to the outward nature of the export model, development depends on the purchasing power and tastes of foreigners. This implies that domestic wages are not a source of effective demand in the economy. Thus, the logic of capitalist accumulation under the agricultural export model encourages cheap labor, which leads to an increasingly regressive distribution of income. This process is self-reinforcing in that the inequalities of land and income, which result from agricultural export expansion, limit the purchasing power and the demand of the local market. As a result, there is no consumer sector or domestic market large enough to support the emergence of an industrial sector, which Nicaragua would need to break its total dependence on primary product exports. Under such circumstances, it is apparent that an agrarian reform to redistribute land and income becomes not solely a matter of social justice, but one of economic necessity (Barry and Preusch 1986, 136).[4]

Somoza's "Agrarian Reform"

Combined with "encouragement" from the U.S. Alliance for Progress, growing tensions in rural areas—which culminated in a number of peasant land invasions in the more densely populated Pacific region—forced the Somoza dictatorship to launch a land-reform program. However, the reform represented little more than a colonization project onto unused lands in the interior; and with little infrastructure, low investment, and poor-quality lands, it did little to increase the productivity and standard of living of the peasantry. Most importantly, despite the land-reform program, export production continued to be the top economic priority. From 1960 to 1976, coffee production increased by 148 percent, sugarcane by 249 percent, cotton by 282 percent, and beef by 268 percent. During this same period, the production of maize, beans, and sorghum increased by only 60 percent, and the average yields of these staple foods showed practically no increase at all during the 1960s and 1970s (Barraclough 1982, 16).

Regardless of Somoza's nominal reform, it was becoming increasingly apparent that the peasantry would get little relief or assistance and that export production would continue to expand. With control over the economic and financial structures and decisions, Somoza had free rein to develop policies in a way that supported the system, contributed to the government's power, and protected his profits and those of his key supporters. Peasants and rural workers would be given no real role in the system other than providing labor as needed. Even the medium-sized landowners, who ironically, controlled the bulk of export production, were increasingly marginalized by the larger export producers and commercial and financial elite associated with Somoza. Thus, although the agricultural export development model may have resulted in rapid economic growth and increased integration in world markets, by having favored only a select few at the expense of the majority of Nicaragua's poor population, it had also created the conditions for a broad-based alliance against the regime. However, the tentative prerevolutionary alliance with these medium-sized export producers, based on a shared discontent with Somoza, would be shaken after the triumph by their differing opinions on how postrevolutionary Nicaragua should be structured. Many private export producers would not respond enthusiastically to the new government's effort to live up to its promises to the peasantry and to improve food security, because private producers would be required to dismantle many of the historical institutions from which they had traditionally benefited.

Initial Debates over
Revolutionary Agricultural Policy

The fundamental goal of the revolutionary government was to reorient the economy to satisfy the basic needs of the majority. One member of the early Planning Ministry staff characterized the Nicaraguan "difference" as follows:

> Our strategy differs from other models of economic development whose first priority is to establish a model of accumulation. Our first objective is to satisfy the basic needs of the majority of the population. This creates a new logic, which we call the "logic of the majority," i.e., the logic of the poor. Instead of organizing the economy from the perspective and interest of the top 5 percent, as was done during the Somoza dynasty, we are trying to organize the economy from the perspective of the majority (Gorostiaga 1982).

Before the revolution, capital had free rein, but now the state intended to assume leadership in the new economy in order to change the political balance between landlord and peasant and between capital and labor. The state was committed to redistributing resources and to raising the standard of living of the poor (Weeks 1985, 171). The state expanded rapidly after the revolution with the intention of shifting the economy away from traditional agricultural export to a more dynamic, nationally integrated development program and of encouraging rapid and sustained economic growth (Spalding 1984, 3). However, reactivation of agricultural export production would be necessary for generating the foreign exchange needed for investment in the new social programs in the form of land, credit, education, health care, and rent reductions, which were to be directed at poor peasants, landless workers, and the urban unemployed. Also, a domestic capital-goods industry was for the most part nonexistent and foreign exchange generated by agricultural exports would provide for essential intermediate and capital goods needed for agricultural, industrial, commercial, and infrastructural development (FitzGerald 1985). Thus, the new government recognized that for immediate economic recovery, it would be crucial to reactivate and maintain this agricultural export production, regardless of the ownership of this sector (Enríquez 1985a, 276).

As a result, the government was forced to depend on the private sector, which had traditionally produced the needed export commodities. Within this context, it chose a "mixed economy" approach in which various forms of property would coexist and in which the new state sector and the cooperative sectors would work with the private producers. The government would simultaneously maintain the "basic-needs" approach; that is, regulate the allocation of resources in line with its political orientation toward satisfying the basic needs of the "popular sectors."

Many in the government argued that combining the two approaches would condition government policies toward addressing basic needs, including food policies, in such a way that, with limited resources to direct to both sectors of agriculture, the options for alleviating the food problem and reorienting the economy toward production for the internal market would be constrained. Food-policy options were also limited by the urgency of increasing the food supply. The liberation struggle itself had worsened an already desperate food situation. The revolution's final offensive in 1979 coincided with the period when fields should have been prepared for planting corn, beans, and other staple foods, and food production was forecast to plummet 40 percent following the victory (Collins 1985, 108). In addition, government programs had increased the demand for food by increasing purchasing power through policies that resulted in more jobs, higher wages, easier access to credit for the *campesinos*, and lower rents for land and urban housing, as discussed below. The government's initial reaction was to import basic grains, but many argued that such a strategy could leave the country vulnerable to pressures from external agents, reflecting yet another constraint on economic policy in general and food policy specifically.

Thus, an "efficiency versus equity" debate began between those in the new government who advocated a "food first," that is, self-sufficiency approach, and those concerned with maintaining the efficient production of agricultural exports to generate much-needed foreign exchange to keep the economy afloat. Proponents of the former approach believed that funneling additional resources to producers of staples would promote a more equitable distribution of food; cut spending on food imports, which would save scarce foreign exchange; and reduce dependency on foreign powers and vulnerability to a food cutoff or boycott. The government was committed to making an adequate diet available to the whole population and to maintaining nutrition levels, and with consumer demand rising, a "food first" model seemed appropriate. Under the export approach, directing resources to export production would allow the country to maintain its foreign exchange earnings, so necessary to sustain petroleum imports and to enable the country to pay its debt.

The national economy was already organized around these exports, the majority grown by private owners with experience in their production and marketing; thus, any shift away from this approach would come at great risk and cost.

In the midst of this debate, in 1981 the Reagan administration abruptly canceled a $9.8 million loan to import wheat from the United States. As a result, there was little disagreement that achieving food self-sufficiency would have to be made a top national priority (Austin, Fox, and Kruger 1985, 19). Such self-sufficiency in basic grains became the cornerstone of the new national food program, Programa Alimentario Nicaragüense (PAN), which was inaugurated soon after the U.S. cutoff. As the initial PAN declaration maintained, the new strategy would be aimed at "achieving food security for the Nicaraguan people through self-sufficiency in basic grains and the creation of a distribution and commercialization system based on the interests and participation of the masses" (PAN 1981).

However, despite its prioritization of food production, the new government did not eliminate the goal of maintaining and increasing agricultural export production, as it recognized the need to generate foreign exchange to be used for the new social programs and to meet their goals of redistributive development. Thus, the revolutionary government chose to incorporate the two approaches into a single economic strategy of "agricultural exporting plus food," to use Vilas's term (1987, 234). Within this strategy, the government would transform property relations and the means of production, increase strategic state investments in export agriculture, cattleraising, and needed infrastructural improvements, and expand and diversify export agriculture with the objective of obtaining the funds necessary to finance agro-industrialization, that is, the processing of local agricultural products to increase the value added to exports. Simultaneously, it would expand cultivation of basic grains to allow the country to improve its food self-sufficiency. Apparently, the goal of good security and improving production for the internal market would be prioritized within an economic strategy that placed agricultural exports at the center of the process of capital accumulation.

An evaluation of Nicaragua's efforts to restructure its agrarian sector through this combined approach allows for a more in-depth understanding of how the contraints of an export-dependent and mixed economy can limit the process of achieving food security.[5] With future economic growth dependent on the continued production of export products, the government would have to continue allocating scarce resources to the export sector, both state and private, which would in turn create competition with the peasantry and with production for the domestic market. Second, because state participation in the production of export crops was limited, meeting production targets for export products depended on the cooperation of the private sector (FitzGerald 1982, 215). Consequently, the government would be forced to maintain a political alliance with the private export producers, while upholding its revolutionary commitment to the rural poor. As we shall see below, the policies that the government tried to implement in order to provide incentives to both food and export producers would become increasingly conflicting, particularly in the face of a growing economic crisis and war; and by 1985, difficult tradeoffs would have to be made between the two sectors.

Increasing Food Production Within a Food/Export Strategy: The Transformation of Agrarian Structures, 1979–1985

One of the most important tools necessary to improve the food security of a country is an agrarian reform to redistribute the country's resources to the previously marginalized population, the peasants and rural workers. Many of the agrarian reforms previously attempted in Latin America have concentrated solely on land distribution. However, a more appropriate, expanded concept of "distribution" would include the distribution of land, farming inputs, and credit, as well as improved access to marketing structures that provide a fair price for peasants' produce (Spalding 1985, 199). Following this expanded definition, revolutionary Nicaragua's attempt to increase food production involved dramatic changes in production, marketing, and financial structures through the redistribution of land, new pricing and market controls, and reforms in credit policy. As PAN's Five-Year Plan states, the government was attempting to "maximize the utilization of available land for basic grain production, using incentives such as credit and guaranteed producer prices for peasant producers as well as for state and private farms" (PAN 1985, 2).

Land Redistribution:
The Agrarian Reform Laws and Titling Program

Phase I: Expropriation of Somoza Properties. The historical pattern of land concentration centered on the growth of export crops and cattle, and one of the new government's first major efforts was to bring more land into food production and to redistribute some of this land. Within 24 hours of the revolutionary takeover, Decree No. 3 confiscated all property belonging to Somoza and his closest associates and gave the government control of approximately 20 percent of the country's agricultural land (Spalding 1985, 206) and 25 percent of the economic production (Conroy 1985a, 53). However, most of the land expropriated during this initial phase was reorganized as state farms due to a reluctance to divide it and turn it over to individual farmers (to be discussed further on). Rather than redistribute this property, the Sandinistas initially attempted to improve the conditions of the peasant producers through generous credit policies and reduced rents (Reinhardt 1987, 17). The state also helped strengthen the Asociación de Trabajadores del Campo (ATC), the rural workers' and peasants' association, which focused primarily on improving working conditions for the rural proletariat rather than on the concerns of independent peasant farmers producing basic grains.

Amidst its first efforts at agrarian transformation, the revolutionary state was trying simultaneously to build the confidence of the private export sector and to encourage its cooperation in production. Despite the expropriation decree, the junta nevertheless promised that the state sector would be "of precise extent and clearly delimited characteristics" and that "properties and activities of the private sector would be fully guaranteed and respected" (Plan for National Reconstruction, as quoted in Gilbert 1983, 10). In addition, Plan 80, the initial revolutionary economic program, placed great importance on the concept of "national unity," an important element of which was the private sector, the "patriotic businessmen" who would continue to receive state support and assistance (Black 1981, 204).

Therefore, in an effort to respect private export property while implementing the first phase of land redistribution, the junta maintained that there would be no upper limit on the size of landholdings. Overall, large estates were mainly unaffected by the reform unless they had been owned by Somoza and his associates. This statement is supported by the fact that in 1981, the state controlled 15 percent of cattle and coffee, 16 percent of cotton, 43 percent of sugar, 55 percent of meat packing, and 91 percent of tobacco, with each case reflecting the ownership pattern of Somoza and his associates (Sims 1981, 5). Apparently, much of the large landholding remained intact, and the government was moving cautiously on demands for additional expropriations, focusing instead on improving rural wages and working conditions (Sims 1981, 5). In early 1981, a World Bank study found sufficient guarantees to conclude that the Nicaraguan government had constructed a "framework wherein the private sector can satisfactorily operate" (*Washington Letter on Latin America*, December 9, 1981, as found in Austin, Fox and Kruger 1985, 17).

The initial decision by the government not to immediately take over more of the export sector was based on two factors. First, the creation of the APP (Area Propiedad del Pueblo, or state-owned territory) out of Somoza's lands required massive organizational efforts and the creation of an administrative apparatus. Because the government had to meet other priorities of reconstruction and the provision of social services, it could not afford to incorporate much more land into the state sector right away. Second, the government knew that it was imperative to maintain a "strategic alliance" with key sectors of the bourgeoisie (Irwin 1983, 127–128). Moreover, both the decision to retain the expropriated land as state farms and the hestiation to expropriate more land indicated that the state was adjusting its agrarian transformation to the reality of an agricultural export-dependent economy. Concerned with protecting export production, the state believed that breaking up the expropriated export farms for redistribution to peasants in order to increase food production would be to "take a historic step backward" by causing a dramatic decrease in export productivity (Reinhardt 1987, 16).[6] Thus, it could be argued that during the first stage of the agrarian transformation, concerns for production efficiency took priority over equity. However, as the lack of production efficiency on the state farms became more evident, such an emphasis would lost its justification and would have to be changed.

Thus, although the first phase of the agrarian transformation may have altered social relations for a segment of the labor force by bringing a significant portion of the agricultural export economy into state hands, the remainder of the landless workforce and the peasants were unaffected by the policy. In addition, the consolidation of the state sector had no effect on food production for domestic consumption because the state farms were primarily export-oriented enterprises (Deere, Marchetti, and Reinhardt 1985, 81–82). Pressure from peasants began to mount for jobs, state services, credit, legal titles, and access to land. In addition, many of the individual peasant farmers began to pull out of the ATC and to join private producer organizations, led by large growers.

This process forced the Sandinistas to reevaluate their original focus on the rural workers, a focus that had been based on their view of the peasantry as essentially a rural proleteriat in formation. They began to reconsider the complexity of Nicaragua's agrarian structure and the importance of the peasantry as *producers* as well as workers and as the source of the basic grains that were vital to the country's food security.[7] This realization led the Sandinistas to agree on the separation of the small landholders from the ATC and to the formation of a separate union, UNAG, the National Union of Farmers and Ranchers (Reinhardt 1987, 17). The recognition of the importance of the peasant producers inspired a debate, which began in 1980, over the quesiton of a new agrarian reform law. This discussion brought out disagreements over the role of the peasantry, over the role of the private sector and private property, over the "path" toward socialism in the mixed economy, and about the type of production units—individual, small farms or coop-eratives—that would be created through the reform (Deere, Marchetti, and Reinhardt 1985, 89–90).

The Agrarian Reform Law of 1981. Despite the government's apparent respect for export property, government guarantees were seemingly insufficient to offset the uncertainty and lack of investor confidence resulting from limitations on the private sector's political influence. Although it was generally realized that profits could be made, private producers were fearful of the FSLN's (Frente Sandinista de Liberación Nacional, or the Sandinista Front for National Liberation) definition of the "logic of the majority," a fear that led them to challenge the regime openly. By 1981 decapitalization had become a serious problem.[8] Com-bined with the pressure from the peasantry, in the form of land invasions led by UNAG, and the growing recognition of the need for food security, such private-sector sabotage convinced the government that a stricter law was necessary in order to make more of the inefficiently used export lands available for food production by the peasantry and to discourage decapitalization.

Therefore, in August of 1981, the government passed the New Agrarian Reform Law, a second, larger step in the land-redistribution process. This new law allowed the government to confiscate property in the event of prolonged abandonment, nonproduction, or decapitalization and to expropriate land that was underused or idle.[9] However, the law affected only plots that were larger than 500 manzanas in the Pacific coastal region and 1,000 manzanas in the interior region (CAHI, 1986b). This law was consistent with the government commitment to economic recovery through the mixed economy. However, it did constitute a structural change by eliminating the option of private owners to withhold their property from productive use (Austin, Fox, and Kruger 1985, 19). As of November 1983, over 436 farms had been expropriated under the new law. Of those, over 63 percent had failed to exploit the land efficiently (Thome and Kaimowitz 1985, 304).

Despite the implementation of the 1981 law, the majority of land and export production still remained in private hands. The law only affected the landholdings of over 500 manzanas, reducing them from 36 percent of farmland in 1978 to 11 percent by 1984 (CAHI 1985b, 13c). However, the majority of Nicaragua's export production had traditionally been in the hands of medium-sized producers—with landholdings between 50 and 500 manzanas—who were thus untouched by the reform. Therefore, in 1984, private producers still accounted for about two-thirds of the production of cotton, coffee, and beef, and private farmers controlled 70 percent of all agricultural land (Thome 1984, 13). This group of medium-sized exporters was thus crucial to the country's economic survival. As a result, the government reiterated that as long as they continued to operate efficiently, maintain investment, and obey labor, health, and other laws, they could keep their businesses forever, and intentionally limited its land expropriations so as not to threaten their security.

With respect to how to distribute the lands that were indeed expropriated, the government recognized that a variety of land-tenure patterns, from production cooperatives to state farms, was inevitable because the historical process of social differentiation, induced by agricultural export development, had created a highly heterogeneous rural social structure (Baumeister and Neira 1984). Nevertheless, due to the difficulties of incorporating the highly dispersed group of small producers of basic grains into the agrarian reform process and of providing them technical and financial assistance, in the implementation of the reform the government encouraged the formation of production or service cooperatives. Although some have argued that this bias toward cooperative formation was not the dominant opinion within the Ministry of Agriculture (Reinhardt 1987, 18), the statistics indicate a preference: of the land redistributed by the end of 1983, 79 percent went to production cooperatives and the remaining 21 percent to individual titles (Thome and Kaimowitz 1985, 304). This emphasis on cooperatives ignored the needs of many of the individual small basic-grains producers, led by UNAG, who were arguing in favor of assigning more individual titles under the reform. Between 1979 and 1984, only 0.7 percent of peasant households received land as individuals (Reinhardt 1987, 20).

Titling Program. The government's initial method of meeting some of UNAG's demands was through a titling campaign begun in 1983. Many individual producers were squatters on public domain lands and were pushing for secure title to the land that they had worked for many years, some since the days of Somoza's reform. Insecure land tenure had prevented many of them from making longer-term investments in basic-grains production, so they produced solely for subsistence rather than for the domestic market. In an effort to provide incentives for their production and participation in the food strategy, in 1983 the Ministerio de Desarrollo Agropecuario y Reforma Agraria (the Ministry of Agricultural Development and Agrarian Reform—MIDINRA) began a program to distribute secure land titles to these settlers. During 1983, 300,000 manzanas were titled through this program benefiting 22 percent of peasant families (MIDINRA 1985). Some have argued that the government's need to maintain the support of UNAG became particularly crucial during 1983–1984 given the upcoming elections and increasing level of contra activity, and thus it was concerned with meeting at least some of UNAG's demands (Thome and Kaimowitz 1985, 308). Nevertheless, it is important to note that the majority of the beneficiaries of the land-titling program were in fact settlers with land in the frontier mountain region whose status was being legalized (Reinhardt 1987, 20). In other words, the titling program did little to redistribute new land to landless peasants; it simply increased the security of many who already had land, albeit illegally. Thus, although significant, the titling program did not constitute a major alteration in land-tenure structures.

In sum, between 1981 and 1984, efforts were made to expropriate and redistribute unused lands and to provide secure titles to the peasantry with the goal of stimulating food production. Yet, there were serious limitations. The 1981 law only affected the landholdings of over 500 manzanas. Medium-sized export producers were unaffected by the law unless they engaged in sharecropping or other debt-service arrangements; as a result, their percentage of total farmland remained the same, 43 percent, between 1981 and 1984. Furthermore, the redistribution during the first 15 months following the 1981 Agrarian Reform law was quite slow, with the actual redistribution of only 30 percent of the expropriated land and the remaining 70 percent being added to the state sector (CAHI 1986a, 5).

Although in 1983 and 1984 an acceleration of the agrarian reform increased the quality and quantity of land available to basic-grains producers, the majority of expropriated land still remained in the state-farm sector, 65 percent in the former year and 57 percent in the latter (CAHI 1986a, 5). One possible reason for the hesitation on the part of the state to redistribute more land was that the revolutionary leaders lacked confidence in the peasants' "traditional" production techniques and culture (CAHI 1985b, 12c). Furthermore, the government's growing concern for protecting the alliance with the national bourgeoisie and for maintaining export production limited the process of agrarian reform, as demonstrated by the data which indicate that only 102,403 manzanas were expropriated in 1983 (DGRA 1986). Of the 290,929 manzanas distributed in 1984, only 46,228 derived from expropriations; the remaining 244,701 manzanas came from state lands or land bought by the state through negotiations with private owners (DGRA 1986). Apparently, the concern for maintaining efficient export production was still taking priority over achieving equity and improving food production through more rapid land redistribution.

Price Support Policies and Intervention into Rural Markets

As Timmer (1986) has pointed out, Latin American governments have often depressed food prices for two reasons (1) to placate urban consumers, usually considered the most politically important group; and (2) to maintain industrial profits, thus stimulating investment and growth, by keeping urban wages lower. Such price freezing often comes at the expense of the basic-foods producers and, thus, of long-term food productivity (Timmer 1986, 20; see also de Janvry 1978, 152–157, and Murdoch 1980, 156–159 for more discussion of "urban bias"). During the Somoza period, the government developed the Instituto Nacional de Comercio Exterior y Interior (the National Institute for Foreign and Domestic Commerce—INCEI) for the specific purpose of holding down the prices of basic foods by releasing large quantities of stored grains as domestic prices began to rise. By restraining price increases in the staples sector, the Somoza state had forced the economically disadvantaged peasant producers to subsidize the rest of the economy or to join the harvest labor force in the agricultural export sector in order to supplement their incomes (Spalding 1985, 212; Saulniers 1987). Therefore, the historical inequalities of the marketing system had left the peasants receiving minimum return from their produce and the urban workers barely surviving on minimal wages while the food brokers prospered.

One of the major objectives of food-pricing policy after the revolution was to eliminate this historical disequilibrium, which has been a disincentive to food production. One of the government's crucial policy instruments was guaranteed producer prices, periodically increased, for a variety of basic food products, including basic grains, beans, milk, meat, and sugar. Producer prices would be controlled through the Empresa Nicaraguense de Alimentos Básicos (the National Foodstuffs Enterprise—ENABAS), an arm of the Ministerio de Comercio Interior (the Ministry of Internal Commerce—MICOIN). Official prices administered through ENABAS increased significantly for the 1981–1982 crop year: maize was up 66 percent and rice 77 percent (CIERA figures, cited in Austin and Fox 1985, 407). Between 1981 and mid-1984 the government tripled its guaranteed price for corn and raised the price for beans, Nicaragua's most important staple food, by 78 percent. Producer prices for sorghum also doubled during this period (Collins 1985, 195). Producers initially proved responsive to these increases, thus temporarily validating the effectiveness of pricing policy as an incentive mechanism (Austin and Fox 1985, 407).[10]

However, there were several difficulties associated with the new pricing policy. First, government guarantees to small farmers of higher prices for food initially contributed to labor shortages in that they provided incentives to individual small farmers to produce on their own land instead of working for agricultural exporters (to be discussed further on). Second, when inflation began to accelerate at unprecedented rates in 1984 and 1985, the incentive effect of the pricing policy became more limited. Although price guarantees protected the peasant producers from the traditional price fluctuations and exploitative exchange relations that had historically undermined their income, prices set for corn and other peasant products were unable to keep pace with rising rural consumer prices. For example, although the producer price for corn and beans had increased sevenfold between 1978 and 1984, the price for a pair of rubber boots had increased 28 times and that of a pair of trousers 140 times (CIERA data, cited in UNRISD 1986, 198). The terms of trade between the countryside and the city were rapidly moving against the former, creating a disincentive to production, particularly of basic foods. In addition, many peasant farmers found it cheaper to buy their food at the government-subsidized consumer prices than to produce it, resulting in an even greater decline in food production (*Mesoamerica*, May 1986:10).

It has been argued that one of the primary reasons for the contradications in producer pricing policy has been that the Nicaraguan government often tended to treat diverse forms of production—peasant, capitalist, cooperative, and state—as one, and in doing so, found it difficult to design policies specifically adapted to the logic of peasant production (UNRISD 1986, 198). The new pricing policy was generalized to suit a variety of agricultural sectors, despite each having a different production logic that would condition the potential effectiveness of the policy. A 1986 survey of 1,000 peasants indicated that the main demand of the peasant producers was for access to basic consumer goods at affordable prices, rather than for higher producer prices. The study also indicated that these peasants calculated the increases in producer prices only in terms of relative changes in input and consumer prices, which provides a rational explanation for their unresponsiveness to the pricing policy (interview with Sonia Aburto, CIERA, August 1986).

Another contradiction that resulted from the producer pricing policy and state intervention in rural markets was that rural marketing structures became increasingly disarticulated. Price controls and state regulation often displaced merchants from commercial activities in rural areas; however, the state was often unable to immediately perform the functions that these agents had performed, thereby restricting access to the food that was being produced. Prior to the revolution, in many cases an individual merchant not only had bought the peasants' produce, but also had provided loans to the small producers and sold them production inputs and consumer goods, in many cases on credit. The government's attempts to replace these functions often decentralized functions among numerous state institutions. This division of functions necessitated extra trips for the peasant producer and often a loss of time in having to deal with different bureaucratic agencies. As Peter Utting (1987) noted, the time lag between the disarticulation of old structures and the consolidation of new ones to replace them reflected a much broader problem associated with the transition process in general and one that the planning process needed to deal with more effectively.

In addition, due to the dispersion of the large number of small-scale basic-grains producers, the government lacked the personnel and technical capacity to control the basic-grains market completely. With an expanding black market, resulting from the widening gap between supply and demand, many producers found government prices less appealing than those of the parallel or black markets; thus, the amount of basic grains that ENABAS controlled was decreasing (*Mesoamerica*, May 1986:2; Saulniers 1987). This phenomenon reflected the difficulty of effectively administering price-control policies and retaining a certain level of market control in the context of a transitional mixed economy where a free market, with potential speculators, influences policy implementation. The tensions resulting from pricing and marketing policies demonstrate that constant attention and flexibility are required of policymakers in economies undergoing transformation in order to determine the appropriate balance of market forces and state control within the economy. Such a balance is of fundamental importance in maintaining the availability of sufficient food for the entire population.

In sum, the policy of fixing prices for food production discriminated against the peasantry and reduced the impact of the other policies aimed at improving their lives and encouraging their participation in increasing food production (Vilas 1987, 235). In an attempt to improve the unequal terms of trade between the countryside and the city and to boost food production, significant price increases were announced for agricultural and livestock products in mid-1984, and even more dramatic increases were announced for these goods in February 1985 (Utting 1987). However, even the higher state prices were unable to compete with those on the black market, where inflation was generating huge price increases. As a result, the state continued to have difficulty in capturing a sufficient portion of the food crop for distribution to the urban areas through "secure" state channels (*Country Report* 1, 1987:13). Furthermore, the producer price increases paled in comparison to the skyrocketing cost of farming inputs and consumer goods in 1985 (interview with Peter Utting, research associate, CIERA, August 1986b). Apparently, the pricing policy would have to be reexamined.

Control over the Financial System and Credit Allocation

It is often argued that redistribution of land alone is insufficient for addressing the needs of the peasantry, without a simultaneous redirection of investment and other resources, particularly credit, to help the small producer. As Austin, Fox, and Kruger point out, "access to credit is the key to other inputs" (1985, 21). In fact, it has been argued that the agrarian reforms of Bolivia, Peru, and Mexico all had little success because they were limited strictly to land redistribution and failed to redirect the crucial financial structures necessary for a complete agrarian transformation.

The revolutionary government of Nicaragua took its agrarian reform a step further. Prior to the revolution, the private agricultural export sector in Nicaragua controlled the provision of agri-production inputs, including credit, fertilizer, seed, and technological assistance. As mentioned previously, large export producers received over 85 percent of the loans made by the financial system to the agricultural sector from 1968 to 1979, leaving the meager remainder for basic-grains producers (Enríquez and Spalding 1985, 12). By consolidating the Sistema Financiero Nacional (The National Financial System—SFN) in 1979, the revolutionary state broke the power of the traditional economic groups and gained control over some of the essential tools necessary to transform the economy. By controlling the allocation of finance, determining investment priorities, and restructuring credit, the government was able to rupture the bond between the agricultural export elites and the financial infrastructure, allowing for a "democratization of credit" and a redirection of financial resources toward food production (Enríquez and Spalding 1985, 36).

The Rural Credit Program. Control of the SFN enabled the government to assume direct control over internal distribution of credit and the allocation of financial resources to both public and private sectors and to direct these resources in accordance with the new political orientation and the basic-needs/mixed-economy approach. Production loans through the Rural Credit Program were the principal instruments used initially to stimulate basic-grains production, 90 percent of which was in the hands of peasants (Spalding 1984, 7). Small- and medium-sized individual producers, as well as cooperative members previously excluded from access to credit, were now incorporated into the financial system. Reflecting the government's new priority of foodstuff production, 313 percent more area planted in basic grains was financed during the 1980–1981 cycle than in the 1977–1978 cycle. Peasant producer holdings under 36 manzanas or in production cooperatives accounted for 92 percent of that acreage (CIERA, from Deere, Marchetti, and Reinhardt 1985, 83). Loans to small farmers multiplied sevenfold between 1979 and 1980 (Sims 1981, 7), and by 1981, 51 percent of corn farmers received credit as compared to 27 percent in 1978–1979 (Spalding 1984, 7). Not only was credit more available, but credit terms were more flexible. In an effort to benefit the basic-grains sector, small farmers were charged 13 percent; to encourage collectivization, cooperatives received the most favorable interest rate, 8 percent, much lower than the rate of inflation (Enríquez 1985a, 275).

This "spilling of credit in the countryside" was criticized in its early stages for its lack of focus and its inefficiency, because, due to limited access to other inputs, production did not increase proportionately (Spalding 1985, 209). Low production levels, exacerbated by the 1982 floods and drought, led to problems with repayment, as small farmers' debts reached massive proportions in 1983 (Austin, Fox, and Kruger 1985, 21). As a result, the government agreed to waive the debts of 38,000 small farmers totaling 350 million córdobas in 1983 (CAHI *Update* 2, no. 13). Nonetheless, despite the subsequent leveling off of lending after 1983, in 1984 small and medium independent farmers and cooperative members obtained sufficient bank credit to plant 372,300 manzanas of corn, beans, and other staple crops, a figure that contrasts sharply with a peak of 20,000 manzanas before the revolution (Collins 1985, 195).

With control of the financial system, the revolutionary government was also able to determine the direction of investments and of scarce foreign exchange. Immediately following the revolution, the quality of most land devoted to basic grains was low, because the peasant producers had been pushed from the more fertile lands by export production and because there was little irrigation or fertilization. Although efforts would be made to transfer food production to more fertile lands, the government also decided to make significant investments in irrigation and fertilizers. It developed the Plan Contigente de Granos Básicos, the Emergency Grain Plan, a capital- and technology-intensive effort to raise basic-grains production on large state farms. Although partially successful, the program's high susceptibility to technical failure and its high import needs made it somewhat inappropriate (interview with Richard Stahler-Sholk, CRIES, July 1986). As a result, in 1986 efforts were being made to modernize peasant production on a smaller scale, with the hope that increased irrigation would lessen the small farmer's vulnerability to unfortunate weather conditions and allow for year-round production and more crop cycles (*Mesoameria*, May 1986:10).[11]

Credit and the Export Sector. With a scarcity of financial resources and many potential peasant recipients, there was an initial concern that the new credit program would reduce the amount of credit available to the agricultural export producers (Spalding 1984, 7). Nevertheless, the government followed through on its credit program, distributing generous quantities of loans between 1980 and 1982. However, in 1982–1983, as economic difficulties began to mount, officials became concerned with the slow rates of repayment of loans by the small farmers and with the need for a sound financial policy. By 1983, it was clear that the country's limited internal resources would not be sufficient to finance national development. Therefore, renewed emphasis was placed on generating foreign exchange, and the government began to target more of the available credit toward the agricultural export sectors once again (Enríquez and Spalding 1985).

In order to appease the private producers, the government continually subsidized export production, as it did basic grains, by keeping interest rates for loans below inflation rates (Spalding 1985, 210). To reduce the private sector's need to risk substantial amounts of its own capital, the February 1985 stabilization plan gave credit advances covering 100 percent of cotton producers' production costs and 80 percent of the expenses for coffee and sugar cultivation. However, a problem arose as some producers began using these low-interest loans to buy dollars on the black market instead of purchasing the prescribed amount of agricultural inputs or using the loans for productive purposes (Enríquez and Spalding 1985, 34). These activities increased tensions between the private sector and the state, and the latter became increasingly fearful that these illegally bought dollars would end up in Miami bank accounts or, worse, in Honduras as funds for the counterrevolutionaries.

Despite the Central Bank's favoring the private export sector with respect to foreign exchange, the export producers demonstrated continuous discontent with the government's financial policy. When the amount of foreign exchange available for production loans began steadily decreasing due to the economic crisis, private producers vociferously complained about insufficient funds to cover costs, blaming government interference and bureaucratic delays in loan dispersals for impeding the production process (Spalding 1984, 15). The private export producers also complained that concentration of credit and investment in basic-grains production left little for export production and thus inhibited their ability to produce. Imports were limited by access to foreign exchange for national needs and development priorities increased while that of the private productive and commercial sectors decreased.

In order to stimulate the private sector, the government had agreed to put up the working capital by providing plentiful credit, to guarantee minimum prices that would allow producers to make a profit, and to subsidize any sudden drops in international market prices, in order to leave producers free to use their money to invest further in production (Collins 1982, 41). However, concern that private producers were absorbing bank resources without proportionate increases in production began to heighten tensions between the state and the private export producers. For example, despite government credits covering 100 percent of production costs, many large cotton producers were unwilling to raise production levels because of what they considered the uncertainty of their status after the agrarian reform (Enríquez and Spalding 1987, 242).

As a result, land cultivated in cotton fell by 55 percent between 1977/ 78 and 1980/81 production cycles (Colburn and de Franco 1985, 281).

Credit Policy in 1985. According to some analysts, redirection of financial policy toward the peasant basic-grains sector was relatively effective in increasing food production. One CIERA study indicated that 50 to 75 percent of the rural groups interviewed for the study reported increases in production and that a significant number of them attributed the increase to improved access to credit and inputs (Utting 1986b). However, despite a concerted effort, the new credit system was unable to reach many of the food-producing peasants dispersed throughout the Nicaraguan countryside. As Enríquez and Spalding point out, this problem began to manifest itself in 1985, when enrollments in the Rural Credit Program leveled off, having succeeded in including only half of the eligible population (1987, 122). Between 1984 and 1985, credit for bean production dropped by almost 100 percent (SFN data from PAN 1987).

The stagnation in the credit program has been attributed by some analysts to the subsistence orientation, low-yield levels, and geographical isolation of much of the peasantry (SFN data from PAN 1987). Others maintain that the state was unable to replace the services traditionally provided by the former intermediaries, who had provided the peasants immediate credit, both in cash and in goods, as well as access to farming inputs and consumer goods (Utting 1986b). In addition, with increasing financial constraints and efforts to curb the fiscal deficit brought to bear by a worsening economic situation, government officials were increasingly concerned about slow recuperation rates of the production loans.

Another factor that contributed to the Rural Credit Program's inability to reach more peasant food producers was that the government had initially tried to prevent credit increases to medium and small producers from eating into available credit for export production. The growing economic crisis only heightened this competition for resources. By 1985 shortages in foreign exchange required that the government rely on monetary issues from the Central Bank to provide money for credit, investment, and subsidies. The fiscal deficit subsequently skyrocketed, and the disequilibria created by an expanding money supply with disproportionate increase in production resulted in an inflationary spiral. The combined effect of these factors was to force the government to trim the fiscal deficit, thus limiting the financial resources available for investments and credit. As a result, difficult decisions over allocation of resources between the food and export sectors were direly needed.

Harvest Labor Shortages

As we have seen, there were a great number of difficulties associated with implementing an agrarian reform and simultaneously encouraging exports. However, one of the more critical problems that clearly illustrates the food/export conflict and warrants more detailed elaboration was the shortage of harvest labor for exports. Although Sandinista food and agricultural policies benefited many peasants and small landholders in the countryside, a perceived negative consequence of these policies was the vast decrease in the number of harvest laborers who were needed to work on the cotton, sugar, and coffee plantations to maintain the agricultural export production. The effect of the agrarian transformation was a disruption of the traditional rural power structures that had guaranteed a sufficient supply of cheap labor for the private export industries; this disruption became more evident during the critical months of the harvest. Thus, a contradiction appeared between the harvest labor demands required to maintain agricultural export production and the basic structural changes in the agrarian sector that grew out of demands for a more equitable distribution of resources (Enríquez 1985a, 266). In fact, some analysts have argued that MIDINRA's initial insistence on a selective reform designed to consolidate existing APP holdings rather than distribute more land to the landless was based on a desire "to avoid the danger that too rapid settlement of the casual labor force might disrupt labor supplies to the export sector" (Irwin 1983, 129).

Agrarian reform policies combined to produce "*campesinización*," the tendency among workers to stay and work on their own small plots of land as opposed to going to work on the agricultural export estates as wage laborers. With the significant increase in the amount of land available to the rural poor and lowered rents, the campesinos had access to a better standard of subsistence, which reduced their need to supplement their income through harvest labor. Credit policies diminished the number of campesinos who would leave their own plots to work on the agricultural export estates (Enríquez 1985a, 272).

Furthermore, in its attempt to satisfy the agro-exporters by holding down wage demands, the government established a wage scale for harvest workers that was ironically too low to provide significant incentive to attract temporary workers, particularly where other traditional forms of economic or political coercion were reduced or eliminated (Enríquez 1985a, 273). One government official concisely summarized the problem: "these and other measures and, more fundamentally, the rupture in the bases which sustained the Somocista model of development, [had] provoked a sudden consequence in the agricultural sector: a shortage of seasonal labor in the coffee and cotton harvests" (Vice-Minister of Agrarian Reform, Salvador Mayorga, cited in Enríquez 1985a, 274).

In dealing with this dilemma, the government could not use economic coercion to force workers to help with the export harvest, because it was precisely this economic coercion and the extreme inequality produced by the prerevolutionary agricultural structure that had fueled the struggle against Somoza and maintained the support of the campesinos for the FSLN. The government's reforms had eliminated much of the need to work in the export harvest. The reforms were basic to the agrarian reform policies and were not likely to be done away with in order to generate a harvest labor supply (Enríquez 1985a, 276). Therefore, the state was forced to implement other short-term methods to alleviate the harvest labor shortage, including a child-care program to free parents for labor during harvest periods and for volunteer labor and the use of university and high-school children during January and February to pick cotton and coffee (Sims 1981, 6). However, as Enríquez accurately points out, reliance on a voluntary workforce could not serve as a long-term solution to labor-shortage problems because the revolutionary enthusiasm that typically follows the initial period of a transformation could not be expected to continue indefinitely (Enríquez 1985a, 277). Thus, the government would have to find other alternatives to meet labor demands of the private and state export sectors in order to encourage their continued cooperation in production of needed export goods, while maintaining and advancing the Sandinistas' commitment to agrarian reform and social equity.

Production Results as of 1985

The government's new agrarian policies initially had positive production results in the staples sector. The greatest success was in rice production, which increased by 93 percent between 1977 and 1982, allowing the country to achieve self-sufficiency in that product by 1983 (MIDINRA 1983). However, because rice production is concentrated primarily on large state and private farms, this increase was more a reflection of the increasing investment in irrigation and fertilizers than of the policies of the agrarian reform. Bean production also registered significant advances, rising 50 percent during the same period (CEPAL 1983). And although output levels for other staple crops began to decline in the 1983–1984 harvest, bean production grew steadily (USDA 1984, 1).

However, basic-grains production often failed to live up to expectations, for, as Minister of Agriculture Jaime Wheelock noted in 1983, Nicaragua was investing 10 times as much in the production of basic grains as it did in the prerevolutionary period, but only attaining an overall 50 percent increase in staples output (*Barricada*, Feb. 28, 1983, cited in Spalding 1985, 215). Corn production, in particular, was a disappointment because, although growth rates were positive during the 1980–1981 harvest, it still lagged far behind other staples. The 1982 floods exacerbated these problems, and in that year corn output fell below pre-1977 levels

(CEPAL 1983). Given the importance of corn in the Nicaraguan diet, this decline presented planners with a serious disappointment. The problems with corn production necessitated increased corn imports in 1982, thus keeping food self-sufficiency out of reach.

In addition, despite the temporary self-sufficiency achieved in rice and beans in 1981 and the fact that production of these two crops was higher in 1984 than during the prerevolutionary period, the output for all food crops began declining by 1985, contributing to food shortages in the face of increasing demand. Production of both rice and beans declined by 10 percent between 1984 and 1985 and corn production registered a slight decline as well (PAN 1987). Between 1984 and 1985, the amount of land in corn production declined 26 percent, from 270,000 to 200,000 manzanas, and that of rice dropped 24 percent, from 62,000 to 50,000 manzanas. During the same period, the area planted in beans also decreased 11 percent, from 120,000 to 106,000 manzanas, and although the drop was not as drastic, it was still great cause for concern (MIDINRA 1987, 22).

The previous examination highlights various factors that were potential contributors to the government's inability to improve food security by 1985. It illustrates the disequilibria that result from contradictions inherent in a revolutionary process that transforms productive and marketing structures within the context of a mixed economy. Although the excalation of the contra war, inflation, the foreign exchange crisis, and unfortunate weather conditions indeed worsened Nicaragua's food problem, a significant amount of responsibility for the continuation of this problem can be attributed to inadequacies and contradictions that emerged from the government's initial pricing and marketing policies and from the continued dependence of the economy on agricultural exports, which had led the government to encourage and protect the export sector, both private and state. The export dependency hampered government efforts to redistribute land to peasants for food production, strained the financial resources available for credit and price subsidies, and reduced the potential alternatives for achieving food security in the face of mounting economic difficulties. Government attempts to maintain the political alliance with the private sector had not only limited the government's ability to promote food production, but the attempts themselves were apparently also proving futile. Cotton production dropped 20 percent between the 1983/84 and 1984/85 cycles, and that of sugar by 18 percent (INEC 1986, 97–98). Although such declines in export production can be attributed to many factors, one of the most significant was that many of the private export producers were taking their land out of production and engaging in decapitalization. In light of the economic crisis wracking the country, increasing instances of such unproductive, "unpatriotic" behavior by the private export producers was encouraging many officials to rethink their priorities.

In addition to the economic crisis, pressures from a growing contra war were also exacerbating the growing tensions between the export and food sectors. To cite one example, MIDINRA had made an effort to shift state livestock production, which traditionally occupied the coastal lands, to more appropriate, traditionally unused lands in the central highlands and frontier regions in order to bring the fertile areas back into basic-grains cultivation (CAHI 1984, 3). However, the war in frontier areas and the slaughtering of herds by the contras stymied the government's attempts to move more cattle out of the Pacific plain. Thus, the escalation of the war was only heightening the government's awareness that difficult decisions about priorities in agriculture, as well as adjustments in policy, would have to be made.

Policy Readjustment: 1985–1986

As we have seen, the government's "national unity" alliance with the private landowners and its concern for maintaining export production restricted its ability to implement the agricultural policies designed to encourage food self-sufficiency, evident in its hesitation to expropriate more land for redistribution and in the continued direction of financial resources toward exports. Until 1985, Sandinista efforts to increase domestic food production focused primarily on increasing the efficiency of land use through liberal credit and technical assistance and on minor redistribution of nonexport lands, primarily marginal state lands. Although the political power of the large landowners was limited, the government's concern for preserving their cooperation meant that their property would be highly protected, restricting further expropriation and redistribution of the food-producing peasantry.

Rising Peasant Discontent

The political pressures from the large commercial producers were not the only political considerations that the Sandinistas had to address with respect to agrarian policies. By the end of 1985, it would become increasingly clear that the peasants' discontent and decreasing participation presented an even greater threat to "national unity" than did the bourgeoisie's. An increasing number of critics of agrarian policy focused their arguments on the limited impact of the 1981 reform on the poorest rural sectors and pointed to the rising discontent as proof of an inadequate policy (CAHI 1985b). At the end of 1985, there were still 105,000 families with little or no land in Nicaragua. Half of these were concentrated in Region IV, the Pacific Masaya region. In 1985, this region also had 30,000 minifundistas, with plots too small to support them (CAHI 1985b). Furthermore, the contra war was increasing the number of landless peasants and farmers, resulting in a flow of displaced peasants out of the countryside either spontaneously or through government relocation programs. By 1986, a total of 250,000 peasants had been resettled, resulting in a severe disorganization of and decline in production (Luciak 1987, 17). Also, a large number of rural poor were still untouched by the agrarian reform after four years. Pressure on the government continued to mount.

In the face of this pressure for land and the growing need to increase food production, the government had few options. Only 11 percent of landholdings in the country fell into the category of over 500 manzanas (or 1,000 in the interior)—the size subject to expropriation under the 1981 law—and most of these lands were being efficiently used and thus could not be expropriated. The only remaining alternative was for the government to negotiate with the private producers and buy their lands. In fact, in 1985 alone, the state acquired 340 properties through negotiations at a cost of more than 500 million córdobas, or 50 million 1985 dollars (Luciak 1987, 18). However, when one notes that total export earnings for 1985 were only $260 million, the feasibility of spending larger sums of money to buy more land for redistribution, particularly during an economic crisis, became increasingly questionable.

One of the major conflicts between the government and many of the independent peasant farmers, represented by UNAG, concerned the government's continued emphasis on cooperatives as the form of production organization. Until 1985, with some exceptions, forming a cooperative was a condition for receiving land; however, many basic-grains producers were unaccustomed to this form of production and thus were untouched by the reform (CAHI 1986a, 4). In addition, the conservative opposition increasingly began using as anti-Sandinista propaganda the fact that during the first three years of the agrarian reform, well over two-thirds of the expropriated land was taken over by the state (CAHI 1986a, 5).

The November 1984 elections demonstrated that the conservatives were not the only ones concerned with the inadequacies of agrarian policy: Sandinista support fell significantly in many of the Pacific departments, including Masaya, that traditionally had been important FSLN strongholds. A strong message indicating need for a policy adjustment was evident in the fact that support for opposition parties in the election was strongest in areas where less than 10 percent of peasantry had received land (CAHI 1985b, 13c). Another reflection of the growing discontent was that many of the politically active peasants who had once volunteered for the militia began to oppose the draft and engage in a "political strike," choosing not to participate in FSLN rallies and in UNAG (CAHI 1985b, 5c). The message became even clearer when, in May 1985, land-poor peasants in Masaya began demonstrations demanding land and invaded several private properties and state farms. These protests represented a crisis that would test the government's commitment to one of its strategic bases of support (CAHI 1985a, 1). The government would have to respond.

Adjustments in Land Distribution in 1985 and the 1986 Agrarian Reform Law

Because of increasing pressures from the contra war and the government's need to maintain support of the peasants, particularly in the war zones, beginning in 1985 the Sandinistas began to reevaluate and transform their agrarian reform policy significantly. An important event in this transformation occurred when the government took the side of the peasants in the Masaya case and opted to redistribute to them the disputed cotton lands held by Enrique Bolaños, president of the Superior Council of Private Enterprise (COSEP). Except for Bolaños, all of the other private producers affected by the Masaya invasions agreed to sell their properties to the state or exchange their holdings for fertile land in regions with no land pressure. Because Bolaños's lands were less than 500 manzanas, MIDINRA had to invoke a "special agrarian reform" clause of the 1981 law and declared the land a "Zone of Agricultural Development Agrarian Reform"; and the land was redistributed to individual peasants (CAHI 1985a, 3).

The government's response to the explosive situation in Masaya reflected its realization that it was no longer possible to protect some of the cotton farms in this region, even to preserve national unity, at the expense of basic-grains production and internal imperatives. The government could no longer ignore UNAG's convincing argument that food shortages were becoming as serious as foreign exchange shortages (CAHI 1985a, 3). In addition to the important Masaya decision, in 1985, 323,196 manzanas of land were redistributed to 15,470 families as individuals or production cooperatives, 23 percent more than the amount redistributed in 1984 (DGRA 1986, 4–6).

Although these figures are important, a more significant aspect of the 1985 redistribution is that it represented a distinct attitudinal shift on the part of the government toward a propeasant direction. In addition, it reflected an apparent recognition by policymakers of the contradictions and inadequacies of the previous policies that had ignored the strong individualistic traits of some Nicaraguan small farmers. They acknowledged that the previous emphasis on collectives was one of the main reasons why they had failed to encourage the participation of many basic-grains producers in the food strategy. The 1985 Agrarian Reform Plan originally indicated that 60 percent of the land that would be redistributed would be given to cooperatives and that only 6 percent would go to individual families. However, in response to the carefully organized pressure from UNAG, the government actually distributed almost half the land to 5,636 individual farmers, three times as many as had received land in the period from 1981 to 1984 (CAHI 1986a, 4). In addition, 95 percent of the expropriated land went to cooperatives and to small and medium individual producers and only 5 percent to the state sector, indicating another shift in the distribution pattern (*Mexico and Central America Report*, March 21, 1986:3). In another interesting trend, 60 percent of the land distributed in 1985 came from the state sector and 40 percent from negotiated sales and expropriations (CAHI 1986a, 4). Apparently, in 1985 the state sector had decreased. Predictions from MIDINRA indicated that this trend would continue and that 39 percent of the land planned for redistribution would come from the state (CAHI 1986a, 1). According to the director of MIDINRA's Department of Land Tenure, the state sector was expected to be reduced to 10 percent by about 1990 (CAHI 1986a, 4).

What appeared to be a new, third phase of the agrarian reform was formalized on January 11, 1986, when a third agrarian reform law was announced. It lowered the 1981 ceilings on land subject to expropriation from 500 and 1,000 manzanas (depending on the region) to 50 and 100 manzanas and authorized the expropriate of land for "public use or social interest." As a result, many landholdings under 500 manzanas, which included many of the medium-sized private export holdings, were no longer exempt from potential expropriation if the land was not "efficiently exploited." In addition, the new law foresaw the possibility of even affecting farms that were efficiently exploited if it was in the "public interest," that is, due to peasant pressure (CAHI 1986b, 1). The new law made it apparent that the government would no longer hesitate to take the type of action it took in the Masaya redistribution if such action was deemed necessary. In fact, as of May 1986, there were thirty cases where the "public interest" clause was invoked (CAHI 1986b, 1).

The 1986 reform plan indicated that 305,202 manzanas would be redistributed, benefiting 16,789 families (DGRA 1986). The then minister of agriculture, Jaime Wheelock, estimated that 20,000 farmers actually benefited from the new policy in 1986 (CAHI May 1986b, 4). Between 1980 and 1986, a total of 4,200,000 manzanas had been reformed, benefiting 93,000 families. Plans for 1987 included the distribution of 192,000 manzanas to 16,500 more families (MIDINRA 1987).

The Impact of the 1986 Agrarian Reform Law on Food and Exports.
Vilas has argued that the text of the 1986 law illustrates a decision on
the part of the government to satisfy the land hunger of the peasantry
without breaking the alliance with the larger landowners, because, by
removing the manzana limits on land subject to expropriation, the law
gave the government the option of expropriating medium-sized properties,
not just those of the larger landowners (1987, 243–244). However, it is
important to reiterate that the most significant element in the alliance
with the private sector was in fact the medium-sized producers, because
they controlled the bulk of export production. By making them subject
to expropriation, the 1986 law appeared to many of these medium-sized
producers as a threat. In a CAHI interview, the president of the Conservative party articulated the views of some of the private landowners.
He complained that the government had "responded politically," that
is, had expropriated the lands of "unfriendly" landowners; and, by doing
so, it had disrupted production on some of the most efficient export
farms (CAHI 1986b, 2). Although the government proceeded cautiously
in some of the most important export-producing regions in recognition
of the politically delicate situation, many landowners expressed considerable uncertainty about their future (*Country Report* 1, 1987:14).

MIDINRA responded to accusations from the bourgeoisie by arguing
that the law had in fact encouraged investment because producers believed
their chances of survival were greater if they ran their farms efficiently.
MIDINRA also argued that many landowners had decapitalized before
the new law was passed and that the failure to cooperate, particularly
among cotton producers, was one of the factors that encouraged policymakers to change the policy (*Country Report* 1, 1987:14; Reinhardt 1987,
32). Thus, one of the central motives behind the reform was indeed a
political one: to cripple the "internal front," the group of private export
producers who intentionally decapitalized or left their land idle in an
effort to hurt the national economy. The price of this move might be
high in terms of export production. However, the price of a loss of
popular support—among the peasantry due to insufficient land redistribution and among the urban poor due to higher costs of scarce food—
perhaps seemed even higher.

By increasing the land pool, the 1986 reform made it much easier to
redistribute land where it was most needed, and the number of small
individual farmers, who were important producers of basic grains,
increased dramatically. Many policymakers predicted that the change
would have a positive effect on domestic food production and would
alleviate food shortages. Despite these optimistic predictions, however,
other policymakers remained uncertain as to what the actual effect of

the new law would be in light of the problems of pricing and marketing problems that had acted as a disincentive to production.

Some officials argued that although the inclination of small farmers might be to cultivate basic grains for domestic consumption, which would ease the food shortages, cultivation of basic grains would lead to a decline in production of export crops, which would hurt foreign exchange earnings. In addition they voiced a concern that the new land distribution would increase the process of campesinización, leaving the large state and private export farms without seasonal laborers. Other officials argued that peasants might abandon basic-grains production in favor of export crops once they recognized that the latter were more profitable, thereby lessening the reform's ability to eliminate food shortages. Apparently, the debate over the agrarian reform will be as lively in the upcoming years as during the initial years of the revolution.

Adjustments in Pricing and Marketing Controls

As noted previously, the policy of fixing prices for food production, combined with the imbalance in supply mechanisms of the marketing system, discriminated against the peasantry and created a disincentive to food production. This limited the impact of the other policies aimed at improving the lives of the peasanty and at encouraging their participation in the food strategy; in addition, it provided political ammunition for the counterrevolutionaries (Vilas 1987, 235). Despite periodic price increases, official price increases were no match for the skyrocketing cost of farming inputs and consumer goods. As discussed earlier, due to the unattractiveness of the official food prices relative to inflation, food producers began selling their produce to the black-market dealers, decreasing the portion of the food crop available for distribution to the urban areas through "secure" state channels. The price disincentives and the difficulties in obtaining farming inputs encouraged many basic-grains producers to withdraw from production all together, to produce for their own subsistence, or to become small-scale speculators and transporters of basic grains on the black market.

In recognition of the inadequate prices, as well as the difficulty of controlling the entire market for corn and beans and capturing the produce of thousands of dispersed small producers, in 1985 the government deregulated the commercialization of corn and beans. Because "honest" private merchants were allowed to buy the producers' goods, the efficiency of the marketing system improved and increased prices provided an important incentive to basic-grains producers. As a result of such deregulation, between 1985 and 1986 the average producer price for corn and beans rose 740 percent and 703 percent, respectively, in sharp contrast to the 106 percent and 271 percent increases between 1984 and 1985 (MIDINRA data as cited in PAN 1987).

To determine who the "honest" merchants were, the government allowed the small producers' organization, UNAG, to select them. In exchange for the freedom to buy the food from the producers, the merchants in turn would agree to sell it to consumers at the official prices, to limit the speculation-induced inflation and the amount of food going to the black market. By deciding to work through the established network of private merchants, the government by this policy reduced the government's expanding bureaucracy. Rather than controlling the entire market, the government chose to concentrate its efforts on controlling the distribution of manufactured and agro-industrial goods, whose procurement was concentrated in relatively few enterprises and thus more easily controlled (Utting 1986a).

The liberalization of the grain market raised concern that peasants would sell more of their produce to the black market, rather than to the government marketing network. In an attempt to deal with this problem, the government made an effort during 1986 to design agreements with peasant producers under which they would sell a certain portion of their crop to ENABAS at official prices in return for guaranteed production inputs and supplies (*El Nuevo Diario*, July 28, 1986; *Meso-america*, May 1986:10).

In addition to the market deregulation, a strong effort was made to improve the marketing network in rural areas by forming new *expendios rurales* and *centros de abastecimiento rural* (CARs), rural supply centers. This policy represented a sincere effort on the part of the government to provide the peasant producers more immediate access to consumer goods at controlled prices, apparently their main concern (Utting 1986a). In addition, during the summer of 1986 the government initiated efforts to create *empresas territoriales*, territorial enterprises, in an attempt to centralize the various bureaucratic functions of buying and selling to fulfill the functions essential to the peasant producers in a more simplified manner (*Barricada*, August 12, 1986).

The farmers' organization, UNAG, has played an important role in assisting the state efforts to capture enough of the market to secure food availability throughout the country, as well as in making state-supplied inputs and services accessible to the widely dispersed food producers. It has helped channel the peasants' produce to the new "campesino stores," the CARs, where they in turn can buy production supplies at low prices (*Central American Report*, 13 (49):392). By the beginning of 1987, these new supply centers were already in operation in regions I and II and were being organized by UNAG itself in other regions of the country (*Central American Report* 14(5):37). UNAG's goal is to help find less bureaucratic means of dealing with the issue of commercialization of basic products than those that the state had originally attempted. As Eduardo Baumeister argued, perhaps UNAG "is attempting to reestablish the form, if not the content, of the role traditionally played by commercial capital in rural areas" (*LASA-NICA Scholars News* 15:7).

Thus, it was apparent that at the end of 1985 the government began adjusting its rural marketing and pricing policies in an attempt to resolve some of the initial contradictions. The 1985 policy changes highlighted the government's willingness to work with the market, not against it, and to operate within the context of a mixed economy, in the instances where its weaknesses were becoming obstacles to an efficient food system. However, problems with bottlenecks in the ENABAS system, bureaucratic inefficiency and delays, and increasing sales by the peasants to the parallel and black markets were still creating difficulties, demonstrating that much remained to be done in this area in the upcoming years.

Adjustments in Credit Policy

Recognizing the destabilizing effects of an expansionist money supply policy in the face of decreasing production and growing speculation, and responding to increasing domestic and international economic problems, the government instituted several adjustments affecting credit and investment policy within its package of economic measures in 1985. Faced with increasingly narrow and difficult choices about which sectors of the economy to protect and which to alter while trimming the fiscal deficit, the government elected to tighten the policy of financing 100 percent of the costs of cotton production and the state farms (Enríquez and Spalding 1987, 124). It also decided to raise interest rates for both borrowers and depositors, designating distinct rates for the borrowers in various agricultural sectors according to its priorities.

It is significant that interest rates for independent producers in the Rural Credit Program increased by only one point, but rates for other borrowers increased by greater amounts (Enríquez and Spalding 1987, 124). Regardless of the low loan repayment rates among the peasantry, the government had chosen not to abandon its political commitment to this sector in an effort to encourage the peasant's continued investments in food production. In addition, despite the financial crisis and the budget cuts, the amount of credit allocated to food production in 1986 increased significantly. Between 1985 and 1986, total credit disbursements for corn production increased by 437 percent, and for rice and bean production by 190 and 157 percent, respectively (SFN data as cited in PAN 1987). Apparently, while making decisions about the redirection of credit and financing, the government gave food production priority over exports.

Concerned with maintaining investment and production, as well as with controlling the inflationary spiral, the government decided to maintain interest rates for all production loans far below the rate of inflation, despite the overall rate increases. Nevertheless, the withdrawal from production by many elements of the private export sector continued to generate a debate among economic planners as to the wisdom of providing these producers with plentiful credit and of subsidizing their production, particularly during the 1988 stabilization measures that forced dramatic budget cuts.

A Food/Export Strategy Within a Process of Transformation: The Constraints

Until 1985, the Nicaraguan government tried to implement its policies of agrarian transformation under the assumption that food and exports were not mutually exclusive and attempted to demonstrate that a flexible approach, through a "mixed economy," could balance the traditionally competing interests of state, peasant, private, and cooperative producers. For the Nicaraguan policymakers, the supposed dichotomy between agricultural exports and internal consumption was not clear-cut because of the important links between the two. In a country where there are few possibilities for the industrial development that could generate the foreign exchange required by the national food system, agricultural exports became an important and necessary element in providing the inputs on which the production and marketing of food for internal consumption depend.[12] Thus, the government was making efforts at improving the efficiency of land on which basic grains were grown, rather than relying solely on expanding production. In this way, it hoped to lessen the possibility of land competition between export producers and producers for the internal market. Furthermore, as of 1986 investments in agriculture were divided equally between export and domestic-consumption production, a strategy that the government hoped would allow the country to increase exports while developing self-sufficiency in food production (Enríquez and Spalding 1987). Producers of beans and corn were using few imported farming inputs so they did not compete with export producers for scarce foreign exchange.

However, by 1985, when food production began to decline amidst increasing demand, it became apparent that many assumptions would have to be reexamined and other unexpected tensions and contradictions would have to be addressed. The revolution had succeeded in dismantling the underlying features of the disarticulated agricultural export model—

which it had inherited—particularly in terms of production, labor, and exchange relations. However, because the new government focused on exports within its own definition of a mixed economy, the revolutionary economic model had resulted in "disarticulations" and problems of its own, which were particularly evident in the food system.

A number of political and economic factors have intervened to constrain the feasibility of the food/export strategy and to limit the government's room for maneuvering between the two agricultural sectors. These factors provide important examples of the kinds of constraints that can limit a government's ability to enhance food security and can determine the evolution of food and agricultural policies within the context of a revolutionary transformation of political, social, and economic structures in a previously underdeveloped economy. For the purpose of reiteration and summarization, I have grouped these constraints into seven categories, most of which are interrelated.

1. As has been shown, the success of food-policy formulation and of the overall economic strategy was conditioned and constrained by an economy based on agricultural exports. As Vilas has argued, the crux of a strategy centered on agricultural exports obviously is its capacity to export and to generate sufficient foreign exchange from those exports to finance investments in food production and other programs (1987, 236). That capacity was threatened by negative trends in international prices, declining productivity in exports, the war, and deteriorating terms of trade. The economic withdrawal of the export bourgeoisie, despite government incentives and stimulants, exacerbated productivity problems and caused further decreases in foreign exchange. These shortages only aggravated the competition for resources between the two agricultural sectors and for the funds available for redistributive programs, tensions that mounted with each passing year. The outlook for improved prices and increased access to international markets is not encouraging; thus, the vicious cycle resulting from the dependency on agricultural exports will not be broken easily.

2. Food policy was conditioned by the political alliances the government was forced to maintain in order to implement its economic strategy successfully. The importance of private-sector cooperation in the revolution required that the government initially move cautiously on its agrarian reform. Despite government attempts at maintaining a good relationship, many of the private exporters held out because of their discontent and discomfort with the political-economic system the revolution was promoting. In 1984, the government's alliance with the small peasant sector began to increase in importance due to growing contra activity and anti-Sandinista propaganda, as well as a recognition of the need to increase production for the internal market. As Nola Reinhardt

points out, the growing economic efficiency of UNAG also meant that the government's concern for maintaining this alliance was not based solely on concerns for equity, but on a desire for efficiency as well (1987, 32). At the First National Conference of UNAG, Jaime Wheelock, minister of agriculture, stated that the campesinos "constitute an irreplaceable, dynamic influence, a real power, one of the pillars of the Revolution" (from Baumeister 1987, 5). Such a statement reflected the growing awareness on the part of the government that the small- and medium-sized producers and cooperatives were indeed economically viable and important actors in the revolutionary model (Baumeister 1987, 5).

3. Historical structural factors limited initial attempts at effective food policy. For example, the country was characterized by a heterogeneous and widely dispersed rural population, which created difficulties in formulating appropriate policies to provide incentives to production. One of the reasons for early policy problems was that the government tended to treat the diverse forms of production organization as one, although each form has its own logic. In addition, it proved very difficult to provide services and assistance to such a widely dispersed population, and many peasants went untouched by the revolutionary policies.

4. Contradictions in the mixed economy affected food policy implementation. In a mixed economy, there will be agents in the free market or in production who will be uncooperative and will undermine price or marketing control policies, particularly during disequilibrium between supply and demand. The attractiveness of the black market detracted from government efforts to implement producer price increases and to distribute food to the areas of the country that had traditionally been without. The government adjusted its marketing policy to attempt to take advantage of the experience and coverage of the "honest" private merchants. However, controlling black market speculation will remain a formidable task, particularly amidst an ongoing debate over state control versus the free marketing of food.

5. Related to the previous tension was the state's frequent inability to fill the gaps created by the displacement of essential agents in the economy, resulting in serious disarticulations in the economy. For example, the preexisting marketing mechanisms, although perhaps exploitative, had been able to reach much of the dispersed basic-grains-producing peasants and were proving difficult to replace. The Nicaraguan case provides an example that dismantling traditional structures is a much less difficult and time-consuming task than the creation of new ones, and that, in revolutionary processes, perhaps the greater struggle comes *after* the overthrow of the old regime.

6. Macro-economic constraints also affected food policy. An increasing fiscal deficit, inflation resulting from declining production and increasing

demand, and a worsening trade deficit and debt crisis were the major factors limiting government efforts at restructuring the food system. Because most of the redistributive programs like credit, subsidies, and investment had been financed by monetary emission, which had contributed to increasing inflation, the Sandinista government forced to cut back on many of these policies in the face of fiscal crisis. Difficult decisions between the two foci of the economic strategy had to be made.

7. Finally, it is important to recognize that the Nicaraguan government's efforts to design and implement necessary food policies, as well as to succeed in its overall development strategy, were made increasingly difficult by the actions of hostile external forces, particularly the United States. It imposed an economic blockade, attempted to close European markets, tried to impede the Contradora process (a series of attempts by the Five Central American presidents to formulate peace accords), and continued military aggression and support of the contra war. The war had dire economic consequences in terms of both human and material resources as well as on actual production of both food and exports. In addition, the U.S. financial war aggravated the foreign exchange crisis, reducing the amount of funds available for allocation to the various sectors. The availability of foreign aid immediately following the revolution enabled the government to distribute funds to "priority areas," including both the bood and the private export sectors; however, aid from the bilateral and multilateral lending institutions decreased as a credit blockade was set in motion by the United States.[13] Therefore, despite attempts by the Nicaraguan government to improve the country's food security and create a viable mixed economy, the difficulties in implementing this novel approach to development and the decision to make adjustments in the strategy were in part the result of actions taken by international opposition forces and were beyond the control of the revolutionary government.

Conclusion

In its food policy changes between 1979 and 1986, the revolutionary government of Nicaragua implemented major programs and restructured the production sector in order to stimulate production of basic grains, not only through land redistribution, but also through a restructuring of the country's pricing, investment, and credit policies. Various factors influenced the development of food and agricultural policies in Nicaragua between 1979 and 1986, including electoral politics, the counterrevolutionary threat, structural contradictions resulting from the new policies, and the balance-of-payments crisis. As Thome argues, the ability of the government to rethink and adjust its policies during the first seven years provides an illustration of its ability to subsume ideological goals in favor of "political pragmatism, economic reality and result-oriented policies" (1984, 16–17). The exigencies of an export-based economy forced policymakers to be sensitive to the needs of the private agricultural export sector while designing, and implementing policies to benefit the peasant producers. Furthermore, policymakers' willingness to allow the free market to play a larger role in the economy and to increase the amount of property in private, rather than state, hands demonstrates an ongoing commitment to a mixed economy and pragmatism in the face of economic pressure, in contrast to the arguments often made that the Nicaraguan economy is becoming completely state run.

In 1985 and 1986, as we have seen, even sharper modifications in the economic strategy were made in an attempt to reorient policies toward increasing production of food for the internal market and to develop the economy on a more self-centered basis. Although the new focus did not in and of itself require that agro-exports be ignored or abandoned, it implied a parallel redirection of the benefits and surpluses of production away from the medium-sized export sector, which had traditionally benefited. Nevertheless, as Vilas has pointed out, until the government is more confident as to what extent production for the internal market can replace agricultural exports as the new center for accumulation, the importance of agricultural exports, although reduced, will remain high (1987, 244). In Fact, in its Plan de Trabajo for 1987, the Ministry of Agriculture reiterated its goal of "working to produce both more foreign exchange [through exports] and more food" (MIDINRA 1987, 32). Apparently, the food/export strategy has not been eliminated, only modified. Thus, the revolutionary government will be forced to continue demonstrating flexibility and ingenuity in dealing not only with the previous tensions, but with additional contradictions, and will have to continue to experiment with the most appropriate means of balancing the needs of the two agricultural sectors.

Notes

Portions of this chapter previously appeared in chapter 8 of a book edited by Michael E. Conroy, with my assistance, *Nicaragua: Profiles of the Revolutionary Public Sector*, published by Westview Press. I wish to thank Westview for permission to incorporate sections of the previous work into the current discussion. I wish to acknowledge the kind cooperation of Jaime Cofré, Anselmo Aburto, and Francisco Guzmán of PAN, Oscar Neira and Sonia Aburto of CIERA, and Luis Enríquez of FAO (Managua) in providing access to important and useful documents during field research in Managua. An earlier draft benefited from insightful comments made by Laura J. Enríquez, Peter Utting, and Michael E.

Conroy. However, none of these individuals bear responsibility for the contents of this chapter, and any errors in fact or interpretation are mine. This chapter should be viewed as a historical analysis in that since the time of writing, in 1987–1988, significant political and economic changes have taken place in Nicaragua.

1. The breakdown of the different commodities as a percentage of total exports is coffee, 25 percent; cotton, 24 percent; beef, 10 percent; sugar, 6 percent; and bananas, 1 percent (Weeks 1985, table 9, 50). When one notes that export earnings represented 33.7 percent of GNP in 1975, the importance of agro-exports to the economy as a whole becomes even more apparent (Weeks 1985, 52).

2. For more detailed information about the agro-export monopoly on financial resources before the revolution, see Enríquez and Spalding 1985.

3. One manzana = .7 hectares or 1.75 acres.

4. As de Janvry maintains, the two underlying foundations of "disarticulated" economies are cheap labor and cheap food, both of which were characteristics of prerevolutionary Nicaragua's agrarian structure. For a thorough discussion of the cheap-food component in Nicaragua, see Frenkel 1987b. For a discussion of the cheap-labor component, also in Nicaragua, see Enríquez 1985b.

5. It is recognized that a complete analysis of food security includes an examination not only of food production, but also of distribution. However, an analysis of the policies that the revolutionary government has undertaken to restructure the distribution side of the food system, although important, is beyond the scope of the current discussion. For an in-depth analysis of those distributional policies, see Austin, Fox, and Kruger 1985; Utting 1987; and Frenkel 1987a and 1987b.

6. Reinhardt is more critical of the FSLN's decision and argues that, because the FSLN was "proexport," its initial hesitation to redistribute reflected an "antipeasant" bias on the part of the FSLN leadership, inherited from the dualistic capitalist agro-export model that historically had prevailed (1987, 15).

7. For an elaboration of this argument and a more in-depth discussion of the Sandinistas' changing conception of the peasantry, see Reinhardt 1987.

8. "Decapitalization" refers to disinventment through such devices as allowing plant and machinery to run down while profits are pocketed or taking out low-interest investment loans and converting the money into dollars to be banked abroad (Gilbert 1983, 44). This economic sabotage was often practiced by cutting back on land in cultivation, laying off workers, selling machinery and livestock, overinvoicing for imported goods, or paying inflated salaries to family members (Collins 1982, 44).

9. "Idle" land was defined as being uncultivated for at least two consecutive years. Land was defined as "underused" when less than 75 percent was sown. Ranchlands were considered underused when there was less than one head of cattle for each 35 acres in the Pacific coastal region or for each 5 acres in the highlands (see Collins 1982, 87–96).

10. The government went to great lengths to avoid placing the burden of these producer prices increases on the consumer by implementing a consumer-

subsidy policy. However, these consumer subsidies were dramatically reduced in 1985 and again in 1986 due to the heavy burden on the fiscal deficit. For a discussion of consumer-subsidy policy, see UNRISD 1986; Utting 1987; and Frenkel 1987a and 1987b.

11. It should also be noted that because much of the country's food cultivation occurred in frontier areas where roads were poor or nonexistent, the revolutionary government also began diverting some of its investment into road construction to these prevously ignored areas. In addition, efforts were made to provide the small staples producers with farming inputs such as seeds, tools, and fertilizers. Furthermore, the government set up and financed training programs for improved farming, storing, and transport techniques to increase yields and decrease losses from spoilage (Collins 1985, 196). However, these and other programs would have to be reconsidered and trimmed in the face of increasing defense costs and a fiscal crisis.

12. Furthermore, what are generally categorized as agricultural export products—cotton, beef, and sugar—are vital not only for generating foreign exchange, but also for providing basic raw materials for some of the food products consumed internally (UNRISD 1986, 206).

13. The IDB and the World Bank provided $238.1 million in loans between July 1979 and December 1981; this amount dropped to $92.1 million between 1981 and 1982 and continued to decline in subsequent years (Enríquez and Spalding 1985, 49). For more detailed information on the economic consequences of U.S. aggression, see FitzGerald 1987.

References and Bibliography

Aburto, Sonia
   1986   Interview with author at CIERA. Managua, July 1986.
Austin, James, Jonathan Fox, and Walter Kruger
   1985   "The Role of the Revolutionary State in the Nicaraguan Food System."
           World Development 13, no. 1 (Jan.): 15–40.
Austin, James, and Jonathan Fox
   1985   "Food Policy." In Nicaragua: The First Five Years, edited by Thomas
           Walker. New York: Praeger, 399–412.
Barraclough, Soló
   1982   A Preliminary Analysis of the Nicaraguan Food System. Geneva: United
           Nations Research Institute for Social Development.
Barry, Tom, and Deb Preusch
   1986   The Central American Fact Book. New York: Grove Press.
Baumeister, Eduardo
   1987   "Economía política en las relaciones entre el estado y el sector privado
           en el proceso nicaragüense." Paper presented at the Seminario sobre
           los Problemas de la Transición en Pequeñas Economías Periféricas,
           Managua, September.

Baumeister, Eduardo and Oscar Neira
1984   "Economía política en las relaciones entre el estado y el sector privado en el proceso nicaragüense." Paper presented at the Seminario sobre los Problemas de la Transición en Pequeñas Economías Periféricas, Managua, September.

Black, George
1981   *The Triumph of the People: The Sandinista Revolution in Nicaragua.* London: Zed Press.

Brockett, Charles
1984   "Malnutrition, Public Policy, and Agrarian Change in Guatemala." *Journal of Interamerican Studies and World Affairs* 26, no. 4 (Nov.).

Bulmer-Thomas, Victor
1983   "Economic Development Over the Long Run—Central America Since 1920." *Journal of Latin American Studies* 15, no. 2 (Nov.): 269–294.

CAHI (Central American Historical Institute)
1983   "UNAG Calls on Nicaraguan Government to Cancel Debt." *Update* 3, no. 13 (June 24).
1984   "Nicaragua's Agrarian Reform." *Update* 3, no. 2 (Jan. 13).
1985a   "Masaya Peasants Prompt Land Expropriations." *Update* 4, no. 23 (July 12).
1985b   "The Nicaraguan Peasantry Gives New Direction to the Agrarian Reform." *Envio* 4, no. 51 (Sept.).
1986a   "Agrarian Reform Undergoes a Change in Nicaragua." *Update* 5, no. 4 (Feb. 7).
1986b   "Reactions to Agrarian Reform Modifications in Nicaragua." *Update* 5, no. 20 (May 21).

CEPAL (Comisión Económica Para América Latina)
1983   *Notas para el Estudio Económico de América Latina, Nicaragua.* Mexico City: CEPAL.

CEPAL/FAO/OIT/SIECA/OCT/OEA
1973   *Tenencia de la tierra y desarrollo rural en Centroamérica.* San José: EDUCA.

CIERA (Centro de Investigación y Estudios de la Reforma Agraria)
1982   *Producción y organización en el agro nicaragüense.* Managua: CIERA.
1983a   *Distribución y consumo popular de alimentos en Managua.* Managua: CIERA.
1983b   *El hambre en los países del Tercer Mundo.* Managua: CIERA.
1986   "Estudio de Ingreso-gasto en nueve municipios." Internal document. Managua: CIERA.

CIERA, PAN, CIDA
1983   *Informe del Primer Seminario sobre Estrategia Alimentaria.* Managua: CIERA.

Colburn, Forrest D., and Silvio de Franco
1985   "Privilege, Production, and Revolution: The Case of Nicaragua." *Comparative Politics* 17, no. 3 (April): 277–290.

Collins, Joseph
  1982   *What Difference Could Revolution Make? Food and Farming in the New Nicaragua.* San Francisco: Institute for Food and Development Policy.
  1985   *What Difference Could a Revolution Make? Food and Farming in the New Nicaragua.* San Francisco: Institute for Food and Development Policy.
Conroy, Michael E.
  1985a   "External Dependence, External Assistance, and Economic Aggression against Nicaragua." *Latin American Perspectives.* Issue 45, vol. 12, no. 2 (Fall): 39–67.
  1985b   "Economic Legacy and Policies: Performance and Critique." In *Nicaragua: The First Five Years,* edited by Thomas Walker. New York: Praeger, 219–244.
Deere, Carmen Diana
  1981   "Nicaraguan Agricultural Policy: 1979–81." *Cambridge Journal of Economics* 5: 195–200.
Deere, Carmen Diana, and Peter Marchetti
  1981   "The Worker-Peasant Alliance in the First Year of the Nicaraguan Agrarian Reform." *Latin American Perspectives* 8, no. 2 (Spring): 40–73.
Deere, Carmen Diana, Peter Marchetti, and Nola Reinhardt
  1985   "The Peasantry and the Development of Sandinista Agrarian Policy, 1979–1984." *Latin American Research Review* 20(3): 75–109.
de Janvry, Alain
  1978   *The Agrarian Question and Reformism in Latin America.* Baltimore: Johns Hopkins University Press.
DGRA (Dirreción General de la Reforma Agraria)
  1986   *Avance y perspectivas de la reforma agraria.* Managua: MIDINRA.
Dorner, Peter, and Rodolfo Quirós
  1983   "Institutional Dualism in Central America's Agricultural Development." In *Revolution in Central America,* edited by Stanford Central America Action Network. Boulder: Westview Press, 200–232.
Durham, William H.
  1979   *Scarcity and Survival in Central America: The Origins of the Soccer War.* Stanford: Stanford University Press.
Enríquez, Laura J.
  1985a   "The Dilemmas of Agricultural Export Planning in Revolutionary Nicaragua." In *Nicaragua: The First Five Years,* edited by Thomas Walker. New York: Praeger, 265–280.
  1985b   "Social Transformation in Latin America: Tensions Between Agricultural Export Production and Agrarian Reform in Revolutionary Nicaragua." Ph.D. dissertation, University of California at Santa Cruz.
Enríquez, Laura J., and Rose J. Spalding
  1985   "Rural Transformation: Agricultural Credit Policies in Revolutionary Nicaragua." Paper presented at the Latin American Studies Association Meeting, Albuquerque, New Mexico, April.

1987 "Banking Systems and Revolutionary Change: The Politics of Agricultural Credit in Nicaragua." *The Political Economy of Revolutionary Nicaragua*, edited by Rose J. Spalding. Boston: Allen and Unwin, 105–125.

FAO (Food and Agriculture Organization of the United Nations)
1986 "Antecedentes sobre la situatión en América Latina y el Caribe." Nineteenth Regional FAO Conference, Jamaica, June.
1977– *Production Yearbooks*. Rome: FAO.
1984

FitzGerald, E.V.K.
1982 "The Economics of the Revolution." In *Nicaragua in Revolution*, edited by Thomas Walker. New York: Praeger, 201–231.
1985 "La economía nacional en 1985: la transición como coyuntura." Paper presented at the Annual Congress of Social Scientists (ANICS), Managua, August.
1987 "An Evaluation of the Economic Costs to Nicaragua of US Aggression: 1980–1984." In *The Political Economy of Revolutionary Nicaragua*, edited by Rose J. Spalding. Boston: Allen and Unwin, 195–213.

Frenkel, María Verónica
1987a "The Evolution of Food and Agricultural Policies During Economic Crisis and War." In *Nicaragua: Profiles of the Revolutionary Public Sector*, edited by Michael E. Conroy, assisted by María Verónica Frenkel. Boulder: Westview Press.
1987b "The Dilemmas of Food Security and Agrarian Transformation in a Revolutionary Context: The Case of Nicaragua." Master's thesis, University of Texas at Austin.

Frenkel, María Verónica, and Gregg L. Vunderink
1985 "The Relationship between the State and the Private Agricultural Export Sector in Post-revolutionary Nicaragua." Paper presented at the Conference of the Institute of Latin American Studies Students' Association (ILASSA), Austin, April. Available from the Central American Writers' Clearinghouse.

Gilbert, Dennis
1983 "The Bourgeoisie and the Nicaraguan Revolution." Paper presented at the Meetings of the Latin American Studies Association, Mexico City, October.

González-Vega, Claudio
1984 "Fear of Adjusting: The Social Costs of Economic Policies in Costa Rica in the 1970s." In *Revolution and Counter-Revolution in Central America and the Caribbean*, edited by Donald E. Schultz and Douglas H. Graham. Boulder: Westview Press, 351–383.

Gorostiaga, Xavier
1982 *Dilemas de la revolución popular sandinista a tres años del triunfo.* Managua: INIES/CRIES.

Harris, Richard L.
1984 "Propiedad social y propiedad privada en Nicaragua." *Cuadernos Políticos* 40 (April-June): 53–67.

IDB (Interamerican Development Bank)
1984–   *Economic and Social Progress in Latin America.* Washington, D.C.: IDB.
1986
INCAP (Instituto de Nutrición de Centroamérica y Panamá)
1969   "Evaluación nutricional de la población de Centroamérica y Panamá: Nicaragua." Guatemala: INCAP.
INEC (Instituto Nacional de Estadisticas y Censos)
1986   *Anuario Estadístico de Nicaragua, 1985.* Managua: INEC.
Irwin, George
1983   "Nicaragua: Establishing the State as the Centre of Accumulation." *Cambridge Journal of Economics* 7: 125–139.
Kaimowitz, David, and David Stanfield
1985   "The Organization of Production Units in the Nicaraguan Agrarian Reform." *Inter-American Economic Affairs* 34, no. 1 (Summer): 51–77.
Lappé, Frances Moore, and Joseph Collins
1977   *Food First: Beyond the Myth of Scarcity.* Boston: Houghton Mifflin.
Luciak, Ilja A.
1987   "Popular Hegemony and National Unity: The Dialectics of Sandinista Agrarian Reform Policies, 1979–1986." *Lasa Forum* 16, no. 4 (Winter): 15–19.
MIDINRA (Ministerio de Desarrollo Agropecuario y Reforma Agraria)
1983   *Informe de Nicaragua a la FAO.* Managua: MIDINRA.
1985   *Plan de trabajo: balance y perspectivas, 1985.* Managua: MIDINRA.
1987   *Plan de trabajo: balance y perspectivas, 1987.* Managua: MIDINRA.
MIDINRA/PAN
1982   "Resumen de políticas de producción y servicios para granos básicos: 1982–83." Managua: MIDINRA/PAN. Mimeo.
Murdoch, William W.
1980   *The Poverty of Nations: The Political Economy of Hunger and Population.* Baltimore: Johns Hopkins University Press.
National Reconstruction Government of Nicaragua
1983   *Economic Policy Guidelines, 1983–1988.* Translated report available at the Central America Resource Center. Austin.
PAN (Programa Alimentario Nicaragüense)
1981   "Programa prioritario de la Revolución: Programa Alimentario Nacional." Managua: PAN. Mimeo.
1985   "Plan quinquenal de alimentación y nutrición." Internal Document. Managua: PAN.
1987   "Caracterización de la situación alimentaria y nutricional del país." Preliminary draft. Managua.
Pérez Brignoli, Héctor, and Yolando Baires Martínez
1983   "Growth and Crisis in the Central American Economies, 1950–1980." *Journal of Latin American Studies* 15, no. 2 (Nov.): 365–398.
Reinhardt, Nola
1987   "Agricultural Exports and the Peasantry in the Agrarian Reforms of El Salvador and Nicaragua." *World Development*, May.

Saulniers, Alfred H.
1987   "State Trading Organizations in Expansion: A Case Study of ENABA."
        In *Nicaragua: Profiles of the Revolutionary Public Sector*, edited by
        Michael E. Conroy, assisted by María Verónica Frenkel. Boulder:
        Westview Press.

Sims, Harold
1981   "Sandinista Nicaragua: Pragmatism in a Political Economy in For-
        mation." ISHI Occasional Papers in Social Change No. 5. Philadelphia:
        Institute for the Study of Human Issues.

Spalding, Rose J.
1984   "State Economic Expansion in Revolutionary Nicaragua." Unpublished
        manuscript from the Central American Writers' Clearing house. Avail-
        able from the Central America Resource Center, Austin.
1985   "Food, Politics, and Agricultural Change in Revolutionary Nicaragua:
        1979–1982." In *Food, Politics, and Society in Latin America*, edited by
        John C. Super and Thomas C. Wright. Lincoln: University of Nebraska
        Press.
1987   *The Political Economy of Revolutionary Nicaragua*. Boston: Allen and
        Unwin.

Stahler-Sholk
1986   Interview with the author at CRIES, Managua, July.

Stanford Central America Action Network, ed.
1983   *Revolution in Central America*. Boulder: Westview Press.

Super, John C., and Thomas C. Wright, eds.
1985   *Food, Politics, and Society in Latin America*. Lincoln: University of
        Nebraska Press.

Thome, Joseph R.
1984   "A Half-Decade of Agrarian Reform in Nicaragua." Paper presented
        at the International Studies Association Convention, Atlanta, March
        30.

Thome, Joseph R., and David Kaimowitz
1985   "Agrarian Reform." In *Nicaragua: The First Five Years*, edited by
        Thomas Walker. New York: Praeger, 299–315.

Timmer, C. Peter
1986   "A Framework for Policy Analysis." In *Food Policy: Frameworks for
        Analysis and Action*, edited by Charles K. Mann and Barbara Hud-
        dleston. Bloomington: Indiana University Press.

UNRISD (United Nations Research Institute for Social Development)
1986   "Urbanization and Food Systems Development in Nicaragua." In *Food
        Systems and Society: Problems of Food Security in Selected Developing
        Countries*. Geneva: UNRISD.

USDA (United States Department of Agriculture)
1984   "Attaché Report: Nicaragua Agricultural Situations Report," no. NU-
        4006. Washington, D.C.: USDA.

Utting, Peter
  1986a   "Limits to Change in a Post-revolutionary Society: The Rise and Fall of Cheap Food Policy in Nicaragua." Unpublished.
  1986b   Interview with the author at CIERA, Managua, Nicaragua, August.
  1987   "Domestic Supply and Food Shortages." In *The Political Economy of Revolutionary Nicaragua*, edited by Rose J. Spalding. Boston: Allen and Unwin, 127–148.
Vilas, Carlos
  1986   *The Sandinista Revolution: National Liberation and Social Transformation in Central America*, translated by Judy Butler. New York: Monthly Review.
  1987   "Troubles Everywhere: An Economic Perspective on the Sandinista Revolution." In *The Political Economy of Revolutionary Nicaragua*, edited by Rose Spalding. Boston: Allen and Unwin, 233–246.
Warnken, Philip F.
  1975   *The Agricultural Development of Nicaragua: An Analysis of the Production Sector*. Columbia: Agricultural Experiment Sector, University of Missouri.
Weeks, John
  1985   *The Economies of Central America*. New York: Holmes and Meier.
Williams, Robert G.
  1986   *Export Agriculture and the Crisis in Central America*. Chapel Hill: University of North Carolina Press.

Periodical and Other Statistical Sources

Barricada, various issues
Central America Report (*CAR*), various issues.
Central American Historical Institute (CAHI), *Updates.*
The Economist Intelligence Unit, *Country Report: Nicaragua, Costa Rica, Panama,* various issues.
El Nuevo Diario, various issues.
INEC biweekly statistical reports.
Lasa-Nica Scholars News: Newsletter of the LASA Task Force on Scholarly Relations with Nicaragua, various issues.
Mesoamerica, various issues.
Mexico and Central American Reports, various issues.
Pensamiento Proprio, various issues.

8

The Results of Mexican
Agriculture and Food Policy:
Debt, Drugs, and Illegal Aliens[1]

Billie R. DeWalt and Kathleen M. DeWalt

Third World nations currently face difficult choices in developing viable food and agriculture policies. In many countries a disturbingly large percentage of the population is inadequately nourished, and most of these countries have increasingly had to resort to imports of basic staples to feed their populations. Paradoxically, however, farmers in many of those same nations often do not have any incentive (and often face many disincentives) to produce the basic staples that would improve the availability of food in the country (for a brief review of some of the problems see Ray 1986).

In order to address the agriculture and food problems, a number of macrolevel policy changes have been encouraged in Third World countries. These policies usually are associated with one end or the other of the political spectrum, but especially in Latin America it is increasingly common for similar proposals to be advocated by both the left and the right. Among the most common and important of the policy solutions advanced have been the following:

1. *The implementation of agrarian reform programs.* Land reform achieved official recognition as a strategy for Latin America in the Charter of the Alliance for Progress, which was signed in Punta del Este in 1961 (see Harrison 1983, 117; de Janvry 1984, 268–269). In 1979, a major world conference concluded that "equitable distribution and efficient use of land . . . are indispensable for rural development, for the mobilization of human resources, and for increased production for the alleviation of poverty" (FAO 1979, cited in de Janvry 1984, 263). Land reform has long been advocated by people on the left, and it has achieved increasing advocacy even among some conservatives (see Rabkin 1985).

2. *The application of modern technology as a major means to boost agricultural productivity.* Growth of productivity through the application of technology has been shown to be the principal means by which economic output can be improved. In the agricultural area, Evenson, Waggoner, and Ruttan have shown that the economic benefits of public research in agriculture are much higher than the rates of return from other kinds of investment (1979). These studies and others call for more public expenditure on research in developing countries and for greater investment in such institutions as the International Agricultural Research Centers.

3. *The adoption of a "comparative advantage" approach.* Since 1930, Latin American countries have experimented with a variety of development strategies including import substitution, statist models, monetarist approaches, and others. Many recommendations concerning the debt crisis that began in the early 1980s suggested that the only way out is for Latin American countries to take on an "outward orientation" and to adopt policies that will stimulate global competitiveness and provide incentives for stimulating exports (for example, Balassa et al. 1986, 24–32). Deregulation, budget deficit reductions, transfer of state enterprises to the private sector, removal of import protection, and establishment and maintenance of competitive exchange rates are among the more specific measures recommended in these reports (Inter-American Development Bank 1984; Balassa et al. 1986). All of these essentially are policies to apply market solutions to economic problems, an approach based on the idea of comparative advantage. The comparative advantage approach argues that those commodities suitable for production because of favorable climate, cost of labor, or whatever should be promoted for export and commodities that other countries can produce more advantageously should be imported.

To gain some appreciation for how such policies may be expected to affect communities in Third World countries, it is important to examine carefully those few cases in which such measures have a long history of implementation. Mexico's food and agriculture policies, and the effects of these on nutrition and rural communities, are among the best documented in the world. Mexico implemented an agrarian reform after its bloody revolution early in the century and began a program to apply modern technology to its agriculture in the early 1940s. For a long period of time its agricultural sector successfully produced export crops (for which the country had a comparative advantage) that earned substantial foreign exchange to finance the development of its industrial sector. Yet, in recent years, several authors have written books and articles alluding to the agricultural crisis that exists in Mexico (see Yates 1981; Barkin and Suarez 1986; Austin and Esteva 1987). From our perspective, the nutrition crisis that is affecting the country is even more critical. The purpose of this chapter is to examine the history of Mexico's crises and to suggest lessons that we might learn from the Mexican case that can inform future agricultural and agrarian policies adopted by Third World nations.

The Effects of the Agrarian Reform

Mexican agricultural policy has not consistently emphasized any one approach to solving the problems of production and provisioning the country. Like all nations, policymaking is a complex undertaking with different approaches being advocated and with the interests of many different groups having to be considered and balanced against the interests of others. This was clearly the case with regard to agrarian reform. Although "Land and Liberty" was the rallying cry for many of the peasants who fought in the Mexican Revolution, because of conservative elements in the new ruling class a significant agrarian reform was not implemented until fifteen years after the cessation of hostilities— not until the 1930s and the presidency of Lázaro Cárdenas. The immediate effects of the reform were increases in agricultural production. Much redistributed land that had not previously been productively used was put into production by the *ejidos*, the communities formed to receive the redistributed land. These communities formed an important source of agricultural production in the years immediately after their formation. In 1940, approximately 51 percent of the value of agricultural production was being produced on the 47 percent of land held by the ejidos (de Janvry 1981, 127). In addition to redistributing the land, Cárdenas had a vision of how the agrarian reform communities could form the basis of a new economic structure in Mexico. As one of his officials put it in 1935:

> We have dreamt of a Mexico of *ejidos* and small industrial communities, electrified, with sanitation, in which goods will be produced for the purpose of satisfying the needs of the people, in which machinery will be employed to relieve man from heavy toil, and not for so-called overproduction (quoted in Hewitt de Alcantara 1976, 4).

Government policy of the time was largely oriented toward the creation of the ejidos, and the expectation was that eventually significant government support would be provided to these small farmers. Unfortunately Cárdenas's vision was not shared by the social groups who gained ascendancy in the government after his presidency ended in 1940.

The Effects of Modern Technology

The war years and those immediately following saw the beginnings of the applications of new technology to try to modernize the agricultural sector. An important element was the Mexican Agricultural Program, a Rockefeller Foundation–sponsored project to apply modern methods of crop production to Mexico. The Mexican Agricultural Program was principally designed to increase the productivity of wheat and maize because these two crops accounted for over 70 percent of the agricultural land in Mexico and were the two most important food crops. The purpose of the effort was

> to increase the production of varieties, the improvement of the soil and the control of insect pests and plant diseases. A corollary goal was to train young men and women in agricultural research and in the development of techniques for promoting the rapid adoption of the new technology (Wellhausen 1976, 128–129).

The program achieved considerable success with wheat; the improvements in this crop became known as the Green Revolution and earned Norman Borlaug the Nobel Peace Prize in 1970. Semidwarf spring wheat varieties that were relatively insensitive to differing day lengths greatly increased the productivity of wheat (see Borlaug 1983). Wheat yields more than quadrupled after 1930, going from only a little over 750 kilograms per hectare to almost 4 tons per hectare in the 1980s (see DeWalt and Barkin 1987, 147). But, as Wellhausen (1976) and Hewitt de Alcantara (1976) emphasized, the miracle seeds were only part of the story. The increases in productivity of the seeds could only be obtained under irrigated conditions, with more fertilizer, more effective control of weeds and insects, mechanized soil preparation and harvesting, and better land-management processes. These requirements "biased" the technology toward larger landholders, and the additional inputs were often made possible by substantial subsidies provided by the Mexican government. Loans, again usually biased toward larger farmers, were provided at subsidized rates for machinery, fertilizer, and pesticides, and irrigation water was provided at a fraction of its cost. The government also invested substantially in other infrastructures like roads, railroads, and storage facilities to handle the wheat. In spite of these subsidies, wheat production did not increase until the government established a guaranteed price for wheat that was well above the world market price. This subsidy, which lasted from 1954–1964, resulted in an increase in hectares sown in wheat, but when the subsidy was removed in 1965, the number of hectares being sown went back to earlier levels, as is

FIGURE 8.1   Hectares of Land Sown, 1940–1984: Maize, Wheat, Sorghum

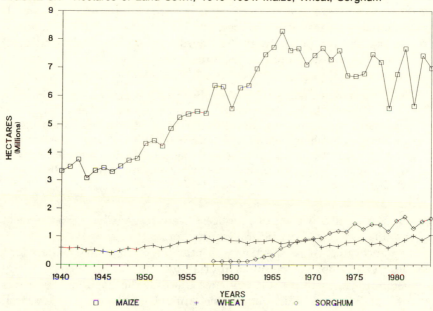

Source: Based on data in DGEA (1981) and INERGI (1987).

shown in Figure 8.1. Thus, the Green Revolution in wheat was made possible more by government subsidies than by the miracle seeds (see Hewitt de Alcantara 1976; DeWalt 1985).

The second important technological factor applied to Mexican agriculture was irrigation. Irrigation was extremely important not only for the increases in wheat productivity but also for the expansion of the agricultural frontier in Mexico. Irrigation made possible the cultivation of many areas of formerly desert land, especially in the arid northeast and northwest regions of the country. Between 1940 and 1979, irrigation absorbed between 70 percent and 99.2 percent of the total annual budget invested in the agricultural sector (see Walsh Sanderson 1984, 118; Barkin and Suárez 1986). The area under irrigation expanded to more than 3 times the area of 1940, and the total area cultivated increased more than 2.5 times over the level of 1940 (DGEA 1982b, 21). By 1985 about one quarter of the land cultivated in Mexico was irrigated. This huge investment in irrigation, however, meant that little of the agricultural budget was available for improving rainfed agriculture. In addition, the irrigated areas were generally made available to commercial farmers and not to small farmers or ejidos.

Irrigation is a technology that creates opportunities for increased productivity as well as increased employment. But simultaneously with the spread of irrigation came a large number of other technological changes. As Esteva (1987) put it, the government's agricultural modernization model essentially gave responsibility for agricultural production to a group of high productivity "enclaves" to which it channeled most of its agricultural development resources. He wrote:

> Thus, things were arranged for the development of commercial agriculture. It settled on the large infrastructure works created by the State . . . in areas that required no large investments for productive improvements; commercial agriculture enjoyed the double incentive of low labor costs and high support prices. It also enjoyed cheap credit, modern subsidized inputs, support for mechanization, reasonably efficient technical assistance and the advances of research (Esteva 1987, 35–36).

By 1950, only 10.5 percent of producers were responsible for 54 percent of the total value of agricultural production.

The government's perspective was that these commercial operations would create employment opportunities for the "unproductive" small farmers. In fact, there is some evidence that this did happen. There was growth of 2.3 percent in cumulative annual employment in modern agriculture between 1950 and 1980 (Couriel 1984, 55). However, although employment in the rural modern sector expanded from 31.7 percent of the total employed in agriculture in 1950 to 51 percent in 1980, there was an *absolute reduction* in the number of self-employed agricultural workers (Couriel 1984, 56). In other words, Mexico was undergoing a transition that was eliminating many of the small farmers, and although employment in the commercial agricultural sector was growing, it was not growing at a fast enough pace to absorb the farmers displaced from rural farm communities.

Simultaneously with the application of these two aspects of technology that were leading to the commercialization of the Mexican agricultural production scene, the government was pursuing food policies that affected agriculture. In 1953 rural support prices were established for basic staples. Theoretically these support prices were to protect the farmers from intermediaries who would make inordinate profits. In fact, the larger farmers inordinately benefited from these support prices. The other effect was that these support prices kept a cap on the prices of basic staples. The government was pursuing the well-known cheap-food strategy—keeping the prices of staples low so that urban industrial wages could also be kept low (see de Janvry 1981, 157–172). The terms of trade for basic staples declined, however, to the point that commercial farmers were no longer interested in growing them. The decade prior to 1973 saw prices for agricultural staples stagnate, and the effects can be seen in Figure 8.1. Although yields increased, the amount of land planted in maize, wheat, and beans declined.

The Comparative Advantage Approach in Mexican Agriculture

These data provide just a few indications of how Mexican agriculture was being radically reorganized. Commercial farmers saw little point (that is, little profit) in growing food staples whose prices were kept at low levels by the government. They used their many government subsidies to reorient their operations toward more profitable crops like strawberries, vegetables, grapes, tobacco, coffee, and agricultural raw materials like cotton. Especially since the mid-1960s, the doctrine of comparative advantage has been a driving force of the Mexican agricultural system (de Janvry 1981, 127). For a very long time, the modern agricultural sector was an important earner of foreign exchange. For much of the 1960s and 1970s until the oil boom, agricultural raw materials and foodstuffs constituted about 70 percent of Mexico's exports (Esteva 1987, 40).

As the stagnation of the basic-grains sector continued, a further reorientation of agriculture occurred as production of livestock and livestock feeds became important. In previous research (see Barkin and DeWalt 1988, 34), we have summarized some of the major trends in Mexican agriculture since 1965. During the same period in which production of food staples like maize, beans, wheat, and rice declined or increased only very slowly, production of oats, alfalfa, soybeans, and other crops to be fed to livestock was booming. This was especially true of sorghum, a case that has been called Mexico's Second Green Revolution (DeWalt 1985). Statistics on sorghum were not collected until 1958 because it was such an unknown crop; but by 1980 it had become the country's second largest crop in terms of hectares planted, and large imports of it also were required. During this same period of time, livestock production also boomed, with production of pigs, chickens, and cattle increasing at rapid rates (see Barkin and DeWalt 1988, 34).

The growth of livestock and livestock-feed production has caused a paradoxical situation. Mexico's total production of grain has increased over *eight times* its level of 1940 due to increased productivity and the expansion into new crops like sorghum. Since 1940 the population has only trebled, yet between one quarter and one third of the population is still undernourished (see DeWalt 1985). The reason is that more and more of the country's grain resources are being fed to livestock rather than serving as food for people. Only about 5 percent of the grains in Mexico in 1960 were fed to livestock; by 1984 this proportion had increased to almost 50 percent (see García Sordo 1985, 8; Barkin and DeWalt 1985). In addition, it is estimated that there are 74 million hectares of pasture devoted to livestock (Yates 1981).

At the same time that large, commercial agriculturalists were losing interest in growing food staples, small farmers were having a difficult time just making a living in farming (see DeWalt and DeWalt 1980). These were the farmers most likely to be growing the basic staples because they had not received subsidies or technical assistance to switch to anything else. They thus continued to grow maize, beans, or switched to crops like sorghum whose cultivation requirements were similar to those of maize or beans. Most found it necessary to find part-time labor opportunities to supplement their incomes. This situation is one with which we became quite familiar during the 1970s from our research in Temascalcingo, a community in the Mexican central highlands (see B. DeWalt 1979; K. DeWalt 1983).

The Effects of Food and Agriculture Policies

The policies followed in Mexico led to a stagnation of the basic-foods sector in the country's agriculture. In many ways, the government was not concerned because it felt that the export of high-value fruits, vegetables, and other agricultural products could pay for any needed imports of staples. By 1980, however, this policy was in a shambles. It was in 1980 that the government established the Sistema Alimentario Mexicano (SAM) in an attempt to return self-sufficiency to the Mexican food system. By 1980 Mexico was importing approximately one quarter of all the wheat, maize, and sorghum needed to meet its needs for food and feed grains. Surveys by the National Nutrition Institute indicated that severe malnutrition was common in many rural areas and that over 27 percent of the population (more than 19 million Mexicans at the time) had a daily calorie and protein intake below the minimum required for physical well-being (Redclift 1981, 13–14). The SAM was going to provide increased subsidies to farmers to increase production and was going to subsidize a "basic food basket" for consumers to try to guarantee an adequate diet to all Mexicans. Unfortunately the cost of such a program was about $3.7 billion in 1980 alone, and because of the economic crisis that hit Mexico in the early 1980s, the program had to be discontinued in 1982.

Since that time, in the popular press and the news media of the mid-1980s, Mexico has become infamous for three things—debt, drugs, and illegal aliens (for example, see Lang with Thornton 1985:30–31). Although there are some other factors involved, each of these can be seen to be

TABLE 8.1   Migration Reported for the Communities in Complete Household Censuses

	Michoacan	S.L. Potosi	Morelos	Tamaulipas
Earn majority of income from agriculture	53%	10%	20%	73%
HH heads who have ever worked outside community	66%	95%	61%	68%
HH heads who have ever worked in United States	25%	80%	15%	23%
Children over 15 still residing in the community	51%	44%	55%	63%
Children over 15 who reside in United States	19%	32%	12%	6%
HH with child in U.S. at time of interview	23%	43%	15%	5%

Source: Compiled by authors based on data collected in the INTSOAMIL/UAM-X Field Project.

related to the failure of the country's agricultural and food policies since 1940.

Some of the problems of the Mexican food and agricultural system can be understood by examining the results of data from four ejido communities that we studied in 1984 (see Barkin and DeWalt 1985; DeWalt and Barkin 1985, 1987; Universidad Autónoma Metropolitana Unidad Xochimilco 1986). The communities are located in the states of Michoacán, Morelos, San Luis Potosí, and Tamaulipas.[2]

The majority of families in all of these communities had access to ejido land, yet our research revealed that agriculture was really a viable economic strategy in only one of the four communities. As Table 8.1 shows, self-assessments of the derivation of income indicated that only in the community in Tamaulipas—a community whose *ejidatarios* each had access to about 15 hectares of irrigated land—were a substantial number of people earning most of their income from farming. Like many small farmers throughout the developing world, people in these Mexican communities had diversified sources of income. In addition to earnings from crops, livestock earnings were quite important (about 30 percent of total income in Morelos), and wage earnings within the communities were significant—between 20 and 25 percent of income in Tamaulipas, Morelos, and Michoacán. (See DeWalt, DeWalt, Escudero, and Barkin 1987, 48 for more detailed information on income sources.)

A common strategy for farmers has been to look for labor opportunities outside of the community. In all of the communities, a majority of the household heads had at some time or another worked outside of their communities. As is shown in Table 8.1, a favorite destination for many of these individuals was the United States. In Derramaderos, for example, 80 percent of the household heads had at one time worked in the United States. This is further reinforced by data on the residences of children. In Derramaderos, 32 percent of the children over fifteen years of age born to families in the community were living in the United States at the time of the interview. Over 43 percent of the families in this community had at least one child in the United States. Although in other communities the numbers were much lower, still 23 percent of the families of the community in Michoacán and 15 percent of the families of the community in Morelos had children in the United States.

Reig has put together the available information on changes in nutritional status for Mexico. His data indicate that, especially in comparing the household income and expenditure surveys from 1963 and 1977, there has been no improvement in the diet of much of the population. There are extreme inequities in access to food. Despite the fact that they spend more than 60 percent of their income on food, the poorest people in the country spend 8 to 10 times less money on food than the wealthy. The result is that, as of 1985, estimates were that between 40 and 50 percent of the population were undernourished or malnourished (Reig 1985, 43).

The nutritional indicators for the communities that we studied show a severity of undernutrition that parallels Reig's data for the nation. Table 8.2 compares nutritional indicators for children by community in 1984. The percentage of children whose weight was less than 90 percent of standard weight for their age suggests some degree of undernutrition at some point in their lives, ranging from about 27 percent in Morelos and Tamaulipas to over 38 percent in San Luis Potosí to a high of 56 percent in Michoacán. Stunting (height for age less than 95 percent of standard), an indicator of chronic undernutrition, characterized 32 percent of children in Morelos and approximately 50 percent in the other 3 communities. The percentage of children whose current weight for height was under 90 percent of standard, an indicator of current nutritional status, was much smaller. It ranged from 5.6 percent in Tamaulipas to 12.5 percent in San Luis Potosí. The overall picture concerning nutritional status in these communities is that between 40 and 50 percent of all the children in these communities appeared to have experienced nutritional stress at some time in their first 5 years of life. Acute undernutrition (as measured by low weight for current height) is less of a problem.

TABLE 8.2 Comparison of Nutritional Indicators for Children Five Years and Under by Community, 1984

	Michoacan	S.L. Potosi	Morelos	Tamaulipas
Number of children (N)	(80)	(56)	(70)	(53)
Height for age				
Average (as a percentage of NCHS standards)[a]	94.8%	95.6%	97.6%	94.7%
Under 95%[b]	51.0%	50.0%	32.0%	47.0%
Weight for age				
Average	91.1%	92.7%	99.5%	96.1%
Under 90%	56.4%	38.7%	27.5%	26.4%
Weight for height				
Average	101.4%	101.6%	104.1%	106.1%
Under 90%	6.4%	12.5%	10.0%	5.6%

[a]Averages compared with NCHS median values for children in the appropriate age, sex, and measurement categories.
[b]This expresses the percentage of children who fall below the percentile of NCHS norms.

Source: Compiled by authors based on data collected in the INTSORMIL/UAM-X Field Project.

As we have indicated, one of the most common strategies for dealing with the nutritional and economic crises within these communities has been migration. Our data from these four rural communities with regard to legal and illegal migration are indicative of what is occurring all over Mexico (see also Cornelius 1976; Camara and Kemper 1979; Dinerman 1982). Estimates of the number of temporary migrants entering the United States from Mexico vary widely; a recent review estimates that short-term Mexican migration provides about half a million work years to the United States. The same source estimates that there may be about 2 to 3 million undocumented Mexicans living in the United States on a longer-term basis (see Gregory 1986, 185). Although Gregory's estimates are lower than many others, the number has been of such a magnitude as to cause significant problems for the United States and to lead to the restrictive immigration reform legislation passed by the Congress in 1986.

It is quite clear from these and other data that most farmers do not consider it worth their while to devote much time to agriculture; it simply does not pay. One indication of this is that large areas of rainfed lands are left uncultivated. We do not as yet have an estimate of this in the communities we studied, but the government estimated that about 9 million hectares of arable land were idle during the 1984 summer crop cycle, in spite of the best rainfall in the past half century.[3]

FIGURE 8.2   Mexico's Trade Statistics, Agricultural and Overall, 1978–1983

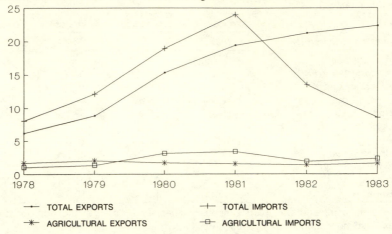

—•— TOTAL EXPORTS   —+— TOTAL IMPORTS

—✳— AGRICULTURAL EXPORTS   —□— AGRICULTURAL IMPORTS

Y AXIS IN BILLIONS OF US DOLLARS
Source: Derived from Banco de México presented in IDB 1986 and Adelski 1987.

Agriculture is also a significant factor in the debt problem. Figure 8.2 gives some indication of the macroeconomic dimensions of the debt crisis in Mexico. Because of the economic crisis, the country has sharply curtailed imports of nonessential goods and services. This has created a surplus in the country's balance of payments that is essential for it to be able to pay its debt-service obligations. However, at the same time that the overall trade surplus during the 1980s has become positive, the trade balance in agriculture has become negative. Although exports of agricultural products have remained at fairly high levels, the country's need to import increasing quantities of basic grains means that agriculture is now a net drain on the country's economy. Imports of agricultural products, principally basic grains, made up 17 percent of total imports in 1983 (see Figure 8.2). In 1984, Mexico's share of agricultural imports made up nearly 25 percent of the total for all of Latin America (IDB 1986, 82)! Thus, we have the paradoxical situation that about one third of Mexico's arable land lies idle (9 million hectares are idle, and about 16 million are cultivated) while the country imports substantial quantities of food.

The principal reason for both the increasing need to import basic grains and the abandonment of land is that small farmers, whose needs have been ignored for so long, have simply found it not worth their while to continue cultivation. Their principal hopes for survival involve either finding an extremely high-value crop for their small plots of land or abandoning agriculture. The first option has led farmers to search for alternative uses for their land. We found that farmers in the four communities we studied in 1984 were experimenting with crops like oilseeds, melons, vegetables, and fruit trees. Unfortunately, for small farmers like these, the likelihood of success with these crops is quite small. It is next to impossible to obtain credit for the inputs needed to grow them, the agricultural extension service in the country provides inadequate technical assistance to small farmers (see Adelski 1987), and the necessary marketing channels are often difficult to establish.

In other areas of the country, some farmers have turned to other cash crops—the cultivation of marijuana or poppies. Private sources seem to be quite efficient in providing the credit, technical assistance, and marketing channels for these crops. Although it is difficult to estimate the amount of production, most observers agree that the flow of illegal drugs from Mexico has increased markedly in the past decade. Most of the profits go to the larger dealers and the government officials who must be paid off to allow the trade to continue to exist, but at least some small farmers are able to make a much better living than they would cultivating any other crop.

The agricultural sector, through its production of drugs and because of its people crossing the border for jobs in the United States, is thus still of key importance in Mexico's economy. Some observers now believe that the foreign exchange earned from drugs and from the remittances of illegal aliens may be more than the earnings of the top two legal sources of foreign exchange—the export of petroleum and the *maquiladora* (border assembly plants) industry (Copeland with Harmes 1987).

Part of the explanation for these strange outcomes of agricultural and food policies lies in the unequal nature of Mexico's development. The government has consistently subsidized the development of the commercial agricultural sector and discriminated against the small-farm sector. Policies have been oriented toward keeping the prices of staple foods cheap (see de Janvry 1981) and toward providing subsidies for the development of the livestock sector (see Barkin and DeWalt 1988). The results of these policies have been to (1) create a large number of rural people who cannot gain a viable livelihood by being involved in agricultural pursuits (or by being involved only on a part-time basis); (2) generate a large number of rural people who cannot afford to consume the products of the "modern" agricultural sector; (3) beget large numbers of these individuals migrating to the already swollen cities of Mexico, or crossing the border into the United States as illegal aliens; and (4) generate a crisis of major proportions in agriculture that has exacerbated Mexico's already severe economic problems.

Thus, it is apparent that none of the three measures (the implementation of agrarian reform programs; the application of modern technology to boost agricultural activity; and the adoption of a comparative advantage approach) that have been advocated to solve food and agricultural problems will necessarily lead to substantial improvement in the situation. Mexico implemented a far-reaching agrarian reform, but then essentially ignored the small-farm sector of the agricultural population. The result is that the agrarian reform communities' share of total agricultural output has been in a steep decline ever since 1940. An agrarian reform without accompanying policies that will allow the small holders to compete is destined to result in problems such as those that have arisen in Mexico. As de Janvry has noted, Mexico is perhaps the clearest example of a country that used land reform as a means of political stabilization yet expected the nonreform agricultural sector to produce the major economic gains (1984, 267).

A perfect example of this concerns innovations in agriculture. Agricultural research in Mexico has been quite successful in raising productivity, but it has exacerbated the gulf in competitiveness between the small and medium-size landholders and the wealthy. Agricultural research has been used in a fashion that magnifies the unequal nature of development in the country. Productivity of some crops by the largest farmers in the country has increased substantially, but the number of malnourished individuals in the country remains at an alarming level. Output of livestock products and high-value crops for domestic and export markets has grown, but this benefits only *those who can afford to purchase such products.*

In the same way, the doctrine of comparative advantage has not been kind to Mexico. The country produces many crops for which it has a climatic and/or wage comparative advantage, and it increasingly imports wheat, maize, and sorghum at the relatively low prices prevailing on the world market. However, as de Janvry has noted in his review of Latin American agriculture: "Agricultural exports and food dependency, while good for the balance of payments and capital accumulation, have a regressive effect on the distribution of consumption, for food imports are biased toward high-income consumers and hardly reach the more remote areas" (1981, 161). In the Mexican case, the situation is no longer good even for the balance of payments.

Mexican agriculture is now one of the most technologically modernized in the Third World. Yet the question that we must ask is whether this modernization has been a positive force or a negative one. It seems apparent to us that a much stronger continuing emphasis by the government on improving rainfed agriculture would have made smaller farmers more competitive in the marketplace.[4] Although this strategy may not appear to be a modernizing one, it would have satisfied three essential needs in the rural Mexican setting. It would have created more *employment*

FIGURE 8.3   Production in Mexico, 1940–1984: Maize, Wheat, Sorghum, Beans

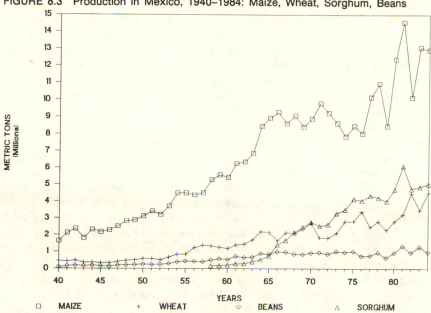

Source: Based on data in DGEA 1987 and INEGI 1987.

for landless people because of the labor-intensive nature of most small-farm agriculture. It would have been more likely to have kept up the *production of staple grains* because these are the crops most likely to be grown by small farmers. And finally, it would have led to a much better *nutritional status* for many poor rural Mexicans. Rainfed agriculture that has been neglected for forty years is unlikely to become productive immediately. However, the results achieved during the period that the SAM was in operation are encouraging. With greater inputs from the government and with higher support prices for grains, Mexican agriculture did respond with higher production as is shown in Figure 8.3.

The conclusion is not that the policies of agrarian reform, agricultural research, and comparative advantage will not work. There may be conditions under which they will be beneficial, but the Mexican case demonstrates how and why they will not necessarily achieve the results intended.

Notes

1. The data presented in this chapter partially derive from research that we conducted in 1984 as part of an agreement between the International Sorghum/Millet Collaborative Research Support Program (INTSORMIL) and the Univ-

ersidad Autónoma Metropolitana—Xochimilco (UAM-X). The purpose of the research was to document the effects that the replacement of maize by sorghum cultivation has had on rural Mexican communities. Sorghum, a crop that was virtually unknown in the country until the late 1950s, had become the second largest crop in terms of number of hectares planted by 1984. Codirectors of the project were David Barkin (UAM-X) and Billie R. DeWalt (Kentucky). We wish to express our appreciation to INTSORMIL, which funded this research through contract number AID/DSAN-G-0149.

2. We chose these communities for reasons related to our study of the replacement of maize by sorghum in rural Mexico. These included the following: First, they are all ejido communities that exist in a very diverse set of ecological circumstances. The communities in Morelos and Tamaulipas have access to irrigation and the others do not. Sorghum cultivation had become quite important in each, and other aspects of agricultural modernization such as credit, mechanization, and technical assistance were prominent features. Second, we wanted to study several regions of Mexico that were less well-known in the ethnographic and community-study literature. All the communities are composed of *mestizos* (a mix of Indian, Spanish, and perhaps other ethnic groups), the dominant culture in Mexico. The community in Tamaulipas is composed primarily of people from the highland areas of Mexico who were resettled in the 1960s when irrigation opened up a sparsely settled area to more intensive exploitation. The community in Michoacán is also composed of resettled people from around Lake Chapala. These individuals were granted land in the early 1960s in the lowlands of the Apatzingan Valley. The community in San Luis Potosí is in a marginal agricultural region much like those in which sorghum grows in other parts of the world. We chose a community in Morelos because at the time of this study sorghum had expanded rapidly in this region from which came significant pressure for agrarian reform during the Mexican Revolution.

Ejidos such as these control almost 50 percent of the land and thus are important components of Mexico's agricultural system. Further details concerning each of the communities may be found in our major report on the research (UAM-X 1986).

3. This figure was cited in a speech by Luis Martínez Villicaña, secretary of agrarian reform, as reported in the Mexican national press during the week of October 15, 1984.

4. During the last several years, there has been a greater effort in Mexico to address the problems of rainfed agriculture. A separate part of the extension system has been established within the office of the Secretary of Agriculture and Hydraulic Resources to deal with rainfed areas. During the SAM years of 1980–1982, the share of agricultural credit going to rainfed lands also increased (see Pessah 1987). Although these are positive trends, it is quite apparent that the agricultural research system in Mexico has yet to produce work that can be transferred to the extension workers in rainfed areas and that, even with increased credit, small holders with rainfed land are not competitive with larger, irrigated operations.

References and Bibliography

Adelski, M. Elizabeth
    1987   "Ejidal Agriculture in Northern Sinaloa, Mexico: Agricultural Re-
            sources, Production, and Household Well-Being." Ph.D. dissertation,
            University of Kentucky.

Austin, James, and Gustavo Esteva, eds.
    1987   *Food Policy in Mexico: The Search for Self-sufficiency.* Ithaca: Cornell
            University Press.

Balassa, Bela, Gerardo Bueno, Pedro-Pablo Kuczynski, and Mario Henrique
Simonsen
    1986   *Toward Renewed Economic Growth in Latin America: Summary, Overview,*
            and Recommendations. Washington, D.C.: Institute for International
            Economics.

Barkin, David
    1982   "El uso de la Tierra Agrícola en México." *Problemas del Desarrollo*
            47/48:59–85.

Barkin, David, and Billie R. DeWalt
    1985   "La Crisis Alimentaria Mexicana y el Sorgo." *Problemas del Desarrollo*
            61:65–85.
    1988   "Sorghum and the Mexican Food Crisis." *Latin American Research*
            Review 23(3): 30–59.

Barkin, David, and Blanca Suárez
    1986   *El Fin de la Autosuficiencia Alimentaria.* Mexico City: Editorial Océano
            y Centro de Ecodesarrollo.

Borlaug, Norman
    1983   "Contributions of Conventional Plant Breeding to Production." *Science*
            219:689–693.

Camara, Fernando, and Robert Van Kemper, eds.
    1979   *Migration Across Frontiers: Mexico and the United States.* Albany: Latin
            American Anthropology Group, State University of New York.

Copeland, Jeff, with Joseph Harmes
    1987   "The Rise of Gringo Capitalism: Mexico Lures American Firms to
            Border Zones." *Newsweek* January 5:40–41.

Cornelius, Wayne
    1976   *Mexican Migration to the United States: The View from Rural Sending*
            Communities. Cambridge: Center for International Studies, Massa-
            chusetts Institute of Technology.

Couriel, Alberto
    1984   "Poverty and Underemployment in Latin America." *CEPAL Review*
            24:39–62.

de Janvry, Alain.
    1981   *The Agrarian Question and Reformism in Latin America.* Baltimore:
            Johns Hopkins.
    1984   "The Role of Land Reform in Economic Development: Policies and
            Politics." In *Agricultural Development in the Third World,* edited by
            Carl Eicher and John M. Staatz. Baltimore: Johns Hopkins, 263–277.

DeWalt, Billie R.
  1979   *Modernization in a Mexican Ejido: A Study in Economic Adaptation.*
          Cambridge: Cambridge University.
  1985   "Mexico's Second Green Revolution: Food for Feed." *Mexican Studies/
          Estudios Mexicanos* 1:29–60.
DeWalt, Billie, and David Barkin
  1985   "El Sorgo y la Crisis Alimentaria Mexicana." In *El Sorgo en Sistemas
          de Produccion en America Latina,* edited by Compton L. Paul and Billie
          R. DeWalt. Mexico City: CIMMYT and INTSORMIL, 153–167.
  1987   "Seeds of Change: The Effects of Hybrid Sorghum and Agricultural
          Modernization in Mexico." In *Technology and Social Change,* 2d ed.,
          edited by H. Russell Bernard and Pertti J. Pelto. Prospect Heights,
          Ill.: Waveland Press, 138–165.
DeWalt, Billie, and Kathleen M. DeWalt
  1980   "Stratification and Decision-making in the Use of New Agricultural
          Technology." In *Agricultural Decision-making: Anthropological Contri-
          butions,* edited by P. Barlett. New York: Academic Press, 289–317.
DeWalt, Billie, Kathleen M. DeWalt, José Carlos Escudero, and David Barkin
  1987   "Agrarian Reform and Small Farmer Welfare: Evidence from Four
          Mexican Communities." *Food and Nutrition Bulletin* 9(3): 46–52.
DeWalt, Kathleen M.
  1983   *Nutritional Strategies and Agricultural Change in a Mexican Community.*
          Ann Arbor: UMI Research Press.
DGEA (Dirección General de Economia Agricola)
  1981   "Consumos Aparentes de Productos Agricolas 1925–1980." *Econotecnia
          Agricola* 5(9).
  1982a   "Consumos Aparentes de Productos Pecuarios (1972–1981)." *Econo-
          tecnia Agricola* 6(9).
  1982b   *Información Agropecuaria y Forestal* 1980. Secretaria de Agricultura y
          Recursos Hidráulicos. Mexico City: DGEA.
  1982c   "Información Económica Nacional." *Boletin Interno* 9, no. 1 (Jan. 6).
  1982d   "Información Económica Nacional." *Boletin Interno* 9, no. 1 (Aug. 11).
Dinerman, Ina
  1982   *Migrants and Stay-At-Homes: A Comparative Study of Rural Migration
          from Michoacan, Mexico.* Center for U.S.-Mexican Studies Monograph
          Series no. 5. San Diego: University of California.
  1987   "Food Needs and Capacities: Four Centuries of Conflict." In *Food
          Policy in Mexico: The Search for Self-Sufficiency,* edited by James Austin
          and Gustavo Esteva. Ithaca: Cornell University Press, 23–47.
Evenson, Robert E., Paul Waggoner, and Vernon Ruttan
  1979   "Economic Benefits from Research: An Example from Agriculture."
          Science 205:1101–1107.
FAO (Food and Agriculture Organization)
  1979   *Report: World Conference on Agrarian Reform and Rural Development.*
          Rome. FAO.

García Sordo, Mario
    1985   "Insuficiente Produccion para Satisfacer la Demanda de Proteinas de Origen Animal." *UnoMasUno* January 9:8.

Gregory, Peter
    1986   *The Myth of Market Failure: Employment and the Labor Market in Mexico.* Baltimore: Johns Hopkins.

Harrison, Paul
    1983   *Inside the Third World: The Anatomy of Poverty,* 2d ed. New York: Penguin Books.

Hewitt de Alcantara, Cynthia
    1976   *Modernizing Mexican Agriculture.* Geneva: United Nations Research Institute for Social Development.

IDB (Inter-American Development Bank)
    1984   *Economic and Social Progress in Latin America: Economic Integration.* Washington, D.C.: IDB.
    1986   *Economic and Social Progress in Latin America: Agricultural Development.* Washington, D.C.: IDB.

INEGI (Instituto Nacional de Estadística, Geographía e Informática)
    1987   *El Sector Alimentario en Mexico, 1986.* Mexico City: INEGI.

Lang, John S., with Jeannye Thornton
    1985   "The Disappearing Border." *U.S. News and World Report* August 19:30–42.

Pessah, Raul
    1987   "Channelling Credit to the Countryside." In *Food Policy in Mexico: The Search for Self-sufficiency,* edited by James Austin and Gustavo Esteva. Ithaca: Cornell University Press, 92–110.

Rabkin, Rhoda
    1985   "A Conservative Case for Land Reform." *National Review* 37 (July 12): 36–40.

Ray, Anandarup
    1986   "Trade and Pricing Policies in World Agriculture." *Finance and Development* September:2–5.

Redclift, Michael
    1981   *Development Policy Making in Mexico: The Sistema Alimentario Mexicano (SAM).* Working Papers in U.S.-Mexican Studies no. 24. San Diego: University of San Diego.

Reig, Nicolas
    1985   "Las Tendencias Alimentarias a Largo Plazo en Mexico: 1950–1984." *Problemas del Desarrollo* 61:9–64.

Stavenhagen, Rodolfo
    1970   "Social Aspects of Agrarian Structure in Mexico." In *Agrarian Problems and Peasant Movements in Latin America,* edited by Rodolfo Stavenhagen. New York: Doubleday.

UAM-X (Universidad Autónoma Metropolitana, Unidad Xochimilco)
    1986   *Los Sistemas Agroeconomicos del Sorgo.* Mexico City: UAM-X.

Walsh Sanderson, Susan R.
   1984   *Land Reform in Mexico: 1910–1980.* New York: Academic Press.
Wellhausen, Edwin J.
   1976   "The Agriculture of Mexico." *Scientific American* 235:128–150.
Yates, P. Lamartine
   1981   *Mexico's Agricultural Dilemma.* Tucson: University of Arizona Press.

9

Popular Participation and Access to Food: Mexico's Community Food Councils[1]

Jonathan Fox

Mexico's post-1982 economic crisis has made an already serious hunger problem worse. The combination of increased unemployment, reduced wages, and the withdrawal of consumer subsidies pushed increasing numbers of families to the brink of disaster. Even before the crisis, however, government studies found that nearly 42 percent of the rural population (approximately 9.5 million people) consumed between 25 percent and 40 percent below the Mexican standard of 2,750 calories per person per day (Montanari 1987, 52).[2]

Government spending increased dramatically during Mexico's 1978–1982 oil-debt boom, and food programs were no exception. Generalized consumer subsidies continued even after the boom collapsed in 1982, partially buffering the first four years of economic crisis; the subsidies were cut in 1986.[3] This study analyzes one of the few major food programs that survived the early 1980s—a massive network of village stores serving Mexico's most remote and poverty-stricken areas. Huge traditional consumer food programs had exclusively benefited city-dwellers, but the Community Food Council program was targeted specifically at the rural poor. This case of community participation in policy implementation shows how the internalization of social conflict within government agencies can directly shape access to food. The discussion begins with an overview of the challenges Mexico's economic crisis poses for food policy and is followed by an analysis of the case.

Food Policy and the Crisis

Three different resources condition household access to food: land, income, and subsidized food-distribution channels.[4] Most hunger is caused by lack of access to one or more of these three resources. Hunger can therefore be fully understood only if all three factors are taken into account.

In Mexico, approximately two-thirds of the malnourished population lives in the countryside. Access to arable land and the means to work it could permit the rural poor to become self-sufficient producers, and stable employment could enable them to purchase an adequate diet in the market. Broadened access to land through an extension of Mexico's long-standing agrarian reform could be a partial solution to the problem of rural hunger, but this path has been blocked by entrenched agribusiness and ranching interests and their powerful allies inside the government.[5] The prospects for increased access to stable jobs are not much better. The reformist Cárdenas administration (1934–1940) emphasized broadening the internal market, but since then the Mexican government's capital-intensive, urban-biased approach to industrialization has created its own set of interests, blocking policy shifts toward significantly increased rural employment.

Although the distribution of land and employment is increasingly well understood, the determinants of access to "nonmarket" food distribution channels, such as government subsidies, have received far less attention.[6] All over the world, consumer food subsidies are extremely politicized. For centuries, abrupt food price increases have been associated with social upheaval. Objective "need" is rarely sufficient to account for food subsidies; "perception of threat" is usually involved. Food-subsidy policies are therefore usually the result of the convergence of interest-group politics and policymakers' understanding of how to maintain political stability.

Generalized food subsidies are usually available to all urban consumers, regardless of need.[7] Governments often rely on generalized subsidies to buffer political conflict and to hold together broad ruling coalitions. If the government keeps urban food prices relatively low, manufacturers are able to keep industrial wages down. These "positive-sum," populist policies for dealing with social problems are increasingly unviable, both politically and economically. Because most Latin American social programs consistently failed to benefit the poorest of the poor even when resources were available, it is difficult to contend that "more of the same" (that is, more conventional government intervention) is the answer to the hunger problem, particularly in the absence of a solution to the international debt crisis. How, then, can governments attack poverty and hunger with programs that can be sustained in the face of long-term economic austerity?

The key to approaching the problem of hunger in the context of powerful political and economic constraints is to develop food policies that channel scarce social resources efficiently and equitably to those in greatest need. "Efficiency" implies service delivery with a minimum of wasteful bureaucracy, and "equity" implies reliable access to food for the lowest-income and most vulnerable populations, without political conditions.

The study of access to government food subsidies is crucial for understanding the prospects for creating a minimal social "safety net" for the lowest-income population in the context of ongoing economic crisis. Unless politically and economically viable "targeted" consumer food subsidies are developed and extended to both city and countryside, the burden of the debt crisis of the 1980s will continue to fall most heavily on Latin America's children, who are today being handicapped by malnutrition.[8]

Enforcing social selectivity in subsidy delivery is easier said than done; the history of social policy in Latin America is replete with examples of programs that failed to benefit the ostensible target groups. It is rarely in the immediate interest of government bureaucrats to deliver scarce resources to low-income, low-status social groups. It is more often in their interest to consume those resources themselves, either directly or by making them available to more powerful social groups in exchange for political or economic rewards.[9] The challenge to any targeted subsidy program is to confront that existing incentive structure and to replace it with one that will encourage equitable and efficient service delivery. One of the most promising alternatives is to entrust the allocation of scarce resources to the organized beneficiaries themselves. Democratic local organizations combine a direct material interest in service delivery with the potential to hold government agencies accountable to low-income communities.

The consolidation of representative local organizations is increasingly recognized to be one of the key factors that turns limited physical and economic resources into successful rural development efforts. Esman and Uphoff's study of over 150 local development associations, cooperatives, and other grassroots organizations in the developing world found that their ability to provide rural citizens with a means of participating in policy decisions was "essential for accomplishing broad-based rural development" (1984, 15). They stress the importance of local organizations as development "intermediaries" that permit the state to reach the grassroots constructively.[10] Mexico's village food-store network opened up one of the most important opportunities for the creation of representative local organizations since Mexico's structural reforms of the 1930s.

Mexico's Rural Food Distribution Program

The Mexican government created a national community-managed rural food distribution program in 1979, just as increased oil and debt income converged to create the illusion of affluence. Mexico's then-hopeful economic situation combined with a shift in the balance of political forces within the state to create an increased commitment to allocate resources to deal with the hunger problem. Reformists still lacked the political clout to confront the interests opposed to either increasing access to land or to reorienting the development model toward a more labor-intensive approach. Private grain traders, many of whom were local oligopolists, presented a more politically vulnerable target. Both government-sponsored and independent research on rural Mexico, moreover, had long emphasized the many ways in which local monopolists kept the rural poor locked in a vicious circle of poverty. Reformist food policymakers therefore chose to intervene actively in rural consumer food markets as a means to broaden access to basic foods.

They created a national network of thousands of community stores that supplied subsidized food to Mexico's lowest-income population, reaching over 13,000 communities by 1986.[11] The government provided the subsidized food and the communities organized the village stores. Most of the program was operated by the National Basic Foods Company (Compañía Nacional de Subsistencias Populares, CONASUPO). CONASUPO, Mexico's second-largest non-financial state enterprise (after the government oil company), buys, processes, and distributes basic foods on a massive scale.

CONASUPO's primary purpose is to appear to further social justice and thereby to legitimate the regime. This goal requires it to respond to peasant demands to some degree. At times this institutional mission creates an environment hospitable to the view that access to food is a right and that the state should encourage peasant allies to fight for that right, within the established political system. This institutional bias was never sufficiently strong, however, to determine whether a reformist approach would actually dominate policy in practice. At issue was which interest groups would benefit more from the government's regulation of grain markets: producers, consumers, or private traders and industrialists. Reformists were only able to intervene on behalf of peasants when the reformists actually controlled policy *implementation*. Throughout the 1970s and 1980s, the balance of power within CONASUPO shifted back and forth between "pro" and "anti-peasant" policy currents, depending on changes in the national political environment.[12] The decision to launch the CONASUPO-COPLAMAR program was the beginning of just such a shift.

The Origins of CONASUPO-COPLAMAR

The National Plan for Depressed Zones and Marginal Groups (Coordinación General del Plan Nacional de Zonas Deprimidas y Grupos Marginados, COPLAMAR) was founded at the beginning of President López Portillo's term (1976–1982). In his inaugural speech, he continued Mexico's long tradition of official populist rhetoric by asking the "pardon" of the "dispossessed and marginalized," even as he presided over a sharp turn toward economic austerity and conservatism. The president had inherited Mexico's most serious economic crisis in decades, and an agreement with the International Monetary Fund sharply limited his freedom of action in the economic arena. But in 1978 López Portillo began to pursue his political agenda, which included a partial liberalization of the electoral system.[13] By 1979, oil income began to come on-stream and Mexico's economy was booming. López Portillo gradually shifted his primary emphasis from renewing the conditions for capital accumulation to revitalizing the regime's neglected social base.

Stock presidential speeches linked the issues of energy and food, stressing their importance to both national autonomy and economic development. Oil received huge investments, consuming much of the foreign exchange it generated, but food and agriculture were neglected during the 1977–1979 period. The apparent resolution of the energy problem created pressures to turn attention to food policy, and in particular, to "do something" about rural poverty and the loss of national food self-sufficiency. In spite of lack of enthusiasm from the major ministries, by late 1979 COPLAMAR officials were able to lobby successfully for increased resource allocation for basic social services, such as rural primary care health clinics and village food outlets in Mexico's lowest-income areas.[14] COPLAMAR made the most progress in those policy areas where it found the most responsive institutional allies, CONASUPO and IMSS (The Mexican Social Security Institute). CONASUPO-COPLAMAR was given a further boost in 1980, when the president announced that Mexico was going to strive to regain national food self-sufficiency. The new Mexican Food System (SAM) strategy was to revitalize peasant rainfed grain production, which had previously been neglected in favor of large-scale, often irrigated production of luxury and export products.[15]

The COPLAMAR and SAM programs were "reforms from above," primarily the result of high-level initiatives from the liberal wing of the political elite.[16] One former high-level COPLAMAR official stressed that the program decision was "completely top-down," with no direct pressure from either official or independent peasant organizations. Those peasant organizations that were pressuring the government were more interested in land rights than in subsidies. Peasant unrest reported during the López Portillo administration was at its lowest level in the two years preceding the COPLAMAR decision (Aguado López et al. 1983, 65).[17] In other words, a high-level government policy current with a long-range view of the need to forestall a *potential* increase in social unrest gained increased influence over policymaking in the context of the oil-debt boom.[18]

CONASUPO-COPLAMAR's Goals:
Policy Innovation and Popular Participation

The stated policy goal was to deliver basic foods at the official price to what CONASUPO-COPLAMAR defined as the "preferred target population." COPLAMAR's national surveys of living standards served as the basis for determining objective need. At least 10,000 rural communities, covering approximately 20 million people, were found to need access to the program's "basic market basket" of subsidized foods. The program's "peasant stores" were considered to have an impact on the population in a radius of five kilometers surrounding the outlet. Because of operational constraints, the program generally limited itself to communities with more than 500 inhabitants and year-round road access (DICONSA 1982, 1–4).

The key shift in government rural food distribution during the López Portillo administration was not the eventual increase in numbers of outlets, but rather the change COPLAMAR induced in how DICONSA, CONASUPO distributors, organized them. Until 1979, most of DICONSA's rural stores were concessions run by private entrepreneurs or other government agricultural agencies. An official DICONSA evaluation concluded, however, that "the enterprise's experience shows one essential operational problem: the guarantee of the final destination and price of the products in the rural stores, which because of their number and isolation complicate supervision. *The operation of concessions*, which face a market in which prices of basic products are 3 or 4 times the official price in the cases of maize, sugar, and beans, *make it practically impossible to avoid corrupt practices* involving the deviation of the products to other stores and industries or their sale at prices above those officially established" (DICONSA 1982, 3, emphasis added). DICONSA tried to deliver subsidized food to the rural poor through the private sector and failed.

CONASUPO-COPLAMAR planners decided that they could serve low-income rural consumers efficiently and equitably only if four conditions were met. First, the program needed *guaranteed supplies* of essential foods. Shortly before the CONASUPO-COPLAMAR network was established, the López Portillo administration had already launched its Alianza line of basic foods—produced by both state and private enterprises for distribution through government channels—making low-cost processed foods (for example, powdered milk, sugar, salt, crackers, flour, pasta, and cooking oil) widely available for both the urban and rural networks.

Second, the network needed its own *storage network*, strategically situated within reach of the target areas. DICONSA's huge warehouses had traditionally been located in the state capitals, whose distance from the rural stores raised distribution costs and whose management made the diversion of subsidized foods to urban consumers and merchants more likely. The oil-debt boom made it possible for the government to build first 200, later rising to 300, large regional warehouses exclusively to serve the village stores.

Third, CONASUPO-COPLAMAR planners decided that one of the lessons of previous efforts was that the network could only rely on *its own transportation network*. Regular DICONSA staff would be unwilling to sacrifice their vehicles, and in many remote areas intermediaries monopolized access to private transportation. CONASUPO-COPLAMAR was able to buy over 3,000 vehicles in the first two years of the program, greatly facilitating both promotion of community organizing and the delivery of food (DICONSA 1982, 7). The creation of an independent infrastructure (that is, warehouses and trucks) gave reformist planners much greater control over operations than they had had in the past, when they depended much more on the existing DICONSA apparatus.

Fourth, planners agreed that *genuine community participation* in policy implementation was essential to guarantee the final destination and price of the food. They concluded from their prior experience with private concessions that "the only valid option was to involve the community itself in the supervision, and even the very management of the operations" (DICONSA 1982, 4). Most governments consider community participation useful only as a means to encourage an upward flow of technical information needed to improve local investments or as a means of sharing project maintenance costs, if they consider it useful at all. CONASUPO-COPLAMAR's community participation procedures, in contrast, were primarily intended to make the bureaucratic apparatus itself more *accountable* to its ostensible clients, that is, to devolve power over policy.[19] The existing staff was too committed to bureaucratic and private interests to implement this policy change; a whole new network of promoters would need to be hired.

The Subsidy Delivery Process

CONASUPO-COPLAMAR was designed to increase peasant bargaining power vis-à-vis private intermediaries. The new "Peasant Stores" were to compete with, but not replace, the high-priced private outlets, selling basic foods at an average of 30 percent below the prevailing rural market price. The CONASUPO-COPLAMAR grain price was higher than the subsidized price of urban tortillas, but the government absorbed large investments in rural distribution infrastructure.

Consumer prices in remote rural areas were often much higher than urban prices for two key reasons: high transportation costs, and frequently inefficient and uncompetitive marketing systems. The effective regulatory impact on rural consumer prices varied in practice according to the region's degree of isolation from urban markets because the more remote the region, the more likely that retail grain markets would be uncompetitive. Grain traders were, however, also often moneylenders whose clients were forced—because of past debt or possible future need for informal credit—to buy from them. This vicious circle of economic dependence was often reinforced by traditional patron-client bonds. Regulation of rural grain markets was therefore not simply a question of increasing economic competition; it would require creating viable alternatives to complex political and cultural, as well as economic, networks of dependence.

The government-supplied village stores only competed with private retailers at the "low end" of the market. Higher-income consumers tended to prefer the more reliable supplies, greater variety, and brand names available from private retailers. The most important product distributed by CONASUPO-COPLAMAR was raw corn, but it tended to be #2 grade animal feed imported from the United States. Organized rural consumers protested that this yellow variety was far inferior to Mexican white corn, particularly since it often arrived in very poor condition. Those who could afford to continued to buy white corn from private outlets. CONASUPO-COPLAMAR therefore competed with private sector retailers in a segmented market, targeting its distribution efforts to the lowest-income consumers.

CONASUPO-COPLAMAR's actual coverage of its target population, essentially the rural bottom third of the income distribution, was determined in part by the geographic distribution of its network. CONASUPO-COPLAMAR built its network primarily in maize-deficit areas in the central and southern parts of the country. The geographic selection process was carried out largely by policymakers who used objective criteria of need, rather than by administrators or politicians who might be more likely to use the allocation process as part of the traditional political patronage system. The pressures from the electorally oriented wing of the political system were powerful, however, and could not be resisted entirely.[20]

Most of the warehouse sites were chosen in consultation with the official National Indigenous Institute (INI), COPLAMAR's close political ally. COPLAMAR also privately consulted autonomous regional peasant organizations. One official directly involved with site selection estimated that about thirty of the locations were deliberately chosen as part of an attempt to provide economic resources and political legitimacy to nascent grassroots democratic peasant organizations. Some of these local movements were operating within the official political party structure, but most were independent of parties. The idea was that the program's procedures for democratizing DICONSA operations would most likely be actively carried out where grassroots mobilization was already in process.

The location of the stores in areas of need was necessary but not sufficient to assure the delivery of basic foods at the official price to the target population. DICONSA judged the performance of its regional branch managers by conventional sales and profit criteria, creating powerful individual and institutional incentives to favor urban over village stores when allocating scarce resources. Branch managers preferred to sell mayonnaise in the state capitals rather than raw corn in the countryside. In addition, organized peasant consumers were a new and not always welcome clientele for DICONSA's officials. Many were indigenous people; Mexico City–based CONASUPO-COPLAMAR officials reported that DICONSA administrators were often quite uncomfortable with being held accountable by people they considered ethnically inferior.

Regional food officials also faced powerful economic incentives to sell subsidized grain illegally to private merchants, who in turn would resell it in remote areas for double or triple the official price. Because CONASUPO made only limited amounts of grain available to the rural distribution program, even during the oil-debt boom, diversion to private intermediaries left the village stores empty. The community participation procedures were designed precisely to create a social force that would counter this built-in temptation for abuse at the operational level.

Rural consumer food subsidies were only effectively delivered when the CONASUPO-COPLAMAR program was able to change the incentive structure that shaped the behavior of operational-level policy implementors. This change was induced by providing political and economic resources to peasant communities for the creation of *social counterweights* to offset the power local elites traditionally wield over the rural development policy implementation process. CONASUPO-COPLAMAR changed the environment: peasant communities had to decide whether to assume the political and economic risks historically associated with

insisting on greater government accountability. As will be discussed
below, a variety of factors intervened to determine the actual degree of
community participation, but the important point here is that *the delivery
of CONASUPO-COPLAMAR's food subsidy required the* collective action
of the community in defense of its immediate material interests.[21]

To encourage grassroots collective action poses a serious dilemma for
reformist policymakers. If beneficiary participation in the implementation
of rural development is genuine, then policymakers cannot be certain
that the participants will use their new power merely to follow a
predictable and docile route through officially established channels. In
the case of CONASUPO-COPLAMAR, reformist policymakers were
willing to take the risks inherent in promoting genuine community
participation in order to offset the power of local elites and traditional
anti-peasant tendencies embedded in government agencies.

CONASUPO-COPLAMAR planners contended that appointing new
representatives of the rural poor to bargain with the government was
the first step toward attacking the roots of rural poverty. They created
an officially legitimate channel for the expression of peasant dissatis-
faction, which permitted reformist policymakers to situate the participation strategy squarely within the framework of the established political
system. At the same time, however, *they attempted to* change *the political
system by inducing the mobilization of a new social force to push for increased
government accountability to the majority of low-income rural citizens.* Only
through this *sandwich strategy* of coordinated pressure on the implementation agency from both above and below would reformist policymakers be able to promote social and economic change.

Policy implementation began with the selection of organizers to
promote the formation of community food-supply committees. Most
COPLAMAR field organizers saw the government's political party as
more often part of the problem than part of the solution. The majority
of organizers were *not*, however, members of opposition political parties.
The recruits tended to be nonpartisan community activists who saw the
consolidation of autonomous grassroots organizations, rather than par-
tisan electoral politics, as the path to social justice and the democratization
of Mexican society.

The promoter's key task was to organize community assemblies to
choose the people who would represent the village in the process of
overseeing and managing DICONSA operations at the village and regional
level. The main purpose of the assemblies was to create a new and
democratic community organization in order to increase the accountability
of government food agencies.

The CONASUPO-COPLAMAR promoters were officially presented
to the municipal and ejido authorities when the program began, but

given the program's objectives it is not surprising that the promoters rarely received a warm welcome.[22] The traditional process for electing authorities in most ejidos and rural municipalities is quite flawed, and entrenched local elites did not welcome the creation of autonomous new interest groups. One former high-level COPLAMAR official estimated that 70 percent of the municipal and ejido leaders opposed the program. In some remote communities promoters had to meet with villagers clandestinely because of the threat of violence from local political bosses (*caciques*) who insisted that all government programs be channeled through them. Although the promoters, as government employees, were relatively immune to cacique repression, the villagers were not.[23]

If a community wanted to install a village store, it had to decide in a formal assembly to administer it according to the guidelines laid out by the CONASUPO-COPLAMAR promoter. The stores were set up on the principle of "co-responsibility"; the community would take responsibility for managing the store, and DICONSA agreed to supply it. The community would find the locale, and DICONSA would supply the working capital with which to buy merchandise. The first step by the assembly was to elect six villagers to a Rural Food Committee (Comité Rural de Abasto) to oversee the management of the store. The assembly was also to elect a store manager, who would be paid a commission from sales (up to 5 percent). The assembly agreed to prepare a locale for the store and to meet monthly to hear reports from the Rural Food Committee about store operations (DICONSA 1982).

The community also agreed to send two representatives, usually the president of the Rural Food Committee and the store manager, to monthly meetings of the Community Food Council (Consejo Comunitario de Abasto) at the regional warehouse that supplied the store. The representatives' task was to oversee the operations of the warehouse and to make sure its several dozen village stores were supplied. These councils were officially considered "one of the fundamental elements for making the CONASUPO-COPLAMAR program one of shared responsibility between the community and the institution" (*Sistema C*, September 1981, 32). The nature of the councils and the scope of their power were the focal points of the political conflict over the program.[24]

The Apparatus Reacts

The CONASUPO-COPLAMAR program created a new force within CONASUPO: a coordinated alliance between reformist Mexico City policy managers and committed field organizers. They in turn allied with organized peasants in their efforts to pressure the rest of the CONASUPO apparatus to carry out the policy. Thus, the program could succeed only insofar as it was able to *internalize social conflict within the agency*. By legitimizing reformist pressures on the bureaucracy from both policymakers above and consumers below, CONASUPO-COPLA-MAR's *sandwich strategy* changed the bureaucracy's incentive structure. At the same time, however, the private and bureaucratic interests that were served by the agency's traditional urban bias continued in their positions of authority, and they did not remain passive in the face of this challenge (see Fig. 9.1).

The reaction of the CONASUPO apparatus to the village store program was crucial to determining what field promoters could and could not do, as well as whether products were actually delivered to village outlets. The response of DICONSA branch managers, who were usually responsible for retail food distribution in an entire state, was central. They could block program outreach, and they allocated resources between urban and rural stores at the state level. DICONSA management usually resisted the attempt to induce powersharing with peasant community representatives, but the key issue was to what degree.[25] This diverse range of scenarios is depicted in Figure 9.1.

The reaction against the community organizing efforts began to mount soon after the program was launched. Commercial interests protested, as well as political authorities that simply feared democratic peasant organization of any kind. The complaints from governors, mayors, ejido commissioners and private traders charged so-called communist infiltration in the program. As one frustrated reformist policymaker put it, "anything having to do with organizing peasants to defend their interests is called communist. Anyone who carries the Constitution under their arm is called a communist" (confidential interview).

CONASUPO-COPLAMAR policymakers handled the political pressure through evasive action, rather than confronting it head-on. At first 50 members of the original field staff of 300 were fired, but by the end of the program's first two years, 400 of a total of 600 were replaced, according to a former top manager. Not all of the approximately 400 were fired; some resigned because they were demoralized by the purges. The remnants of the original staff fought an effective rear-guard action. Reformists were never fully purged, even at the policymaking level, and they defended themselves by moving away from an explicit discussion of social change to a more technical, operational approach. "Promoters" became "Operational Supervisors," as DICONSA's director dealt with the crisis by integrating COPLAMAR staff more into DICONSA's structure. As one of the managers of this shift put it, "we had to learn how to handle groceries."[26]

In spite of the political conflict surrounding the program, the reaction of the traditional power structure inside and outside the bureaucracy

Figure 9.1: Conasupo-Coplamar Food Distribution Operations

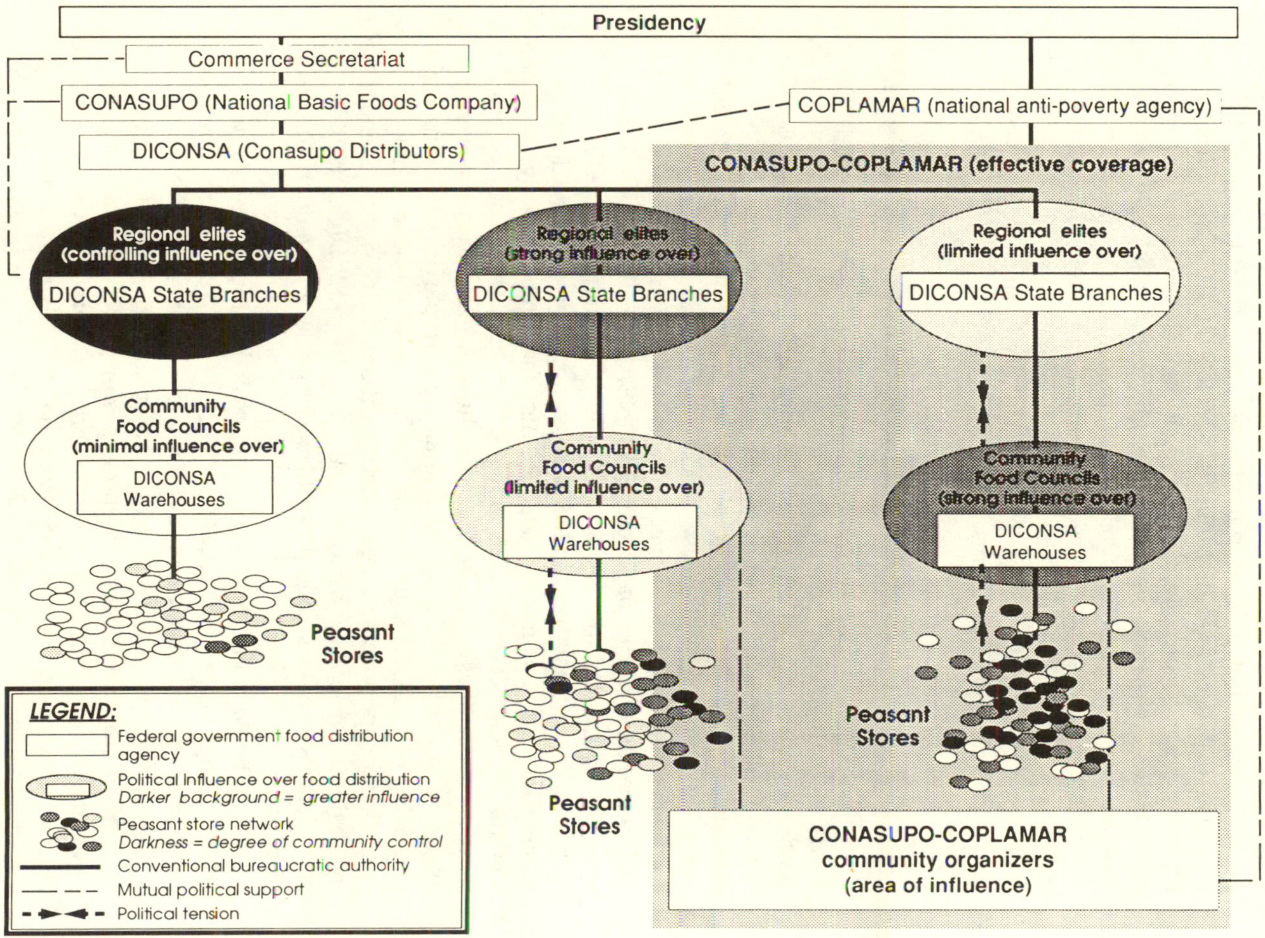

Presidency

Commerce Secretariat

CONASUPO (National Basic Foods Company)

DICONSA (Conasupo Distributors)

COPLAMAR (national anti-poverty agency)

CONASUPO-COPLAMAR (effective coverage)

Regional elites (controlling influence over)

DICONSA State Branches

Community Food Councils (minimal influence over)

DICONSA Warehouses

Peasant Stores

Regional elites (strong influence over)

DICONSA State Branches

Community Food Councils (limited influence over)

DICONSA Warehouses

Peasant Stores

Regional elites (limited influence over)

DICONSA State Branches

Community food Councils (strong influence over)

DICONSA Warehouses

Peasant Stores

CONASUPO-COPLAMAR community organizers (area of influence)

LEGEND:

Federal government food distribution agency

Political influence over food distribution *Darker background = greater influence*

Peasant store network *Darkness = degree of community control*

Conventional bureaucratic authority

Mutual political support

Political tension

was too little, too late to roll back many of the regional movements encouraged by the community participation process. In those areas where promotion was not able to provide the resources for communities to organize, or where food distribution was less of a pressing problem (as in many grain surplus areas), participation failed to take off. In many grain-deficit areas, however, even though operational supervisors either toned down their activities or were replaced, the momentum of the mobilization process did not require "outside agitators" to sustain itself. In many areas of pressing need, where communities had a history of organizing in defense of their interests, the organizing process was taken up by the communities themselves.

The Politics of the Warehouse

CONASUPO-COPLAMAR's integration of community and regional levels of participation turned simple warehouses into focal points for conflict over the allocation of key resources.[27] The important decisions made at the warehouse level involved how to allocate food, trucks, field staff, laborers, and working capital. The communities had the official power to nominate warehouse workers and truck drivers. They were considered community employees, in part to prevent them from unionizing and demanding higher pay from DICONSA, but also to keep their job security dependent on service to the communities. CONASUPO-COPLAMAR officials contended that communities needed leverage to make sure that drivers and loaders did their jobs effectively. Where community food councils were not participatory, these jobs reverted to traditional patronage. Where the councils were effective, however, they fought for and often won the additional right to participate in the hiring and firing of DICONSA employees, including warehouse managers and operational supervisors. These crucial personnel decisions depended on the balance of power between the councils and DICONSA branch managers, which was sometimes tipped by the intervention of Mexico City policymakers.[28]

How often did democratization of food distribution really happen? A wide range of former CONASUPO-COPLAMAR officials, grassroots peasant movement organizers and local leaders, agreed that by the end of the López Portillo administration, approximately 50 of the (then) 200 CONASUPO-COPLAMAR warehouses were effectively supervised by democratic community food councils. Perhaps another 50 were influenced by a process of democratic mobilization. "Effective supervision" of the warehouse does not mean that all the stores in those regions were well-stocked with quality goods. Regional-level participation was necessary but not sufficient for full provisioning, because many resource allocation decisions were made elsewhere in the CONASUPO apparatus. Effective supervision did mean that the basic decisions made at the warehouse level were made by or in consultation with the Community Food Council.

Where Was CONASUPO-COPLAMAR Effective?

The CONASUPO-COPLAMAR program did not openly attack the local power structure, but it created the opportunity for rural citizens to do so. There were, of course, many areas where the caciques themselves, or the official peasant organizations, were able to block or control the program (as illustrated on the left-hand side of Figure 9.1). This is what one would expect from a program that emerged from policymakers' drawing boards in Mexico City, rather than in response to organized demands from below. In those areas where democratic peasant organizations already existed, however, or where the conditions were ripe for their formation, CONASUPO-COPLAMAR usually contributed to their consolidation (for example, in the states of Guerrero, Michoacán, Nayarit, Oaxaca, Puebla, Veracruz, Tabasco, Yucatán, as shown on the right-hand side of Figure 9.1).[29] The resistance generated by this process came not only from local private- or public-sector elites but from powerful interests within CONASUPO itself.

CONASUPO-COPLAMAR worked best where the need for grain was greatest. Participation in the program was most important for rural consumers who lacked access to enough land to be at least self-sufficient. Among Mexico's many such grain-deficit, land-hungry areas, the program worked best where there already was a nascent social movement waiting for the opportunity to grow and spread.

But where do poverty-stricken, oppressed people find the resources with which to mobilize in defense of their interests? This question continues to puzzle social scientists. Many focus on whether the weave of the social fabric encourages people to come together to discuss their problems and to make decisions about how to deal with them. Indigenous culture is one of the most important resources for locally controlled development initiatives (see, for example, MacDonald 1985; Stephen 1988).[30]

Five centuries of conquest have deeply eroded traditional social relations in many areas, yet many indigenous communities of central and southern Mexico still retain vibrant non-Western languages, forms of self-government, and cooperative economic relations. This sense of solidarity is reproduced through continued struggle to defend traditional rights to land and natural resources. The CONASUPO-COPLAMAR program was most successful at encouraging participation where peasants already had the capacity for regionwide democratic mobilization, and those areas were primarily indigenous. The state of Oaxaca experienced some of the most remarkable cases, illustrated graphically on the right-hand side of Figure 9.1.

The Oaxaca Community Food Council Experience

The CONASUPO-COPLAMAR program was particularly well received by the indigenous communities of the impoverished southern state of Oaxaca.[31] The vast majority of Oaxaca's citizens are sub-subsistence rural producers (CEPAL 1982; COPLAMAR 1982). Access to subsidized basic foods, such as raw corn, beans, cooking oil, salt, and sugar, can have a significant impact on the quality of their lives.

The community food councils of Oaxaca first came together in 1982, when 20 (out of then 25) joined together in a statewide coordinating body to negotiate with DICONSA for more and better merchandise and for the freedom to organize autonomously from the government. They first met on the eve of a planned visit by President López Portillo to inaugurate one of the new warehouses. According to one of the food council leaders, "seeing the anomalies which DICONSA always uses to try to fool the campesinos, filling one warehouse full of merchandise to try to make it seem as though all 25 are the same, we all decided to close the warehouses 72 hours beforehand, so they wouldn't have a chance to fill them up at the last minute. We were going to let Lic. López Portillo in, to let him inaugurate the warehouse, but we wanted him to be able to see what the real conditions were." (*El Día*, March 24, 1984). As a result, DICONSA authorities signed a formal agreement with 7 warehouse council presidents, in representation of the 25 Oaxaca councils.

The years 1982 and 1983 were a crucial transition period for the emerging statewide network, which protested continuing supply problems and called for regular audits. The then-conservative state government cracked down, however, and the network fell apart. The leadership soon regrouped, forming the Oaxaca Food Council Coordinating Network in October 1983. By 1985 the network claimed to represent 856 communities, with over 1.4 million low-income rural consumers.[32]

In 1985, the Oaxaca network began to organize the first national organization of democratic community food councils in an effort to form a common bargaining position vis-à-vis DICONSA. The first meeting brought together representatives of over 100 councils, representing about one third of the 12,000 villages served by the program. The increasingly independent-minded movement met with hostility from previously sympathetic top DICONSA authorities, whose countermoves succeeded not only in blocking the consolidation of the national network, but in dividing the Oaxaca network as well. In retrospect, it appears that the Food Council movement was not sufficiently consolidated to sustain a more confrontational approach at the national level.

Once they had been able to organize autonomously on a regional and even statewide level as consumers, Oaxacan peasants took advantage of the new "social energy" and political space to organize as producers as well.[33] In 1984 the Oaxaca Coordinating Network combined community-supplied capital with DICONSA-supplied trucks to supply 18,000 tons of fertilizer to peasant producers throughout the state. They managed to do this at approximately 60 percent of the price charged by the government's agricultural bank (BANRURAL). In spite of operational problems due to lack of administrative experience, the network still outperformed the government bank, which campesinos widely consider to be a parasitic institution. DICONSA authorities withdrew access to government trucks, however, abruptly undercutting the new fertilizer program.[34]

The Oaxaca Community Food Councils' fertilizer distribution experience led them to form their own producers' organizations. By late 1986, at least three Oaxaca food councils had "spun off" nascent autonomous regional producers' organizations. Their goal was to use increased bargaining power to retain a larger share of the value of what they produced for the market.[35] These efforts were particularly important because of the food councils' vulnerability to changes in government policy and loss of elite allies. This experience shows that popular participation, even if apparently narrowly channeled by government programs, can have a range of unexpected consequences, including more autonomous efforts to build democratic economic enterprises to defend poor peoples' food security.

The Community Food Councils and Political Change

Personnel and programs change dramatically in the course of Mexico's presidential transitions, and it was by no means clear that CONASUPO-COPLAMAR would survive 1982. Its co-responsibility approach fit with the new administration's rhetorical emphasis on regional decentralization and "democratic planning." The program's targeted approach also made it quite defensible, because there were many larger and more inefficiently-spent budgets for incoming technocrats to cut. The policy current that oversaw the transition of social programs was sensitive to the potential political cost of withdrawing the state's commitment to supply food to thousands of organized communities.[36] As one reformist policymaker put it, "my ideological struggle was to show that it is cheaper to take up the flag of popular struggles than to confront them head on. In other words, it is cheaper than buying arms" (confidential personal interview). The implication was that if "legitimate" channels were closed off after the participation process had been launched, peasant communities might then seek other means for redress of their grievances.

President López Portillo stepped down in widespread disfavor, and COPLAMAR went down with him, but the rural food distribution program was completely absorbed by DICONSA. It continued increasing in importance within the public grain distribution system in spite of the post-1982 economic crisis. By 1985 the number of rural stores DICONSA considered community-managed had grown to 12,272 and the rural share of DICONSA's basic food distribution had grown to 29 percent, up from 10.5 percent in 1978 (DICONSA 1986a, 9). This increased share indicated that, in relative terms, DICONSA's rural program had become an even more important part of the government's array of rural development policies.[37] Organized rural consumers had won a limited degree of veto power; the program had generated a constituency.

In practice, the program was carried out largely to the degree that peasant communities mobilized in support of policy goals against reluctant administrators. But peasant mobilization usually required active support from reformist policymakers in order to succeed in implementing the reform. Most importantly in the long run, *peasants took advantage of the program's participatory procedures to build their own representative organizations*, whose activities and scope were not limited to the boundaries originally defined by policymakers.

The CONASUPO-COPLAMAR experience suggests that the driving force for more accountable social policy is the *reciprocal interaction* between state reformists and social movements. This outcome depends fundamentally on two key factors. The first is the *capacity of social movements for democratic mobilization*, defined in terms of representativeness and demands for greater government accountability. Their capacity to defend themselves from the twin threats of repression and cooptation depends largely on their degree of autonomy from external interference in their decisionmaking.[38]

Democratic rights must be won, not granted. But some degree of freedom and capacity to organize for these rights is fundamental. The second key factor, therefore, is *the degree to which reformists, strategically located within the state, have the capacity to take democratizing initiatives*. Reformists are defined here as state officials who express their concern for long-term political stability through a willingness to bargain with relatively autonomous social movements. They must be strategically located to be effective (that is, in both the national and the local executive agencies). Otherwise it is unlikely that they will actually control the allocation of significant economic or political resources. The most important political resource they can offer is some degree of protection from both public and private sector repression, which creates space for democratic mobilization. The most important economic resource they can provide is an immediate material incentive for grassroots collective action, which usually requires operational control over policy implementation. These reformists must be strategically located at local as well as national levels in order to assure that they will actually reach grassroots movements.[39]

Conclusions

Mexico's community food councils encouraged widespread grassroots participation in Latin America's most important rural consumer food-subsidy program. In many of Mexico's most impoverished rural areas, the community food councils were the first democratic *regionwide* organizations of any kind. Government rural food distribution efforts succeeded only where peasants were able to mobilize, democratically and autonomously, to offset the power of entrenched regional elites. Remarkably, in spite of political opposition and cutbacks in a wide range of other social programs, the community food councils survived at least the first five years of Mexico's economic crisis. Political mobilization and conflict shaped access to food and permitted the program to survive the transition from heady "positive-sum" economic boom to prolonged "zero-sum" crisis.

Mexico's community food council experience raises the broader question: how can social justice be reconciled with the economic pressures of austerity? The populist approaches of the past are no longer politically or economically viable. Traditionally, "more state" was the solution, as large, privileged bureaucracies subsidized better-off urban sectors first, with at best some trickle down to the largely rural bottom half of the income distribution.

Policies of the past favored generalized subsidies (that is, all urban tortillas, all gasoline, education, etc.). In the context of Latin America's continuing economic crisis, such subsidies can no longer be distributed in terms of a "positive-sum game," where many social groups can benefit to some degree, regardless of need. The challenge to social policy today is to develop *socially responsible selectivity* in resource allocation. For example, if the health budget cannot grow, will resources go to capital-intensive urban hospitals, or to rural primary care? Will the education budget go to ministry bureaucrats or to primary school teachers? If energy resources are limited, will they go to low-cost gasoline for privileged private auto owners, or to mass transportation? If food budgets are limited, will they support basic or nonbasic foods (corn and beans or feedgrains and sugar)? If the economic crisis rules out past patterns of state subsidies for both producers and consumers and the state must keep producer prices up to avoid crop shortfalls, can targeted food distribution programs buffer the impact on the lowest-income population?

How can Latin American states provide for the basic human needs of their most vulnerable populations without reinforcing wasteful bureaucracies? Mexico's Community Food Council experience shows that beneficiary controlled food-policy implementation can allocate increasingly scarce resources efficiently and equitably. The challenge is for "lean states" to channel their increasingly scarce resources toward autonomous, democratic local organizations of the lowest-income populations. Unless these groups have the freedom and capacity to enter the political bargaining process, however, more privileged interests will inherently have priority access to the same limited resources. Hunger cannot be eliminated until the hungry are able to participate effectively in the political conflict over who is to benefit from government action.

Notes

1. This study is based on two years of field research in Mexico and draws from Fox (1986, 1990b). I would like to thank the Inter-American Foundation, the University of California, San Diego's Center for U.S.-Mexican Studies, and the Institute for the Study of World Politics for their generous research support. I would also like to express my appreciation to the many policymakers, rural development activitists, and grass-roots community leaders who shared their time and thoughts with me. Thanks also to Michael Fox of Rebus Technologies for graphic design assistance on Fig. 9.1.

2. With the crisis, the wage share of national income declined from a peak of 40.3 percent in 1976 to 27.7 percent in 1984 (INCO 1986, 7). Workers had to spend an estimated 78 percent of the minimum wage on food in 1984, compared to 55 percent in 1976 (INN 1986). Because underemployment is so widespread and persistent, Mexicans who work full time at the minimum wage are considered in the *upper* half of the income distribution.

3. Even during 1982–1984, when food subsidies increased, the minimum wage fell more than real food prices (except for tortillas). Reliable data on changing consumption patterns are scarce. The National Consumer Institute has done several small surveys of changing consumption patterns and survival strategies in urban areas. Less is known about rural consumption patterns, although some economists suggest that the urban poor and middle classes have suffered the most (Lustig 1990). Any systematic urban/rural comparison would have to distinguish those rural producers who have sufficient access to land and inputs to harvest enough for household needs from the rural majority who do not. The landless and sub-subsistence peasants are likely to have suffered the most significant changes in food consumption, except where government food distribution networks operate or where atypical job opportunities are

available (that is, tourism, narcotics). To my knowledge, Grindle (1988, 1989) has published the only study that specifically documents the effects of the post-1982 crisis at the level of rural communities.

4. Household access is understood to be necessary but not sufficient for equitable distribution among family members.

5. In spite of seventy years of agrarian reform, there are more landless farmworkers today than before the 1910–1917 revolution. Estimates of the farmworker population range up to 5 million. They must travel from one seasonal job to another, rarely earning the minimum wage. Most retain some access to land, but their parcels (as well as government support services) are inadequate to provide year-round subsistence. According to experts at Mexico's National Nutrition Institute, by 1987 approximately 3 million Mexicans had been forced by hunger to migrate to the cities (on both sides of the border) since the economic crisis had begun in 1982. For basic works on Mexico's agrarian reform, see, among many, CEPAL (1982), Esteva (1983), Sanderson (1981), and Warman (1980a, 1980b). For the most comprehensive recent overview of agrarian issues, see Zepeda Patterson (1988). On rural-urban migration, see Arizpe (1978), Grindle (1988) and the many works of the University of California, San Diego's Center for U.S.-Mexican Studies. On landless farmworkers, see Astorga (1985), de Grammont (1986), and Paré (1977).

6. Research is available on the economic costs and impact of consumer subsidies, but few studies are available on their fundamentally political determinants. For economic analyses of consumer food subsidies, see Austin (1981), Timmer, Pearson, and Falcon (1983), and the publications of the International Food Policy Research Institute (for example, Lustig 1986). For further analysis of the politics of food subsidies in Mexico, see Fox (1986).

7. The issue of access to food through subsidies is part of the broader question of which interests governments serve, how they serve them and why. Traditionally, most Latin American government social programs primarily served to consolidate relatively privileged urban political constituencies, through clientelism, concessions to the minority of the urban working class able to organize trade unions, and the creation of middle-class employment opportunities, that is, social-security programs. *Most* government subsidies, however, are usually allocated as economic policy instruments rather than through social programs (that is, low-cost energy, infrastructure, credit, and other inputs for capital-intensive industrial ventures).

8. Of the 2 million children born annually in Mexico, an estimated 100,000 die because of malnutrition-related causes, and another 1 million survive with physical or mental limitations caused by lack of food (INN 1986).

9. Tendler (1982) and Leonard (1982) analyze how the structure of development projects and their degree of vulnerability to local elite monopolization affects the degree to which their benefits are diverted away from the rural poor. As Heaver points out in his study of the politics of the implementation of rural development projects, "new programs and projects must take into account bureaucratic politics, and provide an incentive, in terms of perceived personal advantage, for the bureaucrats [involved] at each level . . . [B]ureaucrats, like

peasants, are rational. It is not often that ignorance and apathy are determinants of behavior, but that existing incentive systems make it in officials' rational self-interest to be apathetic in pursuit of development goals" (1982, iv–v).

10. Esman and Uphoff argue that four factors are crucial for effective rural local organization. They conclude that local membership organizations should: first, have more than one level of organization, to permit effective intermediation between the village and the government and/or private sector. Second, local organizations should complement rather than compete with other development institutions. Third, horizontal and vertical linkages play key roles in increasing the efficacy of local organization efforts. Horizontal linkages bring local organizations with similar interests together, and vertical linkages increase their voice within policymaking circles. Fourth, Esman and Uphoff find that multiple channels for vertical communication are crucial to effective linking of the government and village (1984, 29–30).

11. The number of rural stores increased dramatically, as the CONASUPO-COPLAMAR network expanded and the traditional private concessions were gradually phased out. The rural share of stores rose from 31 percent in 1977 to 81 percent in 1982, when they numbered just over 9,000 (*Informe de Gobierno* 1983, 178). By 1986 DICONSA supplied over 13,000 peasant stores out of a total national network of over 19,000. Except for large shopping centers and trade-union-managed stores, most of the remainder were concessions to private entrepreneurs (DICONSA, unpublished internal memo, 1987).

12. On CONASUPO's early 1970s reform efforts, see Austin (1978); Esteva (1979); and Grindle (1977). For an important overview and critique of CONASUPO's role in Mexico's agro-industrial system, see Barkin and Suárez (1985). On CONASUPO's role in delivering food subsidies, see Lustig and Martín del Campo (1985) and Lustig (1986). On the range of CONASUPO activities during the 1980–1982 Mexican Food System food self-sufficiency strategy, see Austin and Fox (1987) and Fox (1986).

13. Because most political parties were either illegal or did not consider the electoral process legitimate, he had won the presidency unopposed. This lack of even formal competition, combined with the atmosphere of political crisis surrounding the 1976 transition, put the problem of renewing the system's mass political legitimacy squarely on the presidential agenda.

14. See COPLAMAR's five volumes on nutrition, health, housing, education, and the geographic distribution of indicators of "marginality."

15. On Mexico's loss of food self-sufficiency, see, among others, Barkin (1987), Barkin and Suárez (1985); Luiselli (1980); Luiselli and Mariscal (1981); Redclift (1981a,b). Through the late 1970s, academics and political commentarists developed a powerful critique of government bias in favor of large, irrigated, export and industrial farms at the expense of support for peasant rainfed grain farms. The 1980–1982 Mexican Food System strategy gave this critique the legitimacy of official government policy analysis. For overviews of the SAM, see Austin and Esteva (1987); Fox (1986, 1990b); and Spalding (1985).

16. From different points in the food chain, SAM (primarily from the production process) and CONASUPO-COPLAMAR (from marketing) each at-

tempted to attack Mexico's longstanding problem of rural poverty with what policymakers viewed as structural reforms. One of SAM's basic incentives was to raise the government's grain purchase prices, but this measure could hurt low-income rural consumers. As the Price Commission of the policymaking Agricultural Cabinet contended in a 1980 internal proposal, "the increase in the guaranteed price will have a regressive impact on broad sectors of the rural population, since many do not produce enough maize to satisfy their consumption needs. They therefore have to obtain maize in the market, at prices which will surely rise significantly. *We therefore emphatically recommend that CONASUPO, through its CONASUPO-COPLAMAR program, participate widely in depressed areas, maintaining the current maize price there*" (emphasis in original; private, unpublished proposal).

17. As one former middle-level COPLAMAR administrator explained it, "COPLAMAR's intent was to try to control peasant discontent and independent peasant organization, to mediate it or keep it within certain limits. The program was targeted fundamentally to the poor fraction of the peasantry . . . [After the anti-reform backlash of 1976]. The state had to opt, on the one hand, for a line that respected the interests of the agrarian oligarchy through slowing the pace of land redistribution, but on the other hand it had to offer some solution to the situation in the countryside." Aguado López and his colleagues found that mobilization levels began to rise significantly in 1980 and continued to rise in 1981 and 1982. Whatever food-policy reformists' intentions may have been, this pattern is consistent with the hypothesis that the 1980–1982 reformist shift in food policy *encouraged* mobilization, as the possibilities of winning concessions increased.

18. The view of the reformist policymakers themselves is consistent with this approach. According to a top political adviser to the director of CONASUPO's distribution arm (DICONSA), the reasons for the "democratization in these programs is part of a history which goes back further than López Portillo, even further than [former President] Echeverría, back to the [student] movements of 1968, when many of the people who participated . . . went out to work in the countryside after the 2nd of October [the army massacre of several hundred unarmed student protestors]. There were two results. First, there was a political decision at the highest levels to take up the issue of popular participation in a democratic way, since the link between the base and the state had been dislocated, or broken. That was one of the reasons the state tried to recover its social base through a broadening of democratization in certain policies and regions. Second, the people who went out to work in the countryside began to work at the grassroots level to build independent, autonomous social movements. In the case of CONASUPO-COPLAMAR there was a convergence between the government's political expectations and needs and an organizing process which was already going on. I don't think that either the organization and democratization happened spontaneously, or that it came about as a result of the government's political posture, rather that the [reformist] position from above converged with a movement from below" (personal interview). This adviser himself acted as a communications backchannel between government reformists and grassroots movement leaders.

His view shows that the "sandwich strategy" of coordinated pressure from above and below in favor of increased democratization was consciously pursued from both inside and outside the state.

19. Mexico's principal previous effort at integrating community participation into the policy process was the PIDER program, begun in 1973 and later funded by the World Bank. In the case of PIDER, however, participation was ostensibly encouraged only in the selection of community-level public investments, not in the implementation of the projects (and then only several years after the project was launched). As Cernea's detailed study of the participation process in PIDER noted, lack of community involvement in the control and monitoring of the implementation process was one of the key weaknesses of the program (1983, 25, 61). Although in theory PIDER shared COPLAMAR's goal of encouraging participation in order to increase the accountability of government development agencies to their ostensible beneficiaries, it developed no means for consistently doing this in practice (Cernea 1983, 43, 69).

20. Many ruling party politicians lobbied heavily for their localities. The petitioners were usually rejected if the area did not fit COPLAMAR's official definition of need. The decisions were highly centralized by national-level reformists in Mexico City, rather than involving the official participation of politicians more directly responsive to traditional regional elites, such as state governors; governors did manage to intervene to a limited degree. According to one former top COPLAMAR official, of the 200 warehouse sites originally submitted for approval, a total of 9 were vetoed for political reasons, usually by governors who did not want the program's benefits allocated to a contested region.

21. Collective action beyond the immediate community is qualitatively more difficult in rural than in urban areas (Fox 1990a). Populations are more dispersed and horizontal communication is more difficult (Olson, 1985). Individual small holders may be less likely to identify a clearly defined common enemy than, for example, factory or plantation workers. Rural people have nevertheless often overcome these obstacles, particularly when they are bound together by strong cultural bonds and community traditions. The most important obstacle to rural collective action is the intensity of government and private-sector violence used against rural people who come together to identify common problems and act on them. Mexico is one of several developing countries characterized by (relatively) greater political freedom in urban than in rural areas (in 1987, for example, Brazil, Peru, Colombia, Guatemala, El Salvador, Haiti, and the Philippines). On political violence against peasants in two of Mexico's poorest rural states, Oaxaca and Chiapas, see Amnesty International (1986) and Paré (1990).

22. Land-use rights are ceded to ejido agrarian reform communities by the government, but the land is usually worked in individual parcels. Ejidos are politico-economic institutions that act simultaneously as organs of government control and peasant representation (Gordillo 1979, 1988a, 1988b). Approximately half of Mexico's arable land is in the reform sector.

23. At least two community leaders who worked with CONASUPO-COPLAMAR were assassinated (one in Chiapas, another in Tabasco) according

to other community food council leaders. Others were discouraged from participating with beatings and threats (Ortiz Pinchetti 1981).

24. Quantitative national indicators of participation provide a starting point. In the month of July 1982, for example, 95 percent of the community food councils' meetings planned were held. These meetings were attended by 42 percent of the representatives expected, 53 percent of whom were store managers and 31 percent of whom were Supply Committee representatives. The village store managers attended more regularly, in part because they earned their living from commissions and therefore had a direct stake in being supplied. Almost all of the meetings were attended by COPLAMAR field staff, who often used company vehicles to bring community representatives to the meetings. Of those rural food committees represented, 88 percent reported that they were satisfied with the staff support from the promoters. Only 60 percent reported, however, that their petitions were "adequately attended to" by the warehouse staff, indicating the operational bureaucracy's resistance to dealing with organized clients (DICONSA 1982, 13–14).

The data indicate that the pattern of participation did not follow the simple pyramid projected on paper. The participation process was quite uneven, and probably nonexistent in many areas. Many, perhaps most, of the council meetings did not involve the mobilized participation of the majority of communities in those regions. These figures do indicate, however, that after only two years of operation the program had achieved a significant degree of participation in a minority of the villages targeted.

25. Branch manager resistance was very frustrating to the reformist policy-makers in Mexico City, but there was little direct action they could take. Branch managers were usually chosen higher up, by the CONASUPO director in consultation with state governors. According to a former high-level regional administrator, DICONSA branch managers used a wide range of tactics to block community food councils, including such measures as gerrymandering warehouse districts to divide allied communities and preventing agency trucks from bringing community leaders to meetings from outlying areas. The more sophisticated managers would allow the trucks to pick people up for meetings but would have them skip the "troublemakers." Managers were known in some areas to intervene in the internal affairs of village and regional committees, and some were able to block field organizers from working with autonomous peasant organizations. In some cases limited supplies were delivered only to favored and docile villages in an attempt to divide the regional food council and create a clientele for the branch manager.

26. The defensive tone of one of the few official evaluations of the program reveals the political tension by the end of 1982. "The original essence and in fact the only formal goal of the whole Program is to *guarantee the final destination and price* of the products. . . . It is never useless to insist that the entire strategy—especially the community participation—was designed to meet that goal, and *no other* (DICONSA 1982, 19, emphasis in original).

27. Rural development opportunities are often blocked by elites that operate at a regional level, brokering political and economic interaction with the rest

of the country (Bartra 1975; Gordillo 1980, 1986). Few ostensibly participatory social programs effectively generate *regional* participation, which is crucial for creating effective counterweights in defense of peasant interests.

28. Reformist CONASUPO-COPLAMAR policymakers were frequently torn between the institutional imperative to defend the agency's last work over personnel decisions, and their knowledge that the community food councils' enemies were often their opponents as well in the internal power struggle. This institutional imperative was driven in part by the Mexico City management's need to set limits to its conflicts with its own key operational staff. It could push them just so far. If policymakers sacrificed the careers of its middle managers in response to every peasant demonstration or building occupation, the operational staff would themselves rebel, together with their allies in state governments and elsewhere in CONASUPO. As a result, only after intense regional mobilization would the branch office itself be touched. In the event that a branch manager or assistant managers had to be removed under Community Food Council pressure, they were often simply transferred to another region.

29. For a discussion of the importance of the food councils for the redemocratization of an ejido union in southern Nayarit, see Fox and Hernández (1989).

30. For an overview of indigenous movements in Mexico, see Piñeros and Silva (1987).

31. Oaxaca's history has been marked by a traditional rejection of central government authority. Unlike many other regions of Mexico, the revolution did not really happen in Oaxaca (Waterbury 1975). Urban-based elites had traditionally extracted the state's economic surplus more through their control over the terms of trade rather than through direct control over most of the land, and the CONASUPO-COPLAMAR program directly intervened in that power relationship. Economic elites thus had both historical and economic reasons for opposing the program. For an analysis of the power of organized commerce in Oaxaca, see Contreras (1987).

32. For the Coordinating Network's own detailed history of its 1982–1985 activities, see the chronology reproduced in *El Día* (August 31, 1985).

33. The notion of "social energy" follows Hirschman (1984). This process also fits his idea of an "inverted development sequence." These Oaxacan peasants had been unable to organize as producers until they organized as consumers, contradicting economistic assumptions regarding production as necessarily determinative of political outcomes.

34. On BANRURAL, see Austin and Fox (1987); Fox (1986); Gordillo (1988a, b); Rello (1987); Pessah (1987); and Aguilar and Araujo (1984).

35. The strategy of blocking traditional mechanisms of surplus extraction by changing the political as well as the economic terms of trade was primarily articulated on the national level by the National Union of Autonomous Regional Peasant Organizations (UNORCA). The UNORCA network represents an important new political "grey area" in the Mexican countryside, bringing together both nominally official and independent organizations. Many UNORCA producer groups were reinforced by allied community food councils (for example, see Fox

and Hernández 1989). On the UNORCA strategy, see Gordillo (1986, 1987). For analyses of the UNORCA movement, see Bartra (1989), Fox and Gordillo (1989), and Hernández (1989, 1990). For case studies and oral histories of UNORCA network members, see the weekly supplement to the Mexico City daily *El Día*, "Del Campo y el Campesino" (1984–1986).

36. DICONSA's director under President De la Madrid (1982–1988), Raúl Salinas de Gortari, was a rising star in the bureaucracy who had experience promoting rural reform in the rural road-building program during the early 1970s. He is also the brother of Carlos Salinas de Gortari, De La Madrid's secretary of programming and the budget and successor to the presidency in 1988. The Community Food Council program's relatively tolerant approach to bargaining was a crucial forerunner of the "social concertation" policy since promoted more broadly by Salinas and his associate, Manual Camacho. See Salinas de Gortari (1982).

37. After the fall in the price of oil, all global food subsidies began to be rolled back, and by the end of 1986, even the highly sensitive tortilla subsidy was removed. Its elimination was politically managed with the creation of tortilla food stamps (*tortibonos*). The coupons were distributed through CONASUPO food and milk outlets located in primarily low-income neighborhoods, as well as through pro-government trade unions and the ruling political party. The system was modeled on the "social targeting" of the urban liquid milk distribution system, which reaches over 1 million families earning less than twice the minimum wage. The tortilla coupon system was a serious operational challenge for CONASUPO, and the number of coupons distributed during its first year was essentially symbolic, but the coupon system had the potential to grow into an important policy instrument. For a more recent report, see Werner (1988).

38. For further discussion of the issues of representation, participation, and grassroots organization autonomy from the state, see Fox and Hernández (1989).

39. For examples of the published views of reformist food policymakers who played key roles in the CONASUPO-COPLAMAR experience, see Peón Escalante (1988) and Sodi de la Tijera (1988).

References and Bibliography

Aguado López, Eduardo, José Luis Torres, and Gabriela Scherer Ibarra
  1983   "La lucha por la tierra en México (1976–1982)." *Revista Mexicana de Ciencias Políticas y Sociales* July-December:113–114.
Aguilar, Samuel, and Hugo Andrés Aravjo
  1984   Estado y Campesinado en la Laguna: la lucha campesina por la tierra y el excedente. Saltillo, Mexico: UAAAN, *Folleto de Divulgación*, vol. 1, no. 5.
Amnesty International
  1986   *Mexico: Human Rights in Rural Areas*. An Exchange of Documents with the Mexican Government on Human Rights Violations in Oaxaca and Chiapas. London: Amnesty International Publications (also published in Spanish).

Arizpe, Lourdes
  1978   *Migración, Etnicismo y Cambio Económico.* Mexico City: El Colegio de
          Mexico.
Astorga Lira, Enrique
  1985   *El Mercado de Trabajo Rural en México.* Mexico City: Ediciones Era.
Austin, James
  1978   "CONASUPO '76," Teaching course with Robin Hurless. Harvard
          University Business School/School of Public Health.
Austin, James, ed.
  1981   *Nutrition Programs in the Third World.* Cambridge: Oelgaschlager,
          Gunn and Hain.
Austin, James, and Gustavo Esteva, eds.
  1987   *Food Policy in Mexico: The Search for Self-Sufficiency.* Ithaca: Cornell
          University Press.
Austin, James, and Jonathan Fox
  1987   "State-Owned Enterprises as Food Policy Implementors." In *Food
          Policy in Mexico,* edited by James Austin and Gustavo Esteva. Ithaca:
          Cornell University Press.
Barkin, David
  1987   "The End to Food Self-Sufficiency in Mexico." *Latin American Per-
          spectives* 14, no. 3 (Summer): 271–297.
Barkin, David, and Blanca Suárez
  1985   *El Fin de la Autosuficiencia Alimentaria.* Mexico City: Océano/Centro
          de Ecodesarrollo.
Bartra, Armando
  1989   "La apropriación del proceso productivo como forma de lucha." *Pueblo*
          143 (April): 30–34.
Bartra, Roger, ed.
  1975   *Caciquismo y Poder Político en el México Rural.* Mexico City: Siglo XXI.
CEPAL
  1982   *Economía Campesina y Agricultura Empresarial.* Mexico City: Siglo XXI.
Cernea, Michael
  1983   *A Social Methodology for Community Participation in Local Investment:
          The Experience of Mexico's PIDER Program.* World Bank Staff Working
          Papers no. 598, August.
CONASUPO
  1980–   *Sistema C.* Various issues.
  1983
Contreras, Enrique
  1987   "Participación económica y política del comercio organizado de Oax-
          aca." In *Mexico: Problemas Urbano-Regionales,* edited by Guillermo
          Boils. Mexico City: García Valdés/UNAM/IIS.
COPLAMAR
  1982   *Necesidades Esenciales en México.* 5 vols. Mexico City: Siglo XXI.
de Grammont, Hubert C., ed.
  1986   *Asalariados agrícolas y sindicalismo en el campo mexicano.* Mexico City:
          Juan Pablos/UNAM/IIS.

DICONSA
1982   "DICONSA y el programa CONASUPO-COPLAMAR en el contexto del SAM." Paper presented at COPIDER/Harvard Food Policy Workshop, Mexico City, CIESS, October.
1983   *Reglamento de operación del Sistema CONASUPO-COPLAMAR.* Mexico City: DICONSA.
1985   *Reunion nacional de evaluación del Sistema de Distribuidoras CONASUPO.* Mexico City: DICONSA, March.
1986a   *Distribuidora e Impulsora Comercial CONASUPO, s.a. (DICCONSA).* Mexico City: DICCONSA, August.
1986b   *Evolución del sistema de Distribuidoras CONASUPO 1983-1985 y líneas centrales del programa 1986* (General Manager's report). Mexico City: DICONSA, April.

El Dia
1980–   Various issues.
1986

Esman, Milton, and Norman Uphoff
1984   *Local Organizations, Intermediaries in Rural Development.* Ithaca: Cornell University Press.

Esteva, Gustavo
1979   "La experiencia de la intervención estatal reguladora en la comercialización agropecuaria de 1970 a 1976." In *Mercado y Dependencia,* edited by Ursula Oswald. Mexico City: Nueva Imagen/CIS-INAH.
1983   *The Battle for Rural Mexico.* South Hadley, Mass.: Bergin and Garvey.

Fox, Jonathan
1986   "The Political Dynamics of Reform: The Case of the Mexican Food System, 1980–1982." Ph.D. dissertation, Department of Political Science, Massachusetts Institute of Technology.
1990a   Ed., *The Challenge of Rural Democratization in Developing Countries.* London: Frank Cass, Ltd. Also published as *Journal of Development Studies,* July, 1990 26(4). London: Frank Cass.
1990b   "La Dinámica del Cambio en el Sistema Alimentario Mexicano, 1980–82." In *La Historia de la Cuestión Agraria Mexicana* vol. 9, edited by Julio Moguel. Mexico City: Siglo XXI/CEHAM.

Fox, Jonathan, and Gustavo Gordillo
1989   "Between State and Market: The Campesinos' Quest for Autonomy." In *Mexico's Alternative Political Futures,* edited by Wayne Cornelius, Judith Gentleman, and Peter Smith. La Jolla: University of California, San Diego, Center for U.S.-Mexican Studies, 1989, 131–172.

Fox, Jonathan, and Luis Hernández
1990a   "Offsetting the 'Iron Law of Oligarchy': The Ebb and Flow of Leadership Accountability in a Regional Peasant Organization." 13(2): 8–15.

Gordillo, Gustavo
1979   "Estado y sistema ejidal." *Cuadernos Políticos* 21 (July).
1980   "Pasado y presente del movimiento campesino en Mexico." *Cuadernos Políticos* 23 (January).

1986   "Movilización social como medio de producción." *Investigación Económica* 175 (January-March).

1987   "El movimiento campesino en la década de los ochentas." *La Cultura en México* (Supplement of *Siempre*) no. 1296 (February 4): 36–49.

1988a   *Campesinos al asalto del cielo, de la expropriación estatal a la apropriación campesina.* Mexico City: Siglo XXI.

1988b   *Estado, mercados y movimiento campesino.* Zacatecas, Mexico: UAZ/ Plaza y Valdés.

Grindle, Merilee

1977   *Bureaucrats, Politicians and Peasants in Mexico.* Berkeley: University of California Press.

1981   *Official Interpretations of Rural Underdevelopment: Mexico in the 1970s.* Working Papers in U.S.–Mexican Studies, no. 20. San Diego: University of California.

1988   *Searching for Development: Labor Migration and Employment in Rural Mexico.* Ithaca: Cornell University Press.

1989   "The Response to Austerity: Political and Economic Strategies of Mexico's Rural Poor." In *Lost Promises, Debt, Austerity and Development in Latin America,* edited by William Canak. Boulder: Westview Press.

Heaver, Richard

1982   *Bureaucratic Politics and Incentives in the Management of Rural Development.* World Bank Staff Working Papers no. 537.

Hernández, Wis

1989   "Autonomía y desarrollo." *Pueblo* 12, no. 147 (September-October): 40–46.

1990   "Las convulsiones rurales." *El Cotidiano* 7, no. 34 (March-April): 13–21.

Hirschman, Albert

1984   *Getting Ahead Collectively.* New York: Pergamon Press.

INCO (Instituto Nacional del Consumidor)

1986   Política Social, Empleo y Niveles de Vida. Mexico City, unpublished manuscript, June.

Informe de Gobierno

1983   Mexico City: Federal Executive Power 1980–1984.

INN (Instituto Nacional de Nutrición)

1979   *Segunda Encuesta Nacional de Alimentación.* Mexico City: INN.

1986   *Excelsior,* November 14.

INN-CONACYT

1980   *La Alimentación en el Medio Rural.* Mexico City: INN-CONACYT.

Labra, Armando, ed.

1988   *El Sector Social de la Economía, una opción ante la crisis.* Mexico City: UNAM/Siglo XXI.

Leonard, David, and Dale Rogers Marshall, eds.

1982   *Institutions of Rural Development for the Poor, Decentralization and Organizational Linkages.* Institute of International Studies Research Series no. 49. Berkeley: University of California.

Luiselli, Cassio
    1980   "Agricultura y alimentación: premises para una nueva estrategia." In *Panorama y perspectivas de la economía mexicana*, edited by Nora Lustig. Mexico City: El Colegio de Mexico.

Luiselli, Cassio, and Jaime Mariscal
    1981   "La crisis agrícola a partir de 1965." In *Desarrollo y crisis de la economía mexicana*, edited by Rolando Cordera. Mexico City: Fondo de Cultura Económica.

Lustig, Nora
    1984   "Distribution of Income, Food Consumption, and the Fiscal Cost of Alternative Policy Options." In *The Political Economy of Income Distribution in Mexico*, edited by Pedro Aspe and Paul Sigmund. New York: Holmes and Meier.
    1986   *Food Subsidy Programs in Mexico*. Working Papers on Food Subsidies no. 3 International Food Policy Research Institute, January. Washington, D.C.: IFPRI.
    1990   "Economic Crisis, Adjustment, and Living Standards in Mexico: 1982–1985." *World Development* 18, no. 10 (October): 1325–1342.

Lustig, Nora, and Antonio Martín del Campo
    1985   "Descripción del funcionamiento del Sistema CONASUPO." *Investigación Económica* 173 (July-September).

MacDonald, Theodore, ed.
    1985   "Native Peoples and Economic Development, Six Case Studies From Latin America." *Cultural Survival Occasional Paper* no. 16 (January). Cambridge, Mass.: Cultural Survival.

Mejía Piñeros, María Consuelo, and Sergio Sarmiento Silva
    1987   *La lucha indígena: un reto a la ortodoxia*. Mexico City: Siglo XXI/IIS/UNAM.

Montanari, Mario
    1987   "The Conception of SAM." In *Food Policy in Mexico*, edited by James Austin and Gustavo Esteva. Ithaca: Cornell University Press.

Olson, Mancur
    1985   "Space, Agriculture, and Organization." *American Journal of Agricultural Economics* 67, no. 5 (December).

Ortiz Pinchetti, Francisco
    1981   "DICONSA frena la organización campesina y traiciona el programa en cuatro estados." *Proceso* 241 (June 15).

Paré, Louisa
    1977   *El proletariado agrícola en México*. Mexico City: Siglo XXI.
    1990   "The Challenge of Rural Democratization in Mexico." *Journal of Development Studies* 26(4): 79–98.

Peón Escalante, Fernando
    1988   "El papel del Estado en el abasto popular (1910–1986)." In *El Sector Social de la Economía*, edited by Armando Labra. Mexico City: UNAM/Siglo XXI.

Pessah, Raul
    1987   "Channelling Credit to the Countryside." In *Food Policy in Mexico*, edited by James Austin and Gustavo Esteva. Ithaca: Cornell University Press.

Redclift, Michael
    1981a   "The Mexican Food System (SAM): Sowing Subsidies, Reaping Apathy." *Food Policy* 6, no. 4 (November).
    1981b   *Development Policymaking in Mexico: The Sistema Alimentario Mexicano.* Working Papers in U.S.-Mexican Studies no. 24. San Diego: University of California.

Rello, Fernando
    1987   *State and Peasantry in Mexico: A Case Study of Rural Credit in La Laguna.* Geneva: United Nations Research Institute in Social Development (UNRISD). Spanish edition, 1986.

Salinas de Gortari, Carlos
    1982   *Political Participation, Public Investment and Support for the System: A Comparative Study of Rural Communities in Mexico.* Center for U.S.-Mexican Studies, Research Report Series no. 35. San Diego: University of California.

Sanderson, Steven
    1981   *Agrarian Populism and the Mexican State.* Berkeley: University of California Press.

Sodi de la Tijera, Demetrio
    1988   "El sector social en la comercialización: Factor de justicia y eficiencia." In *El Sector Social de la Economía*, edited by Armando Labra. Mexico City: UNAM/Siglo XXI.

Spalding, Rose
    1985   "Structural Barriers to Food Programming: An Analysis of the Mexican Food System." *World Development* 13(12).

Stephen, Lynn
    1988   "Culture as a Resource: Four Cases of Self-Managed Indigenous Craft Production." Paper presented at the Latin American Studies Association meetings, New Orleans, March 17–19.

Tendler, Judith
    1982   *Rural Projects Through Urban Eyes: An Interpretation of the World Bank's New Style Rural Development Projects.* World Bank Staff Working Paper no. 532. Washington, D.C.: World Bank.

Timmer, C. Peter, Walter Falcon, and Scott Pearson
    1982   *Food Policy Analysis.* Baltimore: Johns Hopkins University Press/World Bank.

Uphoff, Norman
    1984   "Rural Development Strategy: The Central Role of Local Organizations and Changing 'Supply Side' Bureaucracy." In *Studies on Agrarian Reform and Rural Poverty*, edited by M.R. Ghonemy, et al. Rome: FAO.

Warman, Arturo
  1980a   *"We Come to Object" The Peasants of Morelos and the National State.*
          Baltimore: Johns Hopkins University Press.
  1980b   *Ensayos Sobre el Campesinado.* Mexico City: Nueva Imagen.
Waterbury, Ronald
  1975   "Non-revolutionary Peasants: Oaxaca Compared to Morelos in the
          Mexican Revolution." *Comparative Studies in Society and History* 17,
          no. 4 (October).
Werner, Louis
  1988   "The Children of Sánchez Revisited." *Seeds* June.
Zepeda Patterson, Jorge, ed.
  1988   *Las Sociedades Rurales Hoy.* Zamora: El Colegio de Michoacán/CON-
          ACYT.

10

Food Security and Regional Development

Jack Corbett

To appreciate fully the perspectives and findings of the preceding chapters it might be useful to step back to the latter half of the 1960s. As agricultural innovations associated with the Green Revolution spread from Mexico to other Third World countries, development experts and national leaders hailed them as a major step forward in the struggle against world hunger. Many also hailed the "Mexican miracle," Mexico's effective use of agricultural exports to assist industrialization and diversification of the economy. Agro-exports, new food-distribution technology and infrastructure, and rapid growth of urban, middle-class markets encouraged investment in and consumption of high-status foods. As multinational corporations promoted First World preferences and eating patterns around the globe, they also facilitated the integration of Third World agri-products with market opportunities in the First World (Williams 1986). Brazil's energetic, calculated advance into the Amazon Basin symbolized efforts to fuse technology, markets, and policy in the pursuit of national development. On occasion uneasy voices questioned the long-term effects, environmental impacts, or socioeconomic consequences of these rapid changes, but in general such concerns were ignored or subordinated to other values.

Despite the optimism of the late 1960s, the 1980s have witnessed a resurgence of concern about the accessibility of adequate food and nutrition (for example, see Valdes 1981; Tullis and Hollist 1986; Hollist and Tullis 1987; Yesilada, Brockett, and Drury 1987). Countries such as India moved from persistent shortfalls in grain production to the occasional surplus; others—including Mexico as cradle of the Green Revolution—watched the volume of food imports mount steadily. Griffin (1987, 17) notes the incongruity of rising per capita food production and malnutrition, an observation echoed in Michael Whiteford's study of Costa Rica reported in this volume. It is easy to point to upheavals in Central American countries such as El Salvador and Nicaragua as significant factors affecting food security. Such explanations are more difficult to sustain for Costa Rica, Mexico, or Brazil. Hollist (1987) summarizes a growing body of evidence showing that Brazil's agricultural development since the 1960s has been paralleled by major problems of malnutrition and food scarcity. Nor are these patterns unique to Latin America, as research in Africa (Bryant 1988), the Pacific Basin (Schuh and McCoy 1986), and Asia (Chisholm and Tyers 1982) attests.

If research demonstrates a persistence of the central problem, new frameworks of analysis call attention to shortcomings in earlier conceptualizations of "food security." In the 1960s it was common to treat malnutrition and inadequate access to food as problems of food supply that would be resolved by increased production or access to world markets. National and household food security were treated as one and the same, with improvements in the former having the same effect on the latter. In retrospect this confidence in the nature and direction of linkages between national and household food accounts was misplaced. At the national level the focus on food security tended to be bound up with concerns for national self-sufficiency and dependency. Some countries, including Mexico (Luiselli Fernandez 1985), were concerned that reliance on food imports, most notably grains, from a few producers would create an undesirable and potentially difficult dependency. The tendency for some American political leaders to talk of the "food weapon" as international political leverage, coupled with the grain embargo against the Soviet Union in 1980 and a later food embargo against Nicaragua, reinforced this anxiety. Political vulnerability aside, many countries felt it would be poor policy to expend scarce foreign exchange on food rather than on imports of machinery, technology, and energy. Food security, therefore, became bound up with the idea of increasing national production of basic foods to reduce reliance on, and vulnerability to, price changes in, international markets. The precise structure of national production was of secondary importance.

A national-accounts approach to food security does not, however, take adequate notice of the circumstances informing household thinking about food requirements. Michael Lipton (1988) points out that individuals are more likely to think in terms of food insecurity, or the strain of providing adequate food for the next meal, the next day, or the next week. This short-term focus stems from low or irregular incomes, uncertain distribution channels, or variable production. As the DeWalts note in this volume, the Mexican food system meets the needs of those with the income to pay the cost; those whose incomes are inadequate to make food purchases or who lack access to distribution networks experience food insecurity, even though national food accounts may be positive. Indeed, there is a certain unhappy irony in the fact that distribution systems for soft drinks and other low-nutrition foods may reach far more people than systems designed to improve nutritional status. The community food councils described by Fox may provide the kind of organizational linkage that effectively ties national policy to household needs, but the key test will be effective performance across time in a way that builds public confidence and encourages support.

Strategic Choices in Food Security Systems

In a general sense there are two fundamental approaches to the creation of food-security systems at the national level. One of these centers on the fundamental principle of supply (produced or purchased); the other emphasizes consumption as its organizing focus. Some food-security programs fall under one of these two by virtue of constituent elements but are without a clearly explicated rationale. In other cases the philosophical position or basic framework has been made quite explicit. A useful juxtaposition of the two approaches may be found in essays by Lattimore (1986) and Luiselli Fernandez and Cruz-Serrano (1986).

Supply-Based Approach

The supply-based approach to food security assumes that if the structural circumstances are appropriate and favorable, food production and/or trade will expand to meet human needs. The primary obstacles to such expansion will be natural (for example, deserts, diseases, distance) or cultural (for example, traditional attitudes or poorly conceived public policies). Obstacles found in nature can be addressed through engineering, whether biological or physical. In Mexico this meant developing new strains of wheat, irrigation systems, and other interventions intended to increase production. In other parts of Central America it might mean coming up with forms of pest control or post-harvest loss management. Ineffective attitudes and policies can be overcome with appropriate incentives, encouragement, and self-discipline in order to find ways to allocate resources as efficiently and productively as possible. The utility of free markets as a means of resource allocation is widely accepted, as is the notion of trade based on differentials in comparative advantage due to factor endowments such as good soils, tropical growing conditions, or seasonality. Overt attempts to manage the supply-based approach should be limited to those that facilitate production or trade, with policy choices made in accordance with sound macroeconomic principles.

Consumption-Based Approach

The consumption-based approach emphasizes meeting basic human needs by responding to aggregations of households or subpopulations such as pregnant and nursing women. This approach springs from attempts to determine key factors such as daily nutritional requirements, then to carry those factors forward, ideally in an integrated fashion, to inform policy choices. One might assess the nutritional needs of the Honduran population and then, on that basis, seek to guide resource allocation or the decisions of groups and individuals in ways that respond to the central concern. Unlike the supply-driven approach, which places individual decisions at the center of the resource-allocation process, the consumption-based approach assumes direct intervention in or structuring of household choices. Subsidies and rationing are policy tools used by the consumption-based approach. The free market may play a role in this approach but it is not accorded center stage, as it is seen as vulnerable to profit-induced distortions and does not allocate scarce resources to those most in need rather than to those with ability to pay.

How do these approaches apply to Central America and Mexico? The supply-based approach has influenced thinking and resource allocation from the creation of CIMMYT (Center for the Improvement of Maize and Wheat) in Mexico in the early 1940s to the expansion of the cattle industry across the region in the 1960s and 1970s to more recent pressures by the International Monetary Fund to reduce public subsidies and facilitate private investment. A recent book by Bruce Jennings (1988) assesses the evolution of organization priorities at CIMMYT. Given its commitment to maximize yields, CIMMYT gave no attention to the dynamics of technology transfer to a heterogeneous agricultural sector, a point also made in this volume by the DeWalts. Subsequent criticisms of the Green Revolution for bias favoring some classes of farmers over others (for example, see Dahlberg 1979; Glaeser 1987) may be justified in terms of the outcome, but it is clear that CIMMYT's concern was to make the technology work, not to consider the social consequences. If society secures maximum production, that is, maximum supply, by concentrating production in the hands of a rather small number of agriculturalists, then allocation of resources to this sector would seem logical.

Thinking about agricultural exports involves the same line of reasoning. As the DeWalts observe, a commitment to the principle that countries should specialize in those products for which they hold a competitive advantage, exchanging them for other goods produced more efficiently elsewhere, has exerted strong influence on trade policy in Mexico and elsewhere. The logic of exchanging El Salvadorean coffee or Honduran bananas for Kansas wheat seems straightforward. This logic assumes that El Salvadorean coffee growers will opt to spend their newly acquired dollars to buy wheat for marketing in El Salvador rather than to invest those same funds in luxury consumption, foreign bank accounts, or political influence. There is little in the history of Central American imports to assure us that agro-export earnings are channeled to meet the food needs of the local population or that local people can afford to pay for imported food, except in those few cases where it proves less costly than local production. In general the supply-based approach fails to incorporate those elements of social structure and political power that dominate public decisions and thus contributes to the poverty, hunger, and malnutrition this volume documents.

Consumption-based approaches to food security "consider food security as the possibility of continuous access to foodstuffs essential for the development and normal functioning of the individuals in a society" (Luiselli Fernandez and Cruz-Serrano 1986, 56). Assured access is a central principle, but modes of access vary and may be vulnerable to a range of disruptive factors. Furthermore, the principle of "access" to food security lacks the abstract and nominally neutral quality to be found in "comparative advantage" or the "market." The latter two principles have been enshrined in capitalism as elements of faith, rarely to be questioned lest one be regarded as an unwelcome skeptic, or worse. "Access" has some vague relationship to notions of social justice and equality, but its significance lies in the ways it is operationalized, not in its adherence to formal theory. In Central America and Mexico consumption-based approaches providing access to food security take one of three forms:

First, and perhaps least honored in the region, is access provided by an *incomes policy* intended to assure citizens of incomes sufficient to purchase food at existing prices. In theory it should be possible to calculate an adequate diet for a model household and legislate minimum wages at rates covering food and other expenditures. In practice this does not happen, just as it does not happen in the United States. The economic stress across the region for most of the 1980s and the need to combat inflation has undermined efforts to sustain the admittedly modest incomes of the majority of the population. Most workers receive the legal minimum wage or below, and their purchasing power has taken a serious battering. Real incomes for Mexican workers receiving the minimum wage dropped 50 percent between 1982 and 1989. Incomes elsewhere in the region have tended to remain stagnant in real terms or to decline slightly. Given the absence of a labor movement able to press for higher wages and the preference of ruling elites for low wages (Brockett 1988, 94), a generalized incomes policy to assure food security is very unlikely.

Second, food security can be addressed in rural areas through a policy package of land, credit, seed, and other inputs intended to improve the position of *small producers.* Unlike the supply-based approach, which stresses maximum production, a small-producer approach to food security emphasizes the value of dealing with poverty and malnutrition among large numbers of rural poor. The aggregate contribution to national food stocks may be minimal, but the primary purpose is to address consumption needs. Small-producer policies were important elements of the post-1979 Nicaraguan reforms (Collins 1985), as they were of the Sistema Alimentario Mexicano in 1980 (Austin and Esteva 1987). Given the persistent problems of rural hunger and malnutrition, policies intended to assist small producers and thereby slow migration to urban areas would seem to merit high priority. In practice, however, the political and economic power of large commercial producers generally channels available resources toward their sector. Even the SAM, explicitly designed to meet the needs of subsistence farmers, had difficulties escaping capture by powerful outside interests. As Stonich demonstrates for Honduras, without policies directed at sustaining and invigorating small producers, the consequences are likely to include accelerating dietary deficiencies and increased pressure on local ecological systems.

Third, and perhaps most common, are various forms of *consumption subsidies.* These vary in scope and implementation, but all subsidies seek to address food security by holding the prices of basic foods below where they would otherwise be. This reduces expenditure pressures on poor consumers and demands for higher incomes. Consumption subsidies, therefore, may be seen as the opposite of the incomes policy intended to enable the poor to pay market prices. Some subsidies may be largely untargeted, meaning anyone who purchases the item in question benefits, and others are geared to specific groups or localities. Mexico, which has had some form of government-supported food subsidy and security program since the late 1930s, has long built its effort around a "basket" of basic commodities supplemented by a highly organized public-sector marketing agent, CONASUPO. The community food councils discussed by Fox build on a long tradition; some might even say CONASUPO (and its antecedents) has been one of the key institutional links between the Mexican government and poor Mexicans since 1937. Elsewhere subsidy programs are more modest, although the emergence of ENABAS in the dual role of guarantor of basic producer prices for some foods and subsidy manager for consumers replicates CONASUPO.

As Fox notes in this volume, subsidies are generally popular with consumers and (assuming the prices paid are at least adequate) with producers as well. Some subsidies are managed by providing producers a guaranteed price in order to take some of the risk from production and then by selling to consumers at a reduced price or without including administration, transportation, or other costs. In the case of imported foodstuffs the subsidy offsets a certain portion of purchase or transportation costs. Some subsidies are directed to food processors to reduce the cost of the final product. Still others come in the form of the overhead absorbed when CONASUPO or other subsidy managers operate their own stores or distribution centers. Yet there are a number of serious drawbacks to consumption subsidies, which have brought them under considerable criticism and policy challenge during the last several years:

1. Lustig (1986) argues that the lack of selectivity or targeting in subsidy programs means many consumers who do not need access to subsidized foods in fact benefit from it when the subsidy takes the form of a general price reduction. Fox makes the same argument, suggesting a principle of "social selectivity" merits consideration, although both he and Lustig recognize some of the difficulties of operationalizing such a concept. Lustig's data suggest that as much as 40 percent of the subsidy accorded to corn benefits those who do not need it.

2. Once the principle of subsidies is established it is very difficult to define boundaries. Lustig's data (1988, 279) demonstrate that in the space of a decade (1971–1979), the share of food subsidy directed to corn, a basic component of the diets of the poor, declined from 70.6 percent to 50.5 percent of food-subsidy allocations; sorghum rose from 0.6 percent to 21.2 percent. Sorghum is heavily used as an ingredient in animal feeds to prepare livestock for the urban market, so in effect pressures to be responsive to middle-class consumers shifted a significant portion of subsidies purported to be advantageous to the marginal consumer away from that sector.

3. Subsidies are popular targets of austerity programs. The Central American countries and Mexico have been forced to turn to the International Monetary Fund for financial assistance and economic stabilization, and a standard portion of the IMF support package involves reduction or elimination of subsidies as a way to reduce overall government spending. At a time when real wages are stagnant or in decline, substantial price increases in basic commodities (which may make up 60 to 80 percent of total family expenditures) come as a heavy blow. Because the Mexican gov-

ernment has been forced to reduce its subsidies for food and other items, it has come under heavy criticism. The bloody 1989 riots in Caracas in the wake of comparable pressures must be taken into account by any government. Yet it is difficult to resist the notion that without selective reductions in food subsidies, other unpalatable cuts in government spending must be made.

The Limits of Production and Consumption Approaches

To return to our general theme, we see in Central America and Mexico two approaches to the dilemmas of food insecurity. With the exception of Nicaragua, the production-based approach is dominant in the region. At present the production-based approach addresses issues of hunger and malnutrition by attempting to promote a community of interest between capitalist agriculture and scientific research, whether basic or applied. The capitalist agro-industrial system—that is, large-scale commercial producers, providers of various inputs, marketers, financiers, and others benefiting from the process—provides the organizational framework and monetary support for systematic application of intellectual resources. This fusion of money and knowledge occupies a powerful position from which to define the policy agenda for any effort to address the causes of hunger and insecurity. However, the production-based approach is largely silent on how to respond to that segment of the population untouched or displaced by its accomplishments. Such people are perceived as externalities who go away in the same fashion that the wildlife disappears as forests are cut or as pesticide-laden waters flow downstream. This perception may be accurate to the extent that people do go away, but social problems remain and are simply transferred to some other aspect of badly stressed national systems. Thus the stage is set for frustration and conflict.

If production-based approaches opt to ignore the human element in food insecurity, then consumption-based approaches race to embrace it. The idea that basic human needs should form the focal point for efforts to address poverty and hunger has both strong emotional appeal and great practical logic, yet even consumption-based approaches have significant limitations and weaknesses. First, to a large degree they are redistributive in nature, requiring the prior availability of resources before they can take effect. An incomes policy requires a stream of income from which a larger rather than smaller share may be diverted. Subsidies by their nature require resources made available from somewhere else. In Mexico during the 1970s subsidies originated through expansion of the public debt or funds generated by petroleum exports, both of which proved to be finite. The fiscal crisis of the 1980s took a heavy toll on subsidies to many system clients, not just the poor. Even investment in small producers may yield only marginal tangible returns, and at times the commitment of resources to small producers represents an effort only to keep the small farmers in place and producing as much as they can reasonably manage under marginal circumstances.

A second drawback to consumption-based approaches to food security is that they are difficult to define as "solutions." Because of political and economic power in the hands of current elites uninterested in structural change, vulnerability to financial crises and decisions made beyond national borders, and no prospect of developing an autonomy capable of confronting other interests in society, institutionalization of consumption-based approaches as an element of system norms is unlikely. Recall that the SAM in Mexico, a tentative effort to address food insecurity, did not survive the presidency of its patron, Jose López Portillo. As Austin and Esteva (1987, 363) remark:

> So what is the overall judgment of SAM's results? Mixed. The production gains were undeniably impressive. But the excessive costliness was impressively undeniable. Self-sufficiency was approached, poverty alleviated, and consumption enhanced, but none to the degree or permanence hoped for. And the fiscal burden proved onerous when the government was faced with the imperative of austerity.

Joseph Collins makes use of the metaphor "food window" (1985, xvi), a means of gaining insight into a society based on the values, behaviors, and expectations associated with the production, distribution, and consumption of food. Addressing the social factors surrounding food security in Central America and Mexico serves as a window through which we observe the complexities and challenges emerging from the competing structures of production and consumption. But in observing the region through this window, we would make a mistake not to notice two shadows that are increasingly likely to affect what we and others see and that will influence our vision of what is to come.

The first of these shadows is the ecological damage noted by Stonich in this volume. As Stonich, Jeffrey Leonard (1987), and others report, the cumulative effects of unrestrained capitalist agriculture and peasant populations desperate to sustain themselves may well destroy much of the biological resource base from Panama to central Mexico. The consequences of deforestation, erosion, pesticide accumulation, and other forms of environmental deterioration are only now becoming apparent, but there are few signs that the present developmental course can be altered in any significant way. At current rates of consumption all of Costa Rica's forests outside public reserves will be cut before the end of the century. To the pressures on El Salvador's resources identified by Durham (1979), pressures largely attributable to the expansion of export agriculture and the displacement of the rural population, we can add the toll of the continuing civil war. Honduras and Guatemala are subject to political and economic forces largely unprepared for, and disinterested in, the need to begin to think in terms of sustainable development rather than energetic accumulation (Browder 1989). The cost and significance of environmental degradation will become apparent only gradually and are masked by migration, commodity price fluctuations, foreign assistance, and other factors. Yet the implications of environmental degradation for the marginal populations presently affected by food insecurity promise to be substantial, and these populations are the least prepared to address the issues.

The second shadow visible through the "food window" is the continuing tension between the production and consumption approaches to food security. Although he uses somewhat different language, Martin Diskin treats much the same concern in his chapter on El Salvador. The apparent indifference, even contempt, of those who control El Salvador's agricultural system for the majority of the population provides little space for policy maneuvering that will effect a lasting resolution (as compared to temporary respites) to the social and political cleavages that plague the country. El Salvador may be the extreme case, but its problems underscore the difficulty of finding ways to deal with food security within the context of existing production and consumption policies. The production preferences of the agricultural elite aggravate the already dismal conditions of the rural poor, as outlined by Diskin. Except for possible food assistance from outside, it is not clear where the resources would come from for food subsidies. There will be no adjustments in existing incomes policy, and a small-producers policy seems implausible. El Salvador may be the extreme, but as Diskin believes, there is nothing in what we see within the current framework that might lead us to expect significant change. Even if a regime more inclined to pursue consumption-based approaches to food security takes power, it is unlikely that the available resources could do more than maintain marginal populations in a precarious limbo.

But perhaps these are only passing shadows, and thoughtful people from across the region may yet deal with the strains of poverty, hunger, malnutrition, and the social challenges that flow from them.

References and Bibliography

Austin, James, and Gustavo Estevo, eds.
   1987   *Food Policy in Mexico.* Ithaca: Cornell University Press.

Brockett, Charles D.
  1988   *Land, Power, and Poverty.* Boston: Unwin Hyman.
Browder, John O., ed.
  1989   *Fragile Lands of Latin America.* Boulder: Westview Press.
Bryant, Coralie, ed.
  1988   *Poverty, Policy, and Food Security in Southern Africa.* Boulder: Lynne
          Rienner.
Chisholm, Anthony H., and Rodney Tyers, eds.
  1982   *Food Security: Theory, Policy, and Perspectives from Asia and the Pacific
          Rim.* Lexington: Lexington Books.
Collins, Joseph
  1985   *Nicaragua: What Difference Could a Revolution Make?* Rev. ed. San
          Francisco: Institute for Food and Development Policy.
Dahlberg, Kenneth
  1979   *Beyond the Green Revolution.* New York: Plenum Press.
Durham, William H.
  1979   *Scarcity and Survival in Central America.* Stanford: Stanford University
          Press.
Glaeser, Bernhard, ed.
  1987   *The Green Revolution Revisited.* London: Allen and Unwin.
Griffin, Keith B.
  1987   "World Hunger and the World Economy." In *Pursuing Food Security,*
          edited by W. Ladd Hollist and LaMond Tullis. Boulder: Lynne Rienner.
Hollist, W. Ladd, and LaMond Tullis, eds.
  1987   *Pursuing Food Security.* Boulder: Lynne Rienner.
Jennings, H. Bruce
  1988   *Foundations of International Agricultural Research.* Boulder: Westview
          Press.
Lattimore, Ralph
  1986   "The Trade Approach to Food Security." In *Food, Agriculture, and
          Development in the Pacific Basin,* edited by G. Edward Schuh and
          Jennifer McCoy. Boulder: Westview Press.
Leonard, H. Jeffrey
  1987   *Natural Resources and Economic Development in Central America.* New
          Brunswick: Transaction Books.
Lipton, Michael
  1988   "Regional Trade and Food Security in Southern Africa." In *Poverty,
          Policy, and Food Security in Southern Africa,* edited by Coralie Bryant.
          Boulder: Lynne Rienner.
Luiselli Fernandez, Cassio
  1985   *The Route to Food-Sufficiency in Mexico.* Center for U.S.-Mexican Studies
          Monograph Series no. 17. San Diego: University of California.
Luiselli Fernandez, Cassio, and Alejandro Cruz-Serrano
  1986   "The SAM Approach to Food Security." In *Food, Agriculture, and
          Development in the Pacific Basin,* edited by Edward G. Schuh and
          Jennifer McCoy. Boulder: Westview Press.

Lustig, Nora
   1986   *Food Subsidy Programs in Mexico.* Working Papers on Food Subsidies
           no. 3. Washington, D.C.: International Food Policy Research Institute.
   1988   "Fiscal Cost and Welfare Effects of the Maize Subsidy in Mexico."
           In *Food Subsidies in Developing Countries,* edited by Per Pinstrup-
           Andersen. Baltimore: Johns Hopkins University Press.
Schuh, G. Edward, and Jennifer McCoy, eds.
   1986   *Food, Agriculture, and Development in the Pacific Basin.* Boulder: West-
           view Press.
Tullis, F. LaMond, and W. Ladd Hollist, eds.
   1986   *Food, the State, and International Political Economy.* Lincoln: University
           of Nebraska Press.
Valdes, Alberto, ed.
   1981   *Food Security for Developing Countries.* Boulder: Westview Press.
Williams, Robert G.
   1986   *Export Agriculture and the Crisis in Central America.* Chapel Hill:
           University of North Carolina Press.
Yesilada, Birol, Charles Brockett, and Bruce Drury, eds.
   1987   *Agrarian Reform in Reverse.* Boulder: Westview Press.

About the Book and Editors

Three children out of every four in Central America and Mexico go hungry, despite abundant arable land, skilled farmers, and a favorable climate. How did this situation develop, and why has it been allowed to persist?

In many Central American countries civil war and social upheaval have meant that crop production lags behind population growth. Food aid and export-led agricultural development strategies, promoted by donor organizations and national governments alike, have only exacerbated the situation. Development strategies such as the extensive promotion of livestock production have caused environmental degradation while failing to provide affordable food for the people.

Harvest of Want demonstrates how hunger and malnutrition can exist simultaneously with growth in agricultural production, especially if crops are destined for foreign markets. The book shows how national and international class interests and power relationships have meshed with donor and debt strategies to create food and nutritional deficits in many Central American and Mexican communities. The contributors conclude that hunger and malnutrition are political, not technical, problems and cannot be solved merely by improving agricultural production practices. What is needed is a social commitment to an equitable distribution of resources and the political will to provide for all groups in society.

Scott Whiteford is professor of anthropology and director of the Center for Latin American and Caribbean Studies at Michigan State University. His publications include *Workers from the North: Plantations, Bolivian Labor and the City in Northwest Argentina* (1981) and *The Keepers of Water and Earth: Mexican Social Organization and Irrigation* (1989), coauthored with Kjell Enge. **Anne E. Ferguson** is assistant professor of anthropology at Michigan State University. She is editor, with Rita Gallin, of *Women and International Development Annual* (Westview Press).

Index